BUSINESS ORGANISATION AND MANAGEMENT

Prof. Dr. Neeru Vasishth
Professor Department of Commerce
Janki Devi Memorial College
University of Delhi

Prof. Dr. Namita Rajput
Professor Department of Commerce
Sri Aurobindo College [Morning]
University of Delhi

KITAB MAHAL

KITAB MAHAL

First Edition : 2024

ISBN : 978-93-92080-99-9

Price : ₹390.00

Head Office

Kitab Mahal Publishers
4655/21, Ansari Road (G. F.)
Daryaganj, New Delhi-110002
Phone : 011-23273230/43526875;
(WhatsApp) 9335107914
Email : kitab_mahal@hotmail.com

Published By : Kitab Mahal, 4655/21, Ansari Road, (G. F.) Daryaganj, New Delhi-110002
Phone : +91 9350075776 Email : kitabmahalpublishers@gmail.com
Visit : www.kitabmahalpublishers.com

Printed by : Avatar Offset, 43/2, Site-IV, Sahibabad Industrial Area, Ghaziabad (U.P.)

Preface

This book is crafted to align with the latest NEP syllabus of B. ComFirst Semester (Minor-I) as prescribed by Rajiv Gandhi University, Arunachal Pradesh. The primary aim of this book is to acquaint the reader with the key concepts that form the fundamental pillar of knowledge, crucial for the beginning businessperson.

The syllabi for the first semester feature content material that seeks to deliver a good mix of theory and practice. It comprises a number of areas of business management, covering the concept and forms of business organisations, foundations of joint stock company related to its formation, principles and functions of management, detailing on concepts related to planning, organising, authority, coordination and control. Every topic is laid down in a manner that would help the reader easily follow the explanations. Questions to reflect on the concepts are given at the end of each chapter.

We are much grateful to Rajiv Gandhi University for their support in following a structured curriculum which forms the framework of this book. The book has been written in student friendly language to make the readers understand the basics of the subject. It is hoped to provide valuable information regarding the basic principles of business organisation and management.

We would like to pay gratefulness to the authors and sites whose work has been consulted in the course of this writing. We also express gratitude to our colleagues whose input has been vital in the formulation and organisation of the issues presented in the book.

Though efforts have been made to make it error-free, errors may still have crept in. Mistakes are deeply regretted and suggestions for improvement are most welcome.

Prof. Neeru Vasishth
neeruvasishth8@gmail.com
Prof. Namita Rajput
namitarajput27@gmail.com

SYLLABUS

COM-MC-1110- BUSINESS ORGANISATION AND MANAGEMENT (Minor Course - 1)

Credit: 04 (4 Lectures + 0 Tutorial + 0 Practical)
Total Credit Hour: 40 hours
Internal Assessment: 20 marks
End Semester Examination: 80 Marks

Total Marks: 100 Marks

Course Outcome: *Students would be able to make use of different management principles in the course of decision making in different forms of business organization*

Module-01: Concept and Forms of Business Organizations: Concepts of Business, Trade, Industry and Commerce- Objectives and functions of Business-Forms of Business Organization- Meaning, Characteristics, Advantages and Disadvantages of Sole Proprietorship; Meaning, Characteristics, Advantages & Disadvantages of Partnership; Kinds of Partners, Partnership Deed, Concept of Limited liability partnership; Meaning, Characteristics, Advantages and Disadvantages of Hindu Undivided Family; Meaning, Advantages and Disadvantages of Co-operative Organization; Social Responsibility, Responsible Business and Ethical Conduct & Values.

Module-02: Joint Stock Company: Joint Stock Company- Meaning, Definition, Characteristics, Advantages and Disadvantages; Code of Business Ethics; Kinds of Companies; Promotion; Stages of Promotion; Promoter-Characteristics & Kinds; Preparation of Important Documents; Memorandum of Association- Clauses; Articles of Association & Contents; Prospectus- Contents; Red herring Prospectus; Statement In lieu of Prospectus (as per Companies Act, 2013).

Module-03: Principles and Functions of Management: Management - Meaning - Characteristics - Fayol's 14 Principles of Management. Functions of Management - Levels of Management - Skills of Management- Scientific Management - meaning, objectives, relevance and criticism.

Module-04: Planning and Organizing: Planning -Meaning, Characteristics, Types of Plans, Advantages and Disadvantages, Approaches to Planning, Management by Objectives (MBO) - Steps in MBO, Benefits and Weaknesses; Organizing - Process,

Contents

Preface

1. Concept of Business (Objectives and Functions) **1-20**

1.1 Introduction 1
1.2 Economic and Non-economic Activities 2
1.3 Types of Economic Activities 2
1.4 Business, Profession and Employment: A Comparison 3
1.5 Business 5
1.6 Features of Business 6
1.7 Additional Features of Business 7
1.8 Objectives of Business 9
1.9 Functions of Business 14

2. Scope of Business **21-34**

2.1 Introduction 21
2.2 Industry (Manufacturing Sector) 22
2.3 Commerce (Service Sector) 24
2.4 Trade 25
2.5 Auxiliaries to Trade 27
2.6 Relationship Between Industry and Commerce 29
2.7 Service Sector 29

3. Forms of Business Organisations **35-60**

3.1 Types of Business Enterprises 35
I. Private Sector Enterprises 35
II. Public Sector Enterprises 35
III. Joint Sector Enterprises 36
3.2 Forms of Private Sector Enterprises 36
I. Non-corporate Form of Business Enterprises 36
1. Sole Proprietorship 37
2. Hindu Undivided Family (HUF) 39
3. Partnership 41

II. Corporate Form of Business Enterprises 36
1. Limited Liability Partnership 51
2. Co-operative Societies 55

4. Social Responsibility **61-74**

4.1 Corporate Social Responsibility 61
4.2 Nature of Corporate Social Responsibility 62
4.3 Levels of Social Responsibility 63
4.4 Historical Perspectives of Social Responsibility 64
4.5 Philosophical Perspectives of Social Responsibility 64
4.6 Principles of Corporate Social Responsibility 65
4.7 Arguments for and Against Corporate Social Responsibility (CSR) 66
4.8 Dimensions of CSR 68

5. Responsible Business and Ethical Conduct and Values **75-96**

5.1 Responsible Business and Ethical Conduct 75
5.2 Ethics 77
5.3 Features of Business Ethics 78
5.4 Need for Business Ethics 78
5.5 Guidelines for Ethical Behaviour 78
5.6 Ethical Activities 79
5.6 Types of Management Ethics 79
5.8 Approaches to Management Ethics 80
5.9 Development of Ethics 80
5.10 Ethical Decision Making 84
5.11 Values 86
5.12 Features of Values 87
5.13 Importance of Values 87
5.14 Innate (Basic) vs. Acquired Values 87
5.15 Values and Beliefs 88
5.16 Types of Values 89
5.17 Factors Affecting Values 91
5.18 Values and Behaviour 92

6. Joint Stock Company **97-10**

6.1 Introduction 97
6.2 Features of a Company 97

6.3 Merits of a Company 98
6.4 Limitations of a Company 99
6.5 Suitability of Company Form of Organisation 101
6.6 Code of Business Ethics 101
6.7 Types of Companies 104

7. Formation of a Company **111-130**

7.1 Introduction 111
7.2 Promotion 111
7.3 Registration/Incorporation 119
7.4 Floatation/Capital Subscription 128
7.5 Commencement 128

8. Documents for Formation of a Company **131-150**

8.1 Documents to be Filed with Registrar of Companies 131
8.2 Memorandum of Association 131
8.3 Articles of Association 136
8.4. Prospectus 141

9. Management Concept and Nature **151-174**

9.1 Management 151
9.2 Features of Management 152
9.3 Importance of Management 152
9.4 Aspects of Management 154
9.5 Nature of Management 155
9.6 Management and Administration 159
9.7 Levels of Management 160
9.8 Managerial Skills 163
9.9 Management Functions 164
9.10 Role of Managers 167
9.11 Functional Areas of Management 168

10. Evolution of Management Thought **175-196**

10.1 Introduction 175
10.2 Management Theories 175
10.3 Pre-Scientific Management Theories 176
10.4 Classical Theory 177

11. Fundamentals of Planning **197-220**

11.1 Meaning 197
11.2 Features of Planning 198
11.3 Importance/Objectives of Planning 199
11.4 Limitations of Planning 200
11.5 Ways to Overcome Limitations 202
11.6 Process of Planning 203
11.7 Features of a Good Plan 205
11.8 Types of Plans 206
11.9 Plans based on Levels 207
11.10 Classification based on Use 208
11.11 Classification based on Time 216
11.12 Classification based on Functional Areas 217

12. Management by Objectives **221-232**

12.1 Meaning of Management by Objectives (MBO) 221
12.2 Components of MBO 223
12.3 Nature of MBO 223
12.4 Objectives of MBO 224
12.5 Need for Management by Objectives 224
12.6 Process of MBO 225
12.7 Merits of Management by Objectives 226
12.8 Limitations of MBO 228
12.9 Effective MBO 229

13. Organising Function **233-254**

13.1 Meaning of Organisation 233
13.2 Nature of Organisation 233
13.3 Process of Organising 234
13.4 Importance of Organising 235
13.5 Organisation Chart 237
13.6 Span of Management 243
13.7 Principles of Organising 251

14. Formal and Informal Organisations **255-266**

14.1 Formal Organisation 255
13.2 Theories of Formal Organisation 256
14.3 Informal Organisation 261
14.4 Formal and Informal Organisations 263

15. Organisation Structure **267-284**
15.1 Organisation Structure 267
15.2 Elements of Organisation Structure 267
15.3 Mechanistic and Organic Structures 268
15.4 Factors Affecting Organisation Structure 269
15.5 Organisation Formats/Theories 272
15.6 Classical Organisation Formats 273
16. Line and Staff Relationships **285-296**
16.1 Introduction 285
16.2 Line and Staff Authority 285
16.3 Features of Line and Staff 285
16.4 Distinction Between Line and Staff 286
16.5 Importance of Staff 287
16.6 Types of Staff 287
16.7 Line and Staff Conflict 289
16.8 Resolution of Line and Staff Conflict 293
17. Authority Responsibility Relationships **297-314**
17.1 Meaning of Authority 297
17.2 Features of Authority 297
17.3 Sources of Authority 298
17.4 Types of Authority 302
17.5 Limitations of Authority 304
17.6 Power 305
17.7 Nature of Power 306
17.8 Sources of Power 307
17.9 Use of Power 308
17.10 Responsibility 309
17.11 Authority and Responsibility 310
17.12 Parity between Authority and Responsibility 310
17.13 Accountability 310
18. Delegation and Decentralisation **315-330**
18.1 Meaning of Delegation 315
18.2 Features of Delegation 316
18.3 Process of Delegation 316
18.4 Forms of Delegation 317

18.5 Importance of Delegation 318
18.6 Principles of Delegation 318
18.7 Elements of Delegation 319
18.8 Barriers to Delegation 320
18.9 Overcome Barriers to Delegation 321
18.10 Centralisation and Decentralisation 323
18.11 Importance of Decentralisation 323
18.12 Limitations of Decentralisation 324
18.13 Factors Affecting Decentralisation 325
18.14 Process of Decentralisation 326
18.15 Degree of Decentralisation 328
18.16 Delegation and Decentralisation 328

19. Co-Ordination 331-340

19.1 Co-ordination 331
19.2 Features/Nature of Co-ordination 332
19.3 Importance/Need for Co-ordination 332
19.4 Limitations in Achieving Co-ordination 334
19.5 Types of Co-ordination 334
19.6 Techniques of Co-ordination 336
19.7 Principles of Co-ordination 337
19.9 Co-ordination—The Essence of Management 339

20. Control Function 341-356

20.1 Meaning of Control 341
20.2 Nature of Control 341
20.3 Importance of Control 342
20.4 Relationship between Planning and Control 343
20.5 Types of Control 344
20.6 Behavioural Aspects of Control 346
20.7 Resistance to Control 347
20.8 Effects of Resistance to Control 348
20.9 Overcome Resistance to Control 348
20.10 Control Process 349
20.11 Focus of Control 351
20.12 Management or Control by Exception 352
20.13 Effective Control System 353

1 Chapter

Concept of Business (Objectives and Functions)

1.1 INTRODUCTION

Human beings perform a variety of activities in their daily lives guided by economic, social, cultural, and religious motives. These activities may be manufacturing, trading, exchange of services, auxiliaries to trade like banking, transportation, insurance etc. or helping a charitable trust, old age home, poor or looking after one's family and friends. These activities can be classified into two categories:

1. Non-economic Activities
2. Economic Activities

1. Non-Economic Activities

Activities undertaken to satisfy the social, cultural, religious, safety, sentimental and emotional needs are known as non-economic activities. They are undertaken to satisfy our higher-order needs of esteem, recognition, and self actualisation and provide self-satisfaction, for example, providing honorary services in a charitable or religious institution, helping the differently abled and old people, volunteering in social or religious camps, serving one's family etc. They are voluntary in nature with no economic motive. They help in part satisfaction of lower-order needs, also, for example, social needs.

2. Economic Activities

Economic activities are performed to earn monetary gain. They are necessary for sustenance of our life. The basic needs of food, clothing and shelter can be fulfilled by pursuing economic activities as they help in earning the livelihood. They also add to our economic wealth and relate to production and distribution of goods and services, like converting inputs into outputs to sell at a gain, buying and selling (trading) goods at a gain, a doctor/lawyer/accountant/teacher providing services for a monetary return etc.

1.2 ECONOMIC AND NON-ECONOMIC ACTIVITIES

The following table highlights differences between economic and non-economic activities:

	Economic Activities	Non-economic Activities
1. Motive	They are undertaken to earn profits or monetary return. They generate wealth and are, thus, the basis for economic development.	They are undertaken to derive satisfaction.
2. Need satisfaction	They satisfy lower-order needs (physiological) of individuals; they may result in part satisfaction of higher-order needs also.	They satisfy higher-order needs of individuals; they may result in part satisfaction of lower-order needs also (social needs).
3. Return	The return is expected in the form of money.	The return is expected in the form of emotional and psychological satisfaction.
4. Cost-benefit analysis	They use scarce economic resources: land, labour, capital etc. A thorough cost-benefit analysis is, therefore, justified before undertaking such activities.	They use human skill, dexterity, emotions and sentiments. It may involve monetary cost but the benefits far outweigh the costs.

1.3 TYPES OF ECONOMIC ACTIVITIES

The economic activities can be divided into the following categories:

1. Business 2. Profession 3. Employment

1. Business

Business is an economic activity carried by the people, for the people. It involves activities such as manufacturing, trading, banking, transport, warehousing etc. to satisfy consumers' needs and earn profits. They also carry the risk of loss. Detailed explanation of the term 'business' is given in the succeeding paragraphs.

2. Profession

Profession means professional achievements in special knowledge as distinguished from mere skill; acquired after attending formal education and training programmes. Profession requires rendering services of personal and expert nature based on professional training and skill. The professionals are members of professional bodies like Bar Council of India (Law). Institute of Chartered Accountants of India (Chartered

Accountants), Indian Medical Council (Doctors), Institute of Company Secretaries of India (Company Secretaries), Institute of Cost and Works Accountants of India (Cost Accountants) etc. They perform professional activities within the framework of these guidelines. Architects, doctors, lawyers, engineers, professors etc. provide services of professional nature.

A profession is characterised by the following ***features***:

1. Professionals have specialised knowledge and training related to their profession.
2. They become members of the professional bodies before they can practice their profession.
3. They base their decisions on general principles.
4. They acquire professional status through performance not through favouritism or other factors irrelevant to work at hand.
5. They are governed by a strict code of ethics that provides norms for members' behaviour to protect their clients.
6. True professionals combine life and work with personal dedication and commitment.

3. Employment

Employment is an economic activity where a person is employed by another person, firm, association of persons, company, corporation, Central or State Government, public body, or a local authority. It involves a contract of employment where the employee gives an oral or written undertaking to the employer to perform the duties assigned to him. The remuneration that employee receives from the employer is called salary and consists of wages, allowances, bonus, perquisites, gratuity, commission etc. A professionally qualified person can also be in employment.

Though the terms 'business', 'profession' and 'employment' are conceptually different, they are complementary and shape the structure of the business enterprise. A business employs people for its smooth conduct and employs the services of professionals like chartered accountants, lawyers, architects etc. to meet the requirements of the legal framework (audit of accounts).

1.4 BUSINESS, PROFESSION AND EMPLOYMENT: A COMPARISON

Though the terms 'business', 'profession' and 'employment' are different, there is close relationship amongst them. To pursue a successful business, the businessman employs people who help in smooth conduct of business operations. Legal framework of the country requires accounts of the business to be audited at regular intervals. This requires the businessman to employ the services of professionals like chartered accountants, lawyers, architects etc. Though different, the three terms are complementary in nature and shape the structure of the business enterprise.

The following table highlights the *differences* between business, profession, and employment:

Factors	Business	Profession	Employment
1. Formation	The entrepreneur decides to form the business by complying with the legal requirements	The professional can exercise profession after his academic training. He acquires membership of the professional body along with the certificate of practice.	A person is employed when he signs an agreement, oral or written, with his employer to work under him.
2. Nature of work	Self-employment	Self-employment	Contract of service under a third person.
3. Type of work	Production and exchange of goods and services to satisfy consumers' needs.	Rendering services of specialised nature.	Perform work as assigned by the employer.
4. Motive	To earn profits (economic)	To charge fees from clients (economic)	To earn salaries or wages (economic)
5. Educational qualification	No formal qualification is required.	Formal training and professional qualification is necessary.	Though professional qualification is not necessary, qualification as required by employers is essential.
6. Financial investment	Depending upon the size of business and nature of activities, investments are made in business. Huge amount of investment is required in large-sized business organisations.	Capital investment is less than what is required to set up a business enterprise.	No capital investment is required.
7. Risk	Substantial risk.	If a professional carries private practice, the element of risk is present.	No risk.

8. Transfer of interest	Interest can be transferred to third parties subject to legal compliance.	Interest cannot be transferred unless the transferee is qualified in the same profession.	Transfer of interest is not allowed.
9. Code of conduct	No formal code of conduct is followed. It may, however, follow the code as prescribed by the business/trade associations like FICCI (Federation of Indian Chambers of Commerce and Industry), CII (Confederation of Indian Industries), AIOE (All India Organisation of Employers).	Professional code of conduct is prescribe by the professional body.	Employer lays down the code of conduct.

1.5 BUSINESS

Business means to remain busy. It includes economic activities related to manufacturing, trading, banking, insurance, transportation etc. to create utilities for consumers. Business includes (a) trade, (b) commerce, (c) manufacture, or (d) any adventure or concern in the nature of trade, commerce or manufacture.

"Business comprises all profit-seeking activities and enterprises that provide goods and services necessary to an economic system. It is the economic pulse of a nation, striving to increase society's standard of living. Profits are a primary mechanism for motivating these activities."

Business is "the organised effort by individuals to produce goods and services, to sell these goods and services in a marketplace, and to reap some reward for this effort."

Business is, thus, a group of persons who organise to produce goods and services to sell at a gain. All business activities have an element of risk. The success or failure of business depends upon the environment in which it operates. How well a business co-ordinate its activities with environmental factors determines how successful that business is.

A business utilises scarce national resources. It is, therefore, necessary that resources are optimally utilised. Profit is the prime motive of pursuing business operations as economic activities.

1.6 FEATURES OF BUSINESS

Business is characterised by the following features:

1. **Goods and Services**: The main feature of business is to provide goods and services that create utility for consumers. It may create form utility (converting raw material into finished goods), time utility (storing goods to sell when consumers want), or place utility (transferring goods from the place of production to the place of consumption). The goods may be consumer goods or producer goods. Consumer goods are meant for final consumption by consumers, like food products or stationary items. Producer goods are used for further production like tools, machines etc. Services are intangibles like gas, electricity, transportation, insurance, warehousing etc.
2. **Exchange**: Goods produced for personal consumption do not constitute business. If the same goods are exchanged with consumers for a price, it is business. A farmer producing grains for personal consumption or a weaver weaving cloth for personal consumption is not doing business. But if the same farmer or weaver produces grains or cloth for sale at profit, their activities are termed as business. The goods may be produced by the business entrepreneur or procured from outside.
3. **Creation of Wealth**: Business uses scarce resources as inputs and converts them into productive outputs required by the society. This adds to capital of the business and wealth of the society.
4. **Profit**: Profit is the main force that drives a business to perform manufacturing or trading activities. Profit is the difference between revenue and cost. Revenue is the total sale value that a business earns on selling the products and cost is the amount incurred in producing the output. Though profit is the main reason for a business to exist, business should also look after the interests of the society. Profit is an important reason for existence and continuity of the business, it is not the role reason.
5. **Continuity**: One-time purchase and sale of goods for profit is not business. If a person buys a pair of shoes and sells it at a profit or sells his land, house

or jewellery at profit, he is not doing business unless he is regularly buying and selling the shoes, land, house or jewellery. Continuity of operations is an important feature of business. A property dealer or a jeweller is doing business as he is performing these transactions regularly. Profit on these transactions is the source of his income.

6. **Risk**: Business operates in the changing, dynamic environment where technological, social, cultural, legal, political, economic, and natural factors directly and indirectly influence the business activities. Though every business forecast changes in the environment, the forecasts can go wrong and business decisions can fail to bring the desired benefits. A business enterprise that risks operating in such an environment and plans its activities scientifically will succeed and earn profits as against those who do not venture into a project for the fear of making losses. Environment has both threats and opportunities. Change in demand, strikes, lockouts, new markets, new customers (market potential) etc. must be explored and planned accordingly. Though it is done with the intent to earn profits, it may even result in losses. Risk is assumed to earn profits, but losses cannot be ignored. The reward for risk is return.
7. **Social Objectives** Business is a socio-economic institution. Profit is the primary objective of business but not the only objective. To achieve the objectives of survival and growth, business must cater to social objectives also. Business is the creation of society, it operates in the society and, therefore, it is ethical that it looks after the interests of the society. Both business and society need each other. Business that helps society in achieving its objectives is more successful than those who maximise their profits at the cost of social interests.

1.7 ADDITIONAL FEATURES OF BUSINESS

The modern business enterprises are characterised by the following features:

1. **Change**: Change is the essence of life. Every product has limited life. Business should accept and implement changes to ensure their success. They operate in the dynamic environment, which is constantly changing, and this change must be accepted by them.
2. **Bigness**: To reap the economies of scale, business enterprises try to reach new heights. Huge capital investment, mass-scale production, large number of

workers, high sales, huge profits, large number of shareholders, huge reserves, huge payments of tax characterise a successful business enterprise.

3. **Diversification:** Big companies have the risk of product failure. Introduction-Maturity-Growth-Decline are the phases of product life cycle. To safeguard against the risk of loss of products in the world of competition, business enterprises diversify their product lines. They produce more than one product to cover the risk of loss in one sector. The TATA group, for example, produces iron and steel, fertilisers, tea, chemicals, textiles, electronics, salt and a number of other goods and services to play safe in the market. Diversification reduces risk, reduces competition, and increases profits of the business.
4. **Globalisation:** Businesses are not confined to national boundaries. Liberalisation policies allow entry of foreign companies in our country and Indian companies in foreign countries. Free flow of capital, technology, manpower, and information systems have increased competition and developed markets at the global level, allowing companies to find cost effective ways to produce their products. Globalisation has developed a single economy, the global economy.
5. **Science**: To grow in the fast-changing environment, businesses are adopting scientific means of production. Modern machines, scientific selection of workers and scientific methods of control contribute to the growth of the business.
6. **Information**: Information related to internal and external environment is an important feature of modern business. Highly developed management information systems and computers are important contributors to fast and easy access to business information. Online information helps businesses operate at the global level.
7. **Government Interference**: Government controls the working of business houses through import restrictions, quota restrictions, limits on foreign investment, double taxation agreements and tax laws etc. Government plays an important role in the development of the business houses. Laws regulate business activities in the social, national, and international interest and businesses work within the constraints of legal framework.
8. **Competition**: Competition is beneficial for consumers as well as the competing firms. "Aggressive home-based suppliers and demanding local suppliers, competing domestic rivals will keep each other honest in obtaining Government

support. Companies are less likely to get hooked on the narcotic of Government contracts or creeping industry protection." *Michael Porter*

9. **Finance**: Finance is the life of a business. A balanced capital structure with optimum mix of long-term and short-term securities helps in meeting the financial requirements of the business.

1.8 OBJECTIVES OF BUSINESS

Objectives are the aims and goals of business houses that help to devise strategies that align with the overall mission and vision of the organisation. These are important for the long-term success and survival of the business and can range from financial gains to social responsibilities. A business must assess and change these objectives according to the changing market conditions, expectations of the society, and the global trends to ensure long-term growth, profitability, and positive contributions to society and the environment.

Economic Objectives

The economic objectives are as follows:

1. **Profit Maximisation:** Business performs the economic activity of transforming inputs into outputs to maximise the profits. The motivational objectives that guides various business activities such as mining, manufacturing, banking, trading etc, is profit maximisation, i.e., to achieve surplus in the value of outputs over inputs. All economic activities are undertaken to earn surplus to meet its goals of survival, growth and goodwill. Profits are the basis for business existence and help it to face market fluctuations and uncertainties like trade cycles, changing demand patterns, etc. *Adam Smith*, a famous economist, believed that entrepreneurs should be allowed to pursue self-interest for the benefit of all.

2. **Market Share:** Long-term stability requires expansion of the share in the market. More market share usually means more revenue and enhances the ability to effectively compete with rivals.

3. **Cost Effectiveness:** Cost reduction through efficient use of resources results in optimisation of operations, effective management of supplies, and technology in investment towards productivity enhancement.

4. **Increase Productivity:** Profits can be maximised if business increases productivity (the ratio of outputs to inputs). Productivity can be increased by optimising the input-output conversion process, i.e., business should plan for optimum allocation of inputs (men, material, money etc.) and optimum production mix (combination of outputs).
5. **Customer Creation:** Customers provide foundation to the existence of the business. Customers can be created if business produces goods of the quality that customers want and sell them at the time, place and the price they want. Thus, they create time and place utility for these goods. Business has to create and ratin customers. Advertising quality goods at affordable prices helps in achieving this objective.
6. **Innovation:** Innovation means to create something new. Business should envision future based on innovation and communicate that vision to organisational members. Innovation is a new idea applied to initiating or improving a process, product or service. It increases production, reduces costs and strengthens the capacity of the business to keep pace with the changing environment. All innovations imply change, but all changes are not innovations. Innovation means improvement in structural, technological, human resource, and cultural components. They lead to business development and enhance its profits and social acceptance.

Non-economic Objectives

As blood is the life of man, so are profits the life of industry, and just as man must maintain life before he can be free to pursue the life's objectives he has set before himself, so profits are necessary to business and are in the proper sense of the word 'primary'. But profits are not the ultimate objects of the responsible company."

—Goyder

There is a growing recognition that business must pursue objectives other than maximising profits and productivity. These are non-economic objectives. Some of the non-economic objectives are discussed below:

I. Organic Objectives

II. Human Objectives

III. Social Objectives

IV. National Objectives

V. Global Objectives

I. Organic Objectives

These are the basic and fundamental objectives necessary for the survival of business firms. They are as follows.

1. **Survival:** Survival ensures that business maintains market standing for a fairly long period of time to meet its objective. Survival is ensured by business capacity to earn profits and build reserves to meet its future demands.
2. **Growth:** Business must grow to maintain competitive strength in the market. Growth means development in products, processes, decision-making ability, adaptability to changing environment, financial and human resources etc. Growth justifies existence of the organisation. It implies expansion and diversification along the same and different products and markets. Sound planning (financial by creating reserves and non-financial by forecasting demand and non-demand factors) helps in optimum utilisation of resources and contributes to corporate growth.
3. **Goodwill:** Business can earn goodwill if it caters to demands of different sections of society; shareholders, consumers, suppliers, workers, government etc. Business that enjoys prestige will be in a strong position to market its goods and earn profits to meet other objectives.
4. **Resources:** Business should generate resources to meet their financial requirements (dividends to shareholders, wages to workers, payment to suppliers, taxes to Government) and add to their reserves to meet their potential investment demands.

II. Human Objectives

Human resource shapes the culture of the business. Human resources are "the total knowledge, skills, creative abilities, talents and aptitudes of an organisation's work force, as well as the values, attitudes approaches and beliefs of the individuals involved in the affairs of the organisation." Without human resources, no can exist. Business must, therefore, develop the human resources.

Following are the important human objectives:

1. **Effective Utilisation of Manpower:** the manpower consists of managers, scientific and research people, executives, supervisors, workers and other people that make up the total business. It should be optimally utilised for benefit of the business. Various human resource activities like human resource planning, recruitment, selection, performance appraisal etc. must be efficiently carried out by the business.
2. **Development of Human Resource:** Business should carry out human resources activities not only for its development but also for development of the human beings. Procurement development, compensation, integration and maintenance are the operative personnel functions carried out by business managers for growth, development and satisfaction of their people.
3. **Participation in Management:** Companies should give responsibilities and challenges to workers for their development. Participation though mutual consultation, communication and understanding maintains healthy industrial relations in the business and results in industrial harmony, commitment to work and high productivity.
4. **Training and Motivation:** Training facilities should be provided to increase on-the-job skills of workers. Positive motivators should be used to energise the behaviour of people. It activates action and leads to effective fulfilment of business goals.
5. **Job Security:** Job security ensures the loyalty of employees, curbs high turnovers, and develops skills that can lead to organisational stability and high productivity.

III. Social Objectives

Business operates in the macro environment that consists of economic and non-economic variables. The key to satisfying goals is customer satisfaction. *Kotler* points out:

"The addition of long-run customer welfare asks the businessman to include social and ecological considerations in his product and marketing planning. He is asked to do it not only to meet his social responsibilities but also because failure to do this may hurt his long-run interest . "Management thinking expects business to pursue the social interests Some of the important social objectives are as follows:

1. **Customer Satisfaction:** Consumer satisfaction and long-run consumer welfare are important requirements of a long-run profitable business. It must provide quality goods to customers at fair prices and create customer patronage.

2. **Remove Sosial Problems:** Business is expected to remove social ills like poverty, casticism, untouchability etc. "Corporations are dependent on acceptance by the society of which they are a part, and for them to ignore social problems might in the long-run be self-destructive."

   There is "an iron law of responsibilities which states that in the long run those who do not use power in a manner that society considers responsibile will tend to lose it." *–Keith Davis.*

3. **Fair trade Practices :** Business provides great service to society by indulging in fair trade practices. Adulteration, hoarding, black-marketing and other anti-social activities should be avoided and business should provide goods and services at fair prices.

4. **Employment Opportunities:** Though automation and mechanisation are the signs of prosperity, providing gainful employment to society should be the endeavour of business organisations. Expansion and diversification generates more jobs in all functional areas (production, human resource, finance, marketing) at all levels.

5. **Environmental Sustainability:** Protecting the environment through sustainability is becoming meaningful. This involves the reduction of carbon footprints and recycling, using renewable resources.

6. **Quality Products and Services:** Offering quality products and services is extremely important for the business to maintain goodwill in the market and among the customers themselves.

IV. National Objectives

It should be the effort of every business to use the resources for national interest. The following national objectives should be followed by the business.

1. **Develop Backward Areas:** The Government provides many tax incentives to establish businesses in backward areas. Business should set industries in backward areas not only to avail these incentives but also to promote national prospects. National priorities aim at balanced regional development where resources in the under developed areas can be exploited and people can be gainfully exploited.

2. **Generate Export Surplus:** A wealthy nation is rich in foreign exchange reserves. To help a country earn these reserves and become self reliant, business should focus on export of goods.
3. **Contribute to Research and Development:** Large corporations have strong resource position and enrich the society by their inventions and innovations. Many business houses have their own technology and engineering institutes that impart training on technical skills to their employees as also to outsiders.
4. **Social Justice:** Business should provide equal job opportunities to men and women, remove inequalities of income and work for upliftment of the society. This ensures justice for all and development of the nation.
5. **Develop Small Enterprises:** Large-scale enterprises should support small enterprises by not competing in the products sold by them. They can use the products of small-scale units as their inputs

V. Global Objectives

1. **International Expansion:** International reach offers a company new growth opportunity and helps it attain economies of scale.
2. **Global Responsibility:** Responsible action in the global arena involves issues such as global warming, human rights, and ethics in cross-border trade.
3. **Cultural Sensitivity:** Respect and understanding of cultural differences have to be observed by companies that are operating in more than one country to maintain better relationships with international customers and partners.

1.9 FUNCTIONS OF BUSINESS

Business performs many functions for its smooth conduct. These functions are inter-related and, thus, their combined performance determines the success of business. Production needs funds and people and, thus, the support of finance and human resource departments. Similarly, marketing department needs to coordinate with production, finance, and human resource departments. The four major functions of business are:

1. Production function 2. Finance function

3. Personnel function 4. Marketing function

1. Production Function

Production management is a system which gives an overview of the production function. It is a "set of components whose function is to transform a set of inputs into some desired output." Three *main components* of the production system are:

(i) ***Inputs***: Inputs help to produce the output. These include the workers, equipment, technical knowledge, information, customers' needs, management, assets etc. Some of the inputs used in the process of transformation are permanent like land, building, machinery, and fixtures while others like raw material and supplies are temporary.

(ii) ***Transformation***: It refers to conversion of inputs into outputs through planning, organising, and controlling of the tools and equipments used to carry out the transformation process. Different types of transformation processes used in the conversion of inputs into outputs are:

(a) Physical transformation in manufacturing activities,

(b) Locational transformation in transportation industry,

(c) Exchange transformation in exchange business,

(d) Storage transformation in warehousing business,

(e) Informational transformation in legal firms,

(f) Physiological transformation in medical profession, and

(g) Gratification transformation in entertainment business.

(iii) ***Outputs***: Outputs are the goods and services produced through transformation of inputs. They also include the by-products of the goods produced, such as pollutants in the form of toxic wastes.

Besides the above discussed basic components of a production system, the environmental factors and feedback mechanism also form its important components. The external environment includes factors such as government regulations, safety regulations, labour laws, economic policies, international policies, etc. The feedback brings information back from the environment to the production manager about the acceptance of goods and services to the consumers. The feedback mechanism indicates changes required in the production system.

The production system is, thus, an open system in continuous interaction with its environment. The diagrammatic representation of the production system is as follows:

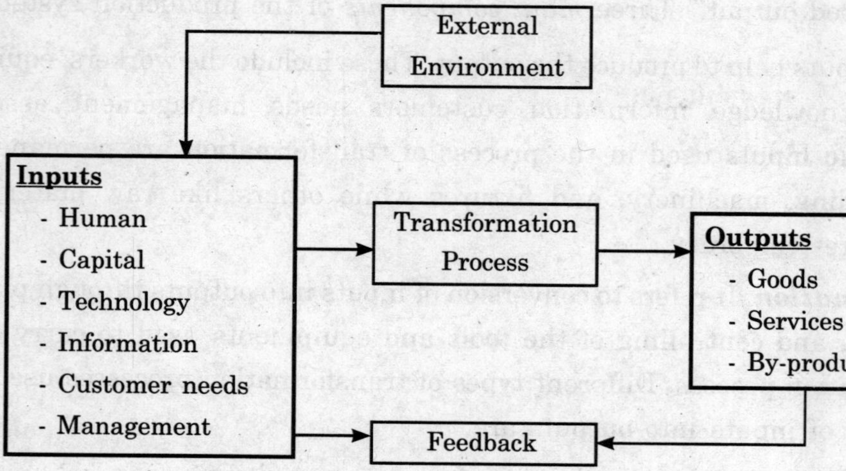

To understand the decisions with respect to effective operations function, areas of operation have been categorised into a hierarchy of operations management decisions, i.e., decisions which are covered in the production/operations management.

(1) Long Range Decisions

i. **Facility Location:** Facility location involves choosing the best sites for buildings, people, materials, and machines to maximise benefits for the company and its stakeholders.

ii. **Product/Process Selection:** Product selection is a strategic decision about "what product to produce – in what form, with what features, and in what quantity." Process selection determines the quality and quantity of manpower needed, the capital required, and the choice of production processes.

iii. **Facility Layout:** Facility layout is the arrangement of workspaces to make it easier to access areas that frequently interact with each other.

(2) Intermediate Range Decisions

i. **Production Planning:** Production planning involves many activities, such as forecasting, managing the supply chain, tracking inventory, and scheduling jobs.

ii. **Controlling Production and Inventory:** It is the process of planning a company's production in advance and controlling the raw materials in inventory needed to produce finished goods.

iii. **Quality Planning:** Quality planning involves setting quality standards and goals, designing a quality control plan and assurance procedures, and creating a quality management plan.

(3) Short Range Decisions

i. **Order Scheduling:** It helps balance customer demands with the ability to meet those demands.

ii. **Worker Assignments:** It means the set of tasks specified for a particular role, outlining an employee's duties and responsibilities within an organisation.

iii. **Quality Control:** Quality control is a procedure to ensure that a manufactured product or service meets defined quality criteria or customer requirements.

2. Finance Function

It deals with matters related to money, both its acquisition and utilisation. It is an essential element of every activity in the business. To carry production smoothly, people are required who have to be paid salaries; equipment are required to enhance organisational productivity and inputs like raw material are required all of which require funds. Similarly, selling requires spending on advertising and sales promotion. The overall production and marketing plans are framed keeping in view the financial position of the organisation. Financial constraints lead to strict operating plans and easy availability of funds lead to liberal operating plans.

Finance managers have a dynamic role to play in making the best use of finance. They are concerned not only with raising of funds, but also with uses of funds with respect to capital investment projects. They make plans which can fit in the changing environment with respect to corporate competition, technological changes, interest rate fluctuations, tax laws changes, economic fluctuations etc. Efficient allocation of financial resources contributes to optimal growth of the economy and satisfaction of individual needs of its members.

3. Personnel Function

Personnel function is "a series of activities related to various aspects of an employee's relationship with the organisation. It is concerned with systems applied to individuals and collectivism." It helps in the management of people by establishing, maintaining, and developing systems which provide the framework of employment. These systems relate to:

i. Employee's joining the organisation—Recruitment and selection.
ii. Management of the employer-employee relationship—Reward, appraisal, development, industrial relations, grievance, and discipline.
iii. Termination of the employer-employee relationship—Retirement, resignation, and dismissal.

The emphasis, in personnel management, is on control of manpower and personnel systems. It is, therefore, a highly compartmentalised system of managing the human resource. Managers device incentive and recognition programmes for benefit of employees and recognise them for their work. This increases employees' morale, communication, and productivity along with decrease in the rate of production errors, labour absenteeism and labour turnover. This also results in phenomenal cost savings and improved management-labour relationships resulting in increased profits and goodwill of the firm.

4. Marketing Function

Most successful companies are customer-focused and heavily committed to marketing. "These companies share an absolute dedication to understanding its purpose and satisfying the needs of customers in well-defined target markets." Their goal is to sell goods and services that provide value to customers and satisfy their needs. Marketing is not confined to any department, it is an "attitude of mind, an approach to business problems that should be adopted by the whole organisation, from the chairman and chief executive down to the lowest levels."

Marketing originated from the concept that customer is the most important person for the company and that survival of every firm depends on retention of its customers in the existing markets and making new and profitable customers in the new markets. *Identification of needs of customers and their satisfaction is the focus of marketing*. Satisfying the needs of consumers is the central core of marketing. A product is considered marketable only if desired by the consumer willing to give up something of value to obtain it. "Value implies worth and relates closely to the idea of usefulness or satisfaction." Thus, firms can sell only those products which give some benefits to the consumer.

Marketing is "a social and managerial process by which individuals and groups obtain what they need and want through creating and exchanging products and value with others." *Philip Kotler*

It is an integrative process that works within the framework of controllable and non- controllable variables. While controllable variables are the product, pricing, promotion and channels of distribution (marketing mix), the non-controllable variables are the technological, social, political, cultural, legal factors etc. that affect the marketing strategies. Marketing attempts to integrate the controllable variables with the non-controllable variables through market research.

Marketing research is "the systematic gathering, recording and analysing of data about problems relating to the distribution and sale of goods." It serves the needs of the organisation by keeping top executives informed about the marketing problems and opportunities and making decisions in response to them. Marketing researchers use statistical and accounting methods in designing studies, collecting, and analysing data and using it for future use.

Questions

I. Long Answer Questions

1. What are economic and non-economic activities? Differentiate between business, profession, and employment.
2. What is business? Explain its features.
3. Business is an economic activity. Explain.
4. Explain the major objectives of Business.
5. Explain the various functions of business

II. Write short notes on:

(i) Economic and non-economic activities.

(ii) Business, profession, and employment.

(iii) Functions of business.

(iv) Finance function.

(v) Marketing function.

(vi) Production function.

(vii) Personnel function.

❑❑❑

Chapter 2

Scope of Business

2.1 INTRODUCTION

The scope of business includes activities ranging from production to distribution of goods and services through productive use of resources. This includes use of scientific know how, technological developments, effective utilisation of funds, coordinating the functional areas, creating harmonious industrial relations, effective marketing, working within regulatory framework of Government and catering to interests of external parties (consumers, suppliers shareholders etc.).

On the basis of functions, business activities can be classified as industry and commerce. While industry deals with manufacturing sector, commerce deals with the service sector Industry and commerce are further branched out in a number of activities that facilitate smooth conduct of business. The spectrum of business activities can be represented as follows:

Spectrum of Business Activities

- Industry (Manufacturing Sector)
  - Extractive (Metals and mining, Oil and Gas)
  - Genetic (Nurseries, Cattle rearing, Dairy farming
  - Construction (Building)
  - Manufacturing (Chemicals, Cement)
- Commerce (Service Sector
  - Trade
    - Internal Trade
      - Wholesale Trade
      - Retail Trade
    - International Trade
      - Export
      - Import
      - Entrepot
  - Auxiliaries to Trade
    - Banking
    - Insurance
    - Communication
    - Warehousing
    - Transportation
    - Advertising and Publicity
    - Packaging

2.2 INDUSTRY (MANUFACTURING SECTOR)

Industry produces goods for final consumption or further production. When goods are used by ultimate consumers, they are known as *consumer goods*, for example, food items, cloth, pharmaceuticals, electronics etc. When goods produced by one industry are used by another industry for further production, they are termed as *producer goods*, for example, machines, tools etc. When goods produced by one industry are used as inputs by another industry whose output is consumer goods, the goods produced by the former industry are known as *intermediate goods*, for example, industry **A** manufactures steel or copper which is the input for industry **B** which produces steel ware or copper ware, steel or copper produced by industry **A** is called *intermediate goods*.

Types of Industries

Industries can broadly be classified into three categories:

1. Primary industries
2. Secondary industries
3. Tertiary industries

1. Primary Industries

Primary industries extract and process materials from natural sources. They also rear plants and animals for reproduction. These industries are of two types:

i. ***Extractive Industries***: Extractive industries extract materials from natural sources such as land, water or air. These materials may be used as final output or inputs by other industries such as manufacturing and construction industries. Minerals, oils fishing, or quarrying are the products of extractive industries. These products may be sold in the market as such (fishing) or used by other indsutries (forest goods) to create other products. These activities are highly mechanised today.

ii. ***Genetic Industries :*** Genetic industries rear plants and animals for reproduction, breeding and multiplication. Breeding of plants in nurseries, cattle rearing, horticulture (garden cultivation), dairy farming, fish hatchery, sericulture etc. are undertaken by genetic industries.

2. Secondary Industries

Secondary industries use the products of primary industries as their inputs and convert them into outputs through construction or manufacturing operations (construction of building using stones). These industries are of two types:

i. ***Construction Industries***: Construction industries are engaged in construction of buildings, roads, dams, bridges, flyovers, railway lines etc. They pursue construction activities at fixed locations. Their products are saleable at fixed sites (immovable products) and cannot be transported to market for sale.

The outputs of manufacturing industries (iron, steel, cement, bricks etc.) and extractive industries (stones, forest products etc.) are the inputs of construction industries.

ii. ***Manufacturing Industries***: Manufacturing industries convert raw material or work-in-process into finished goods. The finished goods may be used for final consumption or further production (machines, tools and equipments). Manufacturing industries use outputs of extractive industries (oil for manufacturing petroleum products) or genetic industries (sugarcane for manufacturing sugar) as their inputs.

Manufacturing industries can be classified as follows:

a. Analytical: Analytical industries analyse the basic material (or product) and separate it into a number of other products. The basic raw material is broken into several other products. Crude oil, for example, is analysed into multiple products like kerosene, petrol, diesel etc.

b. Synthetic: Synthetic industries synthesise two or more products to manufacture a new product. Fertilisers, chemicals, medicines, cement etc. are manufactured by synthetic industries.

c. Processing: Processing industries manufacture a product by performing various processes on the basic input. The input passes through different processes to get converted into final output. Paper or textile are manufactured by processing industries. Crushing of bamboo, conversion into pulp, cleansing of pulp, making of paper, conversion into rims and cutting of paper are the processes involved in the paper manufacturing industry.

d. Assembly line: Assembly line industries assemble the final outputs of different industries and produce a new product. Automobiles, cycles, television sets, air- conditioners etc. are manufactured by assembly-line industries.

3. Tertiary Industries

Tertiary industries provide services to primary and secondary industries to help them perform the business activities smoothly. They smoothen the flow of goods from producers to consumers. They provide services like transportation, banking, warehousing etc. known as auxiliaries to trade. Tertiary industries, thus, form part of the service sector. (For details: see para 2.5).

2.3 COMMERCE (SERVICE SECTOR)

Commerce involves exchange of goods and services from producers to consumers along with wide variety of services, called auxiliaries to trade such as insurance, transportation, advertising publicity, warehousing etc. It is "the sum total of those processes which are engaged in removal of the hindrances of persons (trade), place (transport and insurance), and time (warehousing) in the exchange (banking) of commodities."

Commerce smoothens the flow of goods and services by removing the hindrances that arise in the process of exchange. The following ***hindrances*** can obstruct smooth exchange of goods and services between producers and consumers:

1. Hindrance of Person: Hindrance of person refers to locational gap between producers and buyers, who may not be located at the same place. This gap is reduced by trade where wholesalers and retailers (traders) connect the producers and consumers. Traders buy from producers and sell to consumers.

2. Hindrance of Place: Hindrance of place refers to gap between place of production and place of sale. Goods are generally produced near the sources of raw material and transported to markets for sale. Transportation system through rail, road sea, or air removes the hindrance of place. Packaging and insurance also cover the risk of pilferage or theft and create 'place utility' for goods.

3. Hindrance of Time: Hindrance of time refers to gap between the time when goods are produced and sold. Goods are produced in anticipation of demand and stored for protection against fire theft rain etc. Warehousing removes the hindrance of time. It provides facilities for storage and creates time utility for goods. While the goods are stored, insurance also covers the loss of theft and fire.

4. Hindrance of Exchange: Hindrance of exchange refers to gap arising on account of medium of exchange. When, where, and how payment for goods is to be made are the hindrances of exchange. Banking removes this hindrance as banks collect payment from customers on behalf of producers and finance customers to buy the goods.

5. Hindrance of Knowledge: Hindrance of knowledge refers to informational gap between producers and consumers. Goods cannot be sold unless they are brought to the knowledge of consumers. This hindrance can be removed by advertising, publicity and salesmanship that create awareness amongst consumers and facilitate smooth exchange of goods.

6. Hindrance of Risk: Hindrance of risk refers to the probability of an undesirable outcome arising out of natural (earthquake, flood, rains etc.) or man-made reasons (theft). Insurance removes this hindrance and helps in smooth exchange of goods.

By removing these hinderances, commerce facilitates companies to focus on their core competence, like human resource, financial planning, packaging, designing, and advertising, insurance, transportation etc. Rather than a business performing all these activities under one roof, it specialises on its specific strengths and outsources the rest to other business agencies. These agencies together frame the structure of business and facilitate national and international trade Commerce has reduced distances amongst businesses operating across the globe. On-line business transactions have accelerated the growth of contemporary business.

2.4 TRADE

"Trade in its primary meaning is the exchange of goods for goods or goods for money, in its secondary meaning, it is repeated activity in the nature of business carried on with a profit motive, the activity being manual or mercantile, as distinguished from the liberal arts or learned professions or agriculture."

Trade refers to purchase and sale of goods and services for money. Auxiliaries to trade, such as banking, insurance, transportation, warehousing etc. help in smooth conduct of trade.

1. Internal Trade

It means purchase and sale of goods within the national boundaries. The payment for goods is received in the national currency. It is also known as home trade or domestic trade. Internal trade can be:

i. ***Wholesale Trade:*** Purchase and sale of goods in bulk is known as wholesale trade. Wholesalers are the link between producers and retailers, though in some cases, they sell to ultimate consumers also. They buy goods in large quantities from producers, stock them in warehouses and sell them to retailers in smaller quantities.

ii. ***Retail Trade***: Purchase and sale of goods in smaller quantities is known as retail trade. Retailers buy goods from wholesalers and sell to consumers in smaller quantities. Retailers are the link between wholesalers and final consumers. Departmental stores, chainstores, super bazars are retail organisations. Local shops are the store retailers and hawkers, peddlers etc. are the non-store retailers.

2. International Trade

It means purchase and sale of goods across the national boundaries. Payment for goods is made in the currency of the country from where goods are bought. It is also known as foreign trade. The rules and regulations for international trade are governed by RBI (Reserve Bank of India) in the country.

International trade can take the following forms:

i. ***Export:*** Export means sale of goods across the national boundaries. It sells goods out of the Indian territory.

ii. ***Import:*** Import means purchase of goods from a foreign country into the home country. It means buying goods into the Indian territory.

iii. ***Entrepot:*** It is also known as re-export. It imports goods with a view to export them. Rather than exporting domestic products, entrepot trade exports goods which are first imported in the country and then exported to other countries.

2.5 AUXILIARIES TO TRADE

These are the additional, subsidiary, or allied services that facilitate trade. They help in smooth exchange of goods between producers and consumers by removing various obstacles that arise in the exchange of goods and services. Transportation, banking, insurance, warehousing, packaging, advertising, and publicity are the auxiliaries to trade. Some of these services are discussed below:

1. Banking

According to Banking Regulation Act, 1949, "Banking is the business of accepting for the purpose of lending or investment of deposits of money from the public repayable on demand or otherwise and withdrawable by cheque, draft, order or otherwise."

Banking helps in mobilising savings and lending for productive purposes. Businesses need large funds to buy capital assets and carry out production processes. Banks provide funds in the form of loans, overdrafts, and cash credit. They also discount bills of exchange and provide finance facilities to the holders. Additionally, they facilitate international trade, where trading parties are separated by long distances. Banks release sale documents after collecting payment from buyers, removing the hindrance of finance and exchange.

Besides mobilising individual savings, banks offer several other facilities:

- They provide lockers for the public to keep valuables (jewellery, documents, etc.).
- They control money circulation and check inflation.
- They transfer funds from one place to another and facilitate trade. Traders can make payments through cheques instead of carrying cash.
- They offer credit card facilities to customers. A credit card is a financial tool that allows its holder to pay for goods and services without using cash.

2. Insurance

Insurance is a way of pooling risks. It spreads risk over many people who face similar risks (like life, fire, theft) and who contribute money (called a premium) to a common fund. Payments are made from this fund to those who suffer a loss. Businesses operate in a risky environment with risks from fire, theft, and natural causes. To cover these risks, businesses insure their goods with insurance companies. Insurance companies pay a fixed sum if the event against which the insurance policy is taken happens. Insurance also protects businesses from the loss of goods in transit. Thus, insurance removes the hindrance of risk and promotes trade at both national and international levels.

3. Communication

Producers and consumers are often not in the same place. A business may have offices in different geographical areas. Even within the same office, information needs to be passed across various hierarchical levels. Increasing competition and technological advancements require managers to continuously interact with their superiors and subordinates. Business organisations also interact with outside parties (suppliers, creditors, customers, etc.) and maintain good relationships with their employees. All this requires an effective communication system in the organisation.

"Communication is essentially the ability of one person to make contact with another and to be understood." Globalisation has increased the need for companies to improve products, provide better customer service, and speed up operations. In the information age, advanced telephone systems, computer systems, fax machines, etc. have improved communication.

4. Warehousing

Goods produced are not immediately sold. Production precedes consumption, and until goods are sold, they need to be stored. Storage maintains balance between production and consumption. Warehousing solves the problem of storage. A warehouse is a place where goods are stored. Warehouses provide time utility by making goods available in the market when needed. This removes the hindrance of time.

5. Advertising and Publicity

Advertising and publicity make consumers aware of how products are used. Newspapers, television, radio, telemarketing (marketing through phone calls), displays, contests, and sample distribution help advertise and publicise products. This removes the hindrance of knowledge. Knowing about the availability and usefulness of products creates demand in both existing and new markets.

6. Transportation

It facilitates movement of goods from the place of production to the place of consumption (markets). This removes the hindrance of place. Transportation can be done through air (airplanes), water (ships), road (trucks), and rail (trains). It reduces geographical distance between producers and consumers and helps in the speedy exchange of goods.

7. Packaging

Goods must be properly packed for safe transportation. Packaging protects goods from damage and makes them attractive. Packaging is the box or container that holds the product. It makes the product appealing and easy to handle. Packaging differs from packing. Packaging is the container that reaches the consumer when they buy the product in a store. Packing is the external protective covering for safe transportation. For example, chocolates in a plastic box are packaging, and plastic boxes in cardboard boxes are packing.

2.6 RELATIONSHIP BETWEEN INDUSTRY AND COMMERCE

There is close relationship between industry and commerce that defines the scope of business activities. Industry makes goods available through extraction, genetic processing, manufacturing, or construction. Commerce helps distribute goods (promotes trade) with the help of its ancillary services.

Commerce is broader than trade because it includes trade and its auxiliaries. Industry and commerce are interdependent elements of business that support its survival and growth. Industry without commerce and commerce without industry are meaningless. Commerce removes various barriers to trade and helps in the smooth production and distribution of goods and services to customers. Therefore, without commerce, industry cannot produce goods, and without industry, commerce has nothing to distribute.

2.7 SERVICE SECTOR

A service is intangible and provides satisfaction to the customer. Services cannot be manufactured. They may or may not be tied to a tangible good. Repairs and maintenance are services tied to goods, but consultancy is not tied to goods.

"A service is any activity or benefit that one party can offer to another that is essentially intangible and does not result in the ownership of anything."
– *Philip Kotler*

Transferring goods from producers to consumers requires a wide variety of services like transportation, banking, insurance, warehousing etc. These services may be producer services (trade, transport, communication, financial and business services), government services (public administration, defence, and social goods) and consumer services (personal services like hotels, restaurants, beauty parlours etc.).

The service sector provides various services and plays a rapidly growing role in the modern world. The growing service sector has introduced many innovative services worldwide, branching into areas like transportation, banking, insurance, advertising, publicity, and telecommunication. A variety of services are available to meet the diverse needs of the dynamic business environment, including shareholders, suppliers, customers, creditors, and governments.

The service sector is crucial in raising and investing funds in profitable outlets, producing goods of the right quality and quantity, communicating with consumers, stocking goods in warehouses, and distributing them to consumers near their residences. It helps remove hindrances that obstruct the smooth exchange of goods and services between producers and consumers. Over the last two decades, there have been remarkable changes in the world economy, with many countries shifting from manufacturing sector to the service sector.

In 2022, global services exports reached $7.1 trillion, accounting for 7.1 per cent of world GDP and 23 per cent of total world trade in goods and services. The services sector contributes over 50 per cent to India's GDP. This sector has a unique opportunity for growth due to its labour cost advantages and a rising share of the working-age population. The service sector has the potential to significantly impact the quality of life, especially for the poor and marginalised populations.

Features of Services

1. ***Intangible:*** Services cannot be physically transferred to the buyer as they have no shape, size, colour etc. Comfort of travelling by air cannot be physically transferred. It can only be experienced.
2. ***Simultaneous Production and Consumption:*** Services are produced and consumed simultaneously. Services of a doctor or an electrician are provided only when needed. They cannot be separated from the person who provides them.
3. ***Non-storable:*** Since services are produced and consumed simultaneously, they cannot be stored to be delivered later.
4. ***Availability:*** They are provided near the place of consumers by the service provider as they cannot be transported from the place of production to the place of consumption.

5. ***Perishable:*** The idle capacity of service remains unutilised. If a room in a hotel is not rented, it would mean loss of revenue. This loss cannot be made good later.
6. ***Transfer of Ownership:*** There is no transfer of ownership with services. When a room is booked in a hotel or a ticket in an airplane, ownership is not transferred. Payment is made for the utility and satisfaction derived from the service.

Four A's of Services

1. ***Acceptability:*** Services must be acceptable to the society. Many services have emerged in the recent past which are not readily accepted by the Indian society. Professionally managed old-age homes and wedding management services are not widely acceptable as part of our social and cultural environment. However, day care centres have become acceptable and are picking up fast.
2. ***Awareness:*** It is important to be aware of the services available in society, such as maintenance for housing societies and online bill payment. Without knowing about these services, one cannot utilise them.
3. ***Affordability:*** Services are intangible and do not offer the benefit of ownership. Some people may buy a shirt for ₹1,000 but may hesitate to pay ₹1,000 to an electrician or a plumber for regular maintenance under annual maintenance contracts. Services must, therefore, be affordable and delicately priced.
4. ***Availability:*** Services must be available near the customer. Mobile van services offer useful assistance while driving on the roads, but not many people use them because they may not be readily available. It may take time for the service van to reach the customer due to long distances and traffic jams. Customers prefer services near their residence or where they need them to be acceptable.

Services Provided by the Service Sector

These services represent the auxiliaries to trade. (See para 2.5)

Reasons for Growth of Service Sector

The following reasons are accountable for the growth of service sector:

1. ***Contracting:*** Changes in the economy (specialisation with maturity of the economy) have made it convenient and efficient to contract (outsource) services that were earlier produced in the industry. Industrial firms make great use of

specialist sub-contractors to provide services that were provided by the firms themselves. Several services like legal, accounting and security are contracted out by large industrial firms. This type of outsourcing is called "splintering" of industrial activity. Splintering increases demand for services from the industrial sector and makes service sector grow faster than other sectors.

2. ***Increase in Income:*** As income rises, the demand for services increases faster than for goods. Consumer or personal services like beauty parlours, interior decoration, and health centers are the result of consumers' increasing income.
3. ***High Income Elasticity:*** Income elasticity of demand for services is greater than one. Hence, the demand for services grows faster than the demand for goods as income rises. Demand-led growth of this type results in high prices of services as well as shift of resources into the service sector.
4. ***Technological Advances:*** Service activities have stimulated because of technological advances particularly in case of IT sector (internet), telecommunication (cellular phone services) and financial services (credit cards, ATMs etc.)
5. ***Liberalisation:*** Economic reforms have played important role in accelerating the demand for services. Liberalisation has provided boost to services. In India, policy reforms were made in the 1990s like deregulation, privatisation and opening up to FDI, which promoted the growth of service sector.
6. ***Industrialisation:*** Industrialisation has increased demand for industrial infrastructures like transport, insurance, banking, communication etc. and social infrastructure like education, health care, public goods etc. This has resulted in growth of the service sector.
7. ***High Foreign Demand:*** As a result of Information Technology revolution, services can be delivered over long distances at a reasonable cost. This has increased trade in services worldwide.

   In December 2023, services exports increased by 1.3% to US$ 31.6 billion, led by software, business, and travel services. Imports decreased by 1.2%, leading to record high net earnings of US$ 16.0 billion.
8. ***Urbanisation:*** Increasing urbanisation or movement of people from rural to urban areas has increased the demand for services like communication, banking, public utilities etc.

9. ***Change in Outlook:*** People, in general, have become more concerned about their physical and mental well-being. This has increased the demand for health care and other personal services.

The Government of India acknowledges the significance of boosting growth in the services sector and offers various incentives across diverse fields like healthcare, tourism, education, engineering, communications, transportation, information technology, banking, finance, and management, among others. India's tourism and hospitality sector is projected to earn US$ 50.9 billion through visitor exports by 2028. In October 2021, the PM Ayushman Bharat Health Infrastructure Mission was initiated by the government to enhance the essential healthcare network across India over the next four to five years. India's digital economy is forecasted to hit US$ 1 trillion by 2025. By the end of 2023, the country's IT and business services sector is projected to reach US$ 14.3 billion, showing an 8% growth. The implementation of the Goods and Services Tax (GST) has established a unified national market and lowered the overall tax burden on goods. It is anticipated to cut costs in the long term due to GST input credit availability, leading to reduced service prices. India's software service industry is anticipated to reach US$ 1 trillion by 2030. (https://www.ibef.org/industry/services)

Questions

I. Long Answer Questions

1. Explain the scope of business activities.
2. What do you mean by the manufacturing sector? What kind of industries are covered under this sector?
3. What do you mean by service sector? What type of services are provided by this sector?
4. How does commerce remove various hindrances to trade?
5. Explain the meaning and reasons for growth of the service sector.
6. Define trade. Write the classification of trade.
7. Discuss different aids to trade.
8. How does "Commerce" help in improving the quality of the products and services?
9. Name various hindrances in the distribution process and how commerce helps in removing such hindrances.
10. Define industry and explain various types of industries with suitable examples.

II. Write short notes on:

(i) Extractive industries.

(ii) Banking.

(iii) Service sector.

(iv) Relationship between industry and commerce.

(v) Classification of industries.

(vi) Commerce.

(vii) Hindrance to trade.

❑❑❑

3
Chapter

Forms of Business Organisations

3.1 TYPES OF BUSINESS ENTERPRISES

To carry on the activities of trade, commerce, or manufacture, one or more than one individual come together and mutually agree to set up an enterprise and share its profits and losses in a given proportion. There may be the following types of business enterprises:

i. Private sector enterprises
ii. Public sector enterprises
iii. Joint sector enterprises

I. Private Sector Enterprises

Private sector enterprises are owned and controlled by private individuals with the main motive of earning profits, within the regulatory framework of the government. Private enterprises can be formed as:

- Sole Proprietorship
- Partnership
- Limited Liability Partnership
- Joint Hindu Family Business
- Joint Stock Company
- Co-operative Societies

II. Public Sector Enterprises

Public sector enterprises are owned and managed by the government. They may be in the form of departmental undertakings, public corporations, or government companies. Their motive is to generate employment, check concentration of power and contribute to welfare of the society. These enterprises cover a wide range of activities in heavy industries such as steel, coal, minerals, petroleum, chemicals etc.

III. Joint Sector Enterprises

Joint sector enterprises represent partnership between private and public sector. Their ownership, control and management are shared jointly by the private and the public sector. They represent effective combination of managerial expertise of the private sector and social orientation of the public sector to check concentration of economic power.

"A joint sector enterprise is intended to be a form of partnership between the private sector and the government in which state participation in capital will be not less than 26 per cent, the day-to-day management will normally be in the hands of the private sector exercised by a board of directors on which government is adequately represented."

"Joint Sector Enterprises is an industry and business which is owned, controlled, and managed jointly by private entrepreneurs and the government. Mainly, day-to-day management lies in the hands of the private entrepreneurs and the government exercises control via its representatives present on the board of directors. For example, Maruti Udyog Ltd."

3.2 FORMS OF PRIVATE SECTOR ENTERPRISES

Private sector enterprises can have different forms.

I. Non-corporate Form of Business Enterprises:

1. Sole Proprietorship
2. Hindu Undivided Family
3. Partnership

II. Corporate Form of Business Enterprises:

1. Limited Liability Partnership
2. Cooperative Society
3. Joint Stock Company

(Company form of organisation is explained in chapters 6, 7 & 8)

I. Non-Corporate Form of Business Enterprises

These enterprises do not form as corporates. Their incorporation is not necessarily governed by legal formalities. The popular forms of non-corporate business organisations are sole proprietorship, Hindu undivided family, and partnership.

1. *Sole Proprietorship*

Sole proprietorship is a form of organisation where one person manages the business. He starts the business, arranges for capital privately, undertakes the risk of success/failure of the business and provides the necessary managerial expertise.

The person who carries on sole proprietorship is known as sole proprietor. He does not have to comply with lengthy formalities. He must file Income Tax Return annually and also needs to file GST return if he is registered under GST. He should also deduct TDS and file TDS return if liable for Tax Audit. The Sole Proprietorship requires obtaining a PAN card for a proprietor, opening a bank account in the name of the business, a certificate of registration under the Shop and Establishment Act of the respective state and GST registration.

Features of Sole Proprietorship

Sole proprietorship has the following features:

1. ***Ownership:*** The business is owned by a single owner. He provides the capital and manages it alone.
2. ***Liability:*** The sole proprietor has unlimited liability. If business assets are insufficient to pay the business debts, his personal assets can be used to repay the debt.
3. ***Size:*** The sole proprietary concern is generally small.
4. ***Identity:*** Sole proprietorship and sole proprietor are the same. All assets and liabilities of the business are personal assets and liabilities of the sole proprietor.
5. ***Sole Control:*** The sole proprietor controls all the decisions with respect to products, sources from where funds will be raised etc. He is responsible for all the decisions that he takes. He may, however, appoint a manager to help in business.
6. ***Risk:*** He bears the risk of business alone. He is the sole owner of the profits and bears the losses alone.
7. ***Legal Formalities:*** There are no legal formalities in forming a sole proprietorship. In certain cases, a license is required for starting the business.

Merits of Sole Proprietorship

Sole proprietorship has the following merits:

1. ***Capital:*** Sole proprietorship can be started with limited capital. As the business is not too widespread, sole proprietor can start the business with personal resources or borrowings.
2. ***Formation:*** It is very simple to form a sole proprietary concern. There are no extensive legal formalities.
3. ***Control:*** Sole proprietor has control over business activities. He has complete authority to conduct his business. He is not answerable to anyone except himself. He enjoys complete freedom of conducting the business.
4. ***Profits:*** Sole proprietor is the sole owner of business. He is the sole beneficiary of the profits. This motivates him to increase productivity of business.
5. ***Secrecy:*** A sole proprietor can maintain complete secrecy of accounts. He need not disclose the accounts to outsiders.
6. ***Transfer of Interest:*** A sole proprietor may transfer his business to anyone he likes. There is no restriction either by law or by third persons.
7. ***Decision-making:*** Decision-making is fast as the proprietor need not obtain the consent of others for implementation of decisions.
8. ***Flexibility:*** A sole proprietor enjoys flexibility of operations. He can change from one business to another without complying with legal restrictions.
9. ***Satisfaction:*** For people who do not want to work under others, sole proprietorship is the best form of business enterprise.

Limitations of Sole Proprietorship

Sole proprietorship suffers from the following limitations:

1. ***Liability:*** The proprietor is personally liable for the business debts. His personal property can be used if business assets are insufficient to pay business liabilities. The fear of unlimited liability restrains the sole proprietor from entering into risky business.
2. ***Area of Operations:*** Sole proprietary concerns cannot operate over wide geographical locations. They have limited area of operation.
3. ***Limited Funds:*** A sole proprietor has limited funds to start the business. He can generally not arrange for funds to start a large sized enterprise or expand his business beyond a certain limit.

4. ***Limited Skills:*** In the world of specialisation, managers must be professionally qualified to run the business. They also need assistance of other specialists (marketing, finance etc.) for successful operation of business. A sole proprietor generally lacks professional managerial ability to run his business which restricts its growth and diversification.
5. ***Life:*** The sole proprietary business continues till the proprietor can successfully manage it. In the event of death, illness or insolvency of the sole proprietor, the business also comes to end.

Suitability of Sole Proprietorship

Sole proprietorship is a suitable form of organisation for people who want to start business with limited capital, do not assume high risks and have limited area of operation.

Bakeries, beauty salons, tailor shops, dry cleaners and professions like medicine, accountancy and law are generally organised as sole proprietary concerns.

2. *Hindu Undivided Family (HUF)*

Hindu undivided family comes into existence through status, not through a contract. The Hindu Law defines HUF as a family which consists of all persons descended from a common ancestor and includes their wives and unmarried daughters. Members of the family are called coparceners. The interest in the family property or business passes to three successive generations in the male line. The coparceners, thus, consist of the holder of property, his son, grandson and great grandson. The head of the family is known as 'Karta' who manages the affairs of the family. A joint Hindu family business is, thus, a business carried on by coparceners of the family. The property inherited by a Hindu from his father, grandfather or great grandfather is called the ancestral property.

The High Court held that a daughter can serve as the Karta of a HUF, as the acknowledgement of daughters as coparceners by Section 6 of the Hindu Succession Act includes all aspects of coparcener rights, including the right to become the Karta of the HUF.

Features of HUF

HUF has the following features:

1. ***Formation:*** No legal formalities are required to form an HUF. A joint Hindu family arises by operation of the Hindu Law.

2. ***Membership:*** Formal agreement between coparceners is not required to form an HUF. Membership is acquired by birth.
3. ***Management:*** The management of Hindu undivided business lies in the hands of Karta, the head of the family.
4. ***Liability:*** The liability of Karta is unlimited while that of coparceners is limited to their interest in the family property.
5. ***Number of Members:*** There is no restriction on the number of members. Membership is acquired by birth.
6. ***Secrecy:*** Secrecy is maintained by family members. The accounts need not be disclosed to public or third parties.
7. ***Continuity:*** An HUF is not affected by death, illness or insolvency of its members. It has continuous existence unless all members wish to dissolve the HUF. If Karta dies, the next senior most member becomes the Karta.

   The High Court observed that a woman can serve as the "Karta" of a Hindu Undivided Family (HUF). This upholds the 2016 judgment expanding women's inheritance rights under Section 6 of the Hindu Succession Act.
8. ***Government Interference:*** HUF is free from government interference. Control lies in the hands of Karta. He manages the family the way he wants.
9. ***Sharing of Profits:*** Profits of the business are shared by coparceners. Their share of profit keeps changing with births and deaths of members in the family.
10. ***Absence of Incentive:*** Karta bears unlimited liability for the business and controls the business alone. However, his share of profit is equal. There may not be enough incentive to work.

Merits of HUF

HUF has the following merits:

1. ***Easy to Form:*** It is easy to form and dissolve an HUF. Its formation is governed by Hindu Law and Hindu Succession Act, 1956. It can be wound up as desired by members. There are no legal formalities involved.
2. ***No Government Interference:*** There is no government interference in managing the HUF. The family members operate the business as they want.
3. ***Control:*** Control lies with the head of the family. The coparceners work with commitment and dedication under the expert guidance of Karta.

4. ***Membership:*** There are no legal formalities for acquiring membership. Membership is acquired by birth.
5. ***Secrecy:*** Secrecy is shared by the family members. There is no disclosure of accounts to outside parties.
6. ***Continuity:*** Business continues irrespective of death, illness or insolvency of any family member. The business is, therefore, more stable than sole proprietorship.
7. ***Liability:*** Except Karta, liability of members is limited to their share in the family business. Their personal assets cannot be used to pay the business debts.
8. ***Family Status:*** Business is conducted by members with loyalty, commitment and dedication. This brings name and fame to the ancestral family property.

Limitations of HUF

HUF suffers from the following limitations:

1. ***Liability of Karta:*** Karta has unlimited liability. His personal assets can be used to pay business debts. He is, thus, unlikely to take risky ventures.
2. ***Limited Capital:*** The family has access to limited funds. The share of property gets divided with every new member while capital is not contributed by them. The business continues with the ancestral property. There is, thus, limited scope for expansion.
3. ***Area of Operation:*** The area of operation is limited because of limited capital.
4. ***Restriction on Transfer:*** The business cannot be transferred to third persons unless agreed by all the family members.
5. ***Ability of Karta:*** As the business is practically managed and controlled by Karta, if the Karta is not proficient to run the business, there is risk of incurring losses. He believes more in stability than innovations and creativity.

Suitability of HUF

Particularly where joint families do not want to take independent jobs or businesses, HUF is a suitable form of organisation. It provides economic, emotional, and social security to members and also a pride of being part of the joint family business.

3. *Partnership*

On expansion of business, the sole proprietor may find it difficult to provide additional funds and managerial skills. He may prefer to convert his business into partnership. Partnership is, thus, expansion of sole proprietary business.

Two or more persons carry on business and share its profits and losses in a given ratio. They jointly contribute capital and managerial skills to run that business. The terms and conditions on which partners agree to work are contained in an agreement known as partnership deed.

Features of Partnership

Partnership firm has the following features:

1. ***Two or More Persons:*** There must be minimum two persons to form a partnership. The maximum number of people prescribed for a partnership firm is 50.
2. ***Agreement:*** Partnership comes into existence through an agreement. There is oral or written agreement amongst partners to start a business and share its profits or losses.
3. ***Profit Sharing Ratio:*** The partnership agreement is generally supported by a partnership deed. The deed specifies the ratio in which partners agree to share profits and losses of the partnership firm.
4. ***Relationship:*** Each partner is principal as well as agent of the firm. The business of partnership firm can be carried by all or any partner on behalf of others. As an agent, he can bind other partners to his acts. Each partner is, thus, bound by the acts of other partners.
5. ***Liability:*** Partners of the firm have unlimited liability. They are jointly and severally liable for debts of the firm. Their personal assets can be used to pay the firm's debts.
6. ***Formation:*** Partnership is governed by the provisions of Indian Partnership Act, 1932.
7. ***Control:*** The business is controlled by all the partners. They are jointly and severally liable for management and control of the business.
8. ***Secrecy:*** Secrecy of accounts is maintained amongst partners. Accounts need not be disclosed to outsiders.
9. ***Transfer of Interest:*** A partner can transfer interest in the business through consent of other partners.
10. ***Registration:*** Registration of the firm is not compulsory though partners may opt for registration with the Registrar of firms because of the merits of registration.

Merits of Partnership

A partnership firm has the following merits:

1. ***Easy to Form:*** It is easy to form a partnership firm. Partners can enter into agreement and form a partnership firm. The registration, though desirable, is not compulsory. It can easily be wound up as desired by partners.
2. ***Finance:*** The fund-raising capacity of partnership firm is more than that of sole proprietorship or Hindu undivided family. New partners can be admitted raising funds. It can, therefore, operate at a scale wider than sole proprietorship or HUF.
3. ***Numbers of Members:*** Only 2 members can form a partnership firm.
4. ***Secrecy:*** Accounts of the partnership firm are known only to its partners. They need not be published and disclosed to general public.
5. ***Co-operated Effort:*** Since profits are shared by partners in the ratio of their capital contribution, all partners co-operate to increase efficiency and profits of the partnership firm.
6. ***Flexible:*** It is a flexible form of organisation. Business can be easily changed. Admission and retirement of partners is also at the will of the partners. There is no legal restriction on admission or retirement except for the maximum number of partners.
7. ***Managerial Skill:*** Partnership firm has the benefits of synergy. Total contribution by partners is more than the sum of their individual contribution. The firm benefits from pooled managerial skills of the partners.
8. ***Sharing of Risk:*** Risk is shared by all the partners unlike a sole proprietor who bears the loss of business alone.

Limitations of Partnership

Partnership firm suffers from the following limitations:

1. ***Liability:*** The liability of partners is unlimited. As their personal assets can be used to pay business debts, partners prefer to do safe and secure business.
2. ***Transfer of Interest:*** A partner cannot withdraw from the partnership firm without the consent of other partners. He is not free to transfer his interest in the business.
3. ***Access to Financial Resources:*** As the maximum number of partners is restricted, they operate at small or medium scale of operations.

4. ***Stability of Tenure:*** Partnership can be dissolved on insolvency, lunacy, or death of any partner. It can be easily dissolved at the will of partners. Any of the partners can demand dissolution of the firm.
5. ***Disharmony:*** Disharmony or lack of trust and confidence amongst partners can affect operations of the partnership firm.
6. ***Public Support:*** As accounts of partnership firm are not disclosed to the public, it may lack public support.

Suitability of Partnership Firm

It is suitable for business operations that require moderate amount of capital, pooling of managerial skills and risk of unlimited liability by owners. Hotels or stationery business and professional firms such as chartered accountancy, architecture, legal and management consultancy, medicine etc. are usually organised as partnership firms.

Partnership Formation

Partnership Deed: A partnership is formed when two or more partners enter into an oral or written agreement to carry on a business and share its profits and losses in a given ratio. This agreement is generally in writing to avoid conflicts amongst partners. When this instrument is in writing, it becomes a legal document by which any right or liability can be imposed upon partners. This written agreement is known as *partnership deed.* It contains details of the firm and terms and conditions that partners have to follow. It can be altered by mutual consent of partners. The contents of this deed are not disclosed to public.

Contents of Partnership Deed: A partnership deed contains the following clauses:

1. Name of the firm.
2. Business carried on by the firm.
3. Place where business is carried on.
4. Names and addresses of partners.
5. Amount of capital contributed by each partner.
6. Interest to be paid on capital contribution.
7. Share of partners in profits of the firm (profit sharing ratio).
8. Salary or commission payable to partners.

9. Amount that can be withdrawn by partners.
10. Interest to be charged on drawings.
11. Duties, rights and obligations of partners.
12. Interest to be paid on loan given by the partner to the firm.
13. Ways of solving disputes amongst partners.
14. Provision for preparation and audit of accounts.
15. Provision for dissolution of the firm and settlement of accounts.

Registration of Partnership: A partnership firm can be registered with the Registrar of firms of the State where the firm is situated under the requirements of the Partnership Act, 1932. Though it is not compulsory for a firm to get registered, it is desirable to do so as there are many advantages of registration. A firm may get registered at the time of formation or any time during its existence.

Procedure for Registration: If partnership firm opts for registration, it follows the following procedure:

The firm shall apply for registration to the Registrar of Firms in a prescribed form along with the prescribed registration fee. The application form should contain the following particulars:

1. Name of the firm.
2. The firm's principal place of business.
3. Names of other places where the firm carries on business.
4. Date when partners are admitted to the partnership firm.
5. Names and permanent addresses of the partners.
6. Duration of the partnership firm.

The application form should be signed by all the partners. If the Registrar is satisfied with the authenticity of the form, he will register the firm. He enters the name in the register of firms. Upon doing so, the firm becomes a registered firm from the date when entry is made in the register of firms. The registrar subsequently issues a certificate of registration which is a conclusive evidence or proof of registration of the firm.

Merits of Registration: Registration has the following merits:

1. The firm can file a suit against partners in the court of law.
2. Partners can file a suit against each other in the court of law.

3. Partners can obtain information from the Registrar's office before joining the firm.
4. A partner can retire from the firm by simply informing the Registrar.

Effects of Non-registration: A firm that does not register suffers from the following limitations:

1. The firm cannot file a suit against partners.
2. It cannot file a suit against third parties for recovery of its claims.
3. Partners cannot file a suit against each other or the firm for enforcement of their claims.

Types of Partnership Firms

Partnership firms can be of the following types:

1. ***Partnership at Will:*** This partnership firm is created at the will of partners. It does not specify the period for which it is formed. Any partner can give notice that he wants to withdraw from the firm and the firm, thus, dissolves. Partnership at will is, therefore, formed when partners want to form and dissolves when the partners want to dissolve it.
2. ***Particular Partnership:*** This partnership firm is formed for a particular period or venture. When that period or venture ends, the partnership firm comes to an end.
3. ***Limited Partnership:*** With at least one or more partners with unlimited liability, rest of the partners have liability limited to the amount of capital contributed by them. Their personal assets cannot be used to pay the firm's debts. These partners cannot take part in management of the firm or act on behalf of the firm or other partners. They can, however, inspect the books of account of the firm. They can withdraw or transfer their interest any time they want with the consent of partners with unlimited liability.
4. ***General Partnership:*** The liability of every partner is unlimited except that of the minor. Share of minor partner is limited to his capital contribution. Personal assets of rest of the partners can be used to pay the firm's debts.

Types of Partners

Partners can be of the following types:

1. ***Active Partners:*** These partners contribute capital and participate in management of the firm. They are the actual partners of the firm. Their

liability is limited. Once they retire, they give public notice of the fact. Thus, they become free from liabilities of the firm.

2. ***Sleeping Partners:*** They are also known as dormant partners. They contribute capital but do not take part in management of the firm. They share profits and losses of the firm and have unlimited liability. They need not give public notice of their retirement.
3. ***Limited Partners:*** These partners have interest limited to their share in capital contribution. They share profits/losses of the firm, but do not take part in its management.
4. ***Partners in Profits Only:*** These partners share only profits of the firm but not its losses. They do not take active part in management though their liability for the firm's debts is unlimited.
5. ***Nominal Partners:*** These partners only lend their name for benefit of the firm. They neither contribute capital nor take part in management of the firm. They do not even share profits or losses of the firm, but they are liable to third parties for the firm's acts like other partners. These partners may or may not charge money from the firm for lending their name. Nominal partners can be partners by estoppel, or partners by holding out.
   (i) **Partners by Estoppel:** They represent as partners by words (spoken or written) or conduct. Since outside public believes them to be partners, they become liable to outsiders for acts of the firm. For example, X tells Y that he is partner of a firm to which Y gives a loan amount of ₹50,000. If the firm is unable to repay the loan to Y, Y can recover the same from X as partner by estoppel. X is liable for debts of the firm. He cannot refuse that he is not a partner.
   (ii) **Partners by Holding Out:** They are people who have been made to believe to the outsiders that they are partners of the firm. While this fact is being disclosed to others, they do not deny the same. A, a partner of a partnership firm, says to Y that X is partner of the firm. X hears this but does not refuse. X becomes liable for the debts of the firm. In either case (partners by estoppel or holding out), the nominal partner becomes liable for the debts if the third party proves that he acted upon the fact that nominal partner (X) is partner of the firm.
6. ***Minor as a Partner:*** A partner who is not yet 18 years of age is a minor partner. A minor partner can enter into benefits of partnership firm. He can share profits of the firm and inspect the books of account but cannot enter

into contracts on behalf of the firm, take part in management or file a case against the firm for getting his share of profits. The share of partner is limited to capital contributed by him. To the extent of his capital contribution, he has right to share the profits. On becoming major, if the partner wants to leave the partnership firm, he has to give public notice thereof. If he does not do so, he becomes active partner of the firm with effect from the initial date of joining. He can take part in management of the firm and his liability also becomes unlimited, like that of other partners.

Rights, Duties and Liabilities of Partners

The rights and obligations of partners are described in the partnership deed. In the absence of a bonafide partnership deed, provisions of the Partnership Act regarding rights and obligations apply.

Rights of a Partner

The rights of a partner are as follows:

1. Right to take part in day-to-day management of the firm.
2. Right to be consulted and heard while taking decisions regarding the business.
3. Right of access to books of account and call for the copy of the same.
4. Right to share the profits equally or as agreed upon by the partners.
5. Right to get interest on capital contributed by the partners to the firm.
6. Right to avail interest on advances paid by the partners for business purpose.
7. Right to be indemnified in respect of payments made or liabilities incurred for protecting the firm from losses.
8. Right to use partnership property exclusively for partnership business, not himself.
9. Right as agent of the firm and implied authority to bind the firm for any act done in carrying the business.
10. Right to prevent admission of new partners/expulsion of existing partners.
11. Right to continue unless and otherwise he himself ceases to become partner.
12. Right to retire with the consent of other partners and according to the terms and conditions of deed.
13. Right to sue for dissolution of the firm.

14. Right to do all such acts in the time of emergency which would protect the firm from losses.
15. The outgoing partner has a right to carry on similar business operations without the use of firm's name.

Duties of a Partner

The duties of a partner are as follows:

1. ***To carry on the business for common advantage***: Every partner is bound to carry on business of the firm for common advantage of everyone. The partner must use his knowledge and skills in the conduct of business to secure maximum benefits for the firm. He has duty to work hard and conduct business in the best and common interest of the firm.
2. ***To be just and faithful to each other:*** Every partner must be just and faithful to other partners of the firm. He must observe utmost good faith and fairness towards other partners in business activity.
3. ***To render true accounts:*** Every partner must render true and proper accounts of his co-partners. Every entry in the books must be supported by vouchers. Explanations should be provided if demanded by other partners.
4. ***To provide full information:*** Every partner must provide full information to co-partners regarding activities affecting the firm. No information should be concealed or kept secret.
5. ***To attend diligently to his duties:*** Every partner is bound to attend duties diligently and act honestly and faithfully for the business of the firm.
6. ***To work without remuneration:*** A partner is not entitled to receive any kind of remuneration for taking part in the conduct of the business, though in practice, the working partners are generally paid remuneration as per agreement, and commission in some cases.
7. ***To indemnify for loss caused by fraud or wilful neglect:*** If any loss is caused to the firm because of partner's wilful neglect or fraud against third party, such partner must indemnify the firm for the loss.
8. ***To hold and use partnership property exclusively for the firm:*** The partners must hold and use partnership property exclusively for the purpose of business and not for their personal benefit.
9. ***To account for personal profits:*** If a partner makes any personal profit from partnership transactions or use of property of the firm or business connection

with the firm or the firm's name, he must account for such profit and pay it to the firm.

10. ***Not to carry any competing business:*** A partner must not carry any business competing with business of the firm. If he does so and earns any profit, he must account for the profits and pay it to the firm.
11. ***To share losses:*** It is the duty of the partners to bear the losses of the firm. Partners share losses as per profit sharing ratio or equally when there is no agreement.
12. ***To act within authority:*** Every partner is bound to act within the scope of his authority. If he exceeds authority and the firm suffers any loss, he shall have to compensate the firm for such loss.
13. ***Duty to be liable jointly and severally:*** Every partner is jointly and individually liable to third parties for all acts of the firm while he is a partner.
14. ***Duty not to assign his interest:*** A partner cannot assign or transfer his interest to an outsider without the consent of other partners.

Liabilities of a Partner to Third Parties

The following are the liabilities of a partner to third parties:

1. ***Liability of a partner for acts of the firms:*** Every partner is jointly and severally liable for all acts of the firm done while he is a partner. The creditors of the firm can sue all the partners jointly or individually.
2. ***Liability of the firm for wrongful act of a partner:*** If any loss or injury is caused to any third party or any penalty is imposed because of wrongful act or omission of a partner, the firm is liable to the same extent as the partner. However, the partner must act in the ordinary course of business of the firm or with authority of his partners.
3. ***Liability of the firm for misutilisation by partners:*** Where a partner acting within his apparent authority receives money or property from a third party and mis-utilises it or a firm receives money or property from a third party during business and any of the partners mis-utilises such money or property, the firm is liable to make good the loss.
4. ***Liability of an incoming partner:*** An incoming partner is liable for the debts and acts of the firm from the date of his admission into the firm. However, the incoming partner may agree to be liable for debts prior to his admission. Such

agreement will not empower the prior creditor to sue the incoming partner. He will be liable only to other co-partners.

5. ***Liability of a retiring partner:*** A retiring partner is liable for the acts of the firm done before his retirement but a retiring partner may not be liable for the debts incurred before his retirement if an agreement is reached between the third parties and the remaining partners of the firm discharging retiring partner from all liabilities. After retirement, the retiring partner shall be liable unless a public notice of his retirement is given. No such notice is required in case of retirement of a sleeping or dormant partner.

II. Corporate Form of Business Enterprises

Organisations formed as corporate enterprises must comply with legal formalities for their incorporation and functioning. The popular forms of corporate organisations are:

1. Limited Liability Partnership
2. Co-operative Societies
3. Joint Stock Company

(See chapter 7)

1. *Limited Liability Partnership*

Limited Liability Partnership is governed by the Limited Partnership Act, 2008. If an LLP is not registered under the Act, it will be considered as Partnership under the Indian Partnership Act, 1932 provided other conditions under the Act are satisfied.

Limited Liability Partnership (LLP) is a corporate structure that combines the flexibility of a partnership and advantages of limited liability of a company. It is an alternative corporate business form that provides the benefits of limited liability of a company, but its members have the flexibility of organising their internal management based on a mutually arrived agreement (as in case of a partnership firm). Since LLP contains elements of both 'corporate structure' and 'partnership firm structure' it is called a hybrid between a company and a partnership. Being a flexible structure, it is useful for small and medium enterprises, in general, and for the enterprises in services sector, in particular.

Every LLP shall have at least two partners and shall also have at least two individuals as Designated Partners, one of whom shall be resident in India. The duties and obligations of Designated Partners shall be as provided in the law. It has a separate legal entity, distinct from its members.

LLP is governed by an agreement in writing which must be filed with the Registrar of companies in the prescribed form and manner along with the prescribed fees. It shall state the name of its proposed business in the incorporation document.

Features of Limited Liability Partnership

LLP has the following features:.

1. **Separate Legal Entity:** It is a body corporate, and a legal entity separate from its partners. It is liable to the full extent of its assets, but the liability of the partners is limited to their agreed contribution in the LLP.
2. **Number of Members:** It is formed by two or more persons, for carrying on a lawful business with a view to make profit. They subscribe their names to an incorporation document and file the same with the Registrar.
3. **Perpetual Succession:** LLP has a perpetual succession. Death or insolvency of a partner does not dissolve the LLP. It can be wound up by the Tribunal under circumstances as prescribed in the Act.
4. **LLP Agreement:** The mutual rights and duties of partners of an LLP amongst themselves and between the LLP and its partners are governed by an agreement between partners or between the LLP and the partners subject to provisions of the LLP Act, 2008.
5. **Designated Partners:** Every LLP shall have at least two partners and have at least two individuals as Designated Partners, one of whom shall be resident in India. The duties and obligations of Designated Partners shall be as provided in the law.
6. **Accounts**: It shall maintain annual accounts reflecting its true and fair situation. A statement of accounts and solvency shall be filed by every LLP with the Registrar every year. The accounts of LLPs shall also be audited unless any class of LLPs is exempt from this requirement by the Central Government.
7. **Investigation of Affairs:** If required, the Central Government has powers to investigate the affairs of an LLP by appointing competent Inspector for the purpose.
8. **Conversion of Specific Forms:** A firm, private company or an unlisted public company can be converted into LLP in accordance with the provisions of the Act.

With effect from the date of certificate of registration issued by the Registrar in this regard, the conversion shall become valid as specified in the LLP Act. With effect from the date of registration specified in the certificate of registration, all tangible and intangible property, assets, interests, rights, privileges, liabilities, obligations relating to the firm, or the company shall vest in the LLP. The firm or the company, shall be deemed to be dissolved and removed from the records of the Registrar of Firms or Registrar of Companies, as the case may be.

9. **Public Document:** The LLP agreement is a public document. A copy of it can be obtained from the registered office of the LLP on payment of prescribed fee.
10. **Name:** It shall have the words 'limited liability partnership' or 'LLP' as last words of its name.
11. **Provisions of Partnership Act:** The Indian Partnership Act, 1932 shall not be applicable to Limited Liability Partnerships.

Merits of LLP

LLP has the following merits:

1. ***Limited Liability***: The liability of the partner in LLP is limited to his contribution. LLP discharges its liabilities from its own assets.
2. ***Flexibility***: It is an alternative corporate business form that gives the benefits of limited liability of a company and the flexibility of partnership.
3. ***Continuity***: It continues to exist irrespective of changes in partners.
4. ***Independent Entity***: It can enter into contracts and hold property in its own name. As it is a separate legal entity, it is liable to the full extent of its assets. However, liability of the partners is limited to their agreed contribution in the LLP.
5. ***Personal Liability***: No partner is accountable for unauthorised actions of other partners. Thus, individual partners are protected from joint liability created by wrongful acts of other partners. The LLP, however, is not relieved of the liability for its other obligations as a separate entity.

Limitations of LLP

The only limitation of forming an LLP is that it cannot come out with its own IPO and raise money from the public which a company form of organisation can do.

Distinction between Company, Partnership Firm and LLP

Features	Company	Partnership firm	LLP
Registration	Compulsory registration required with the ROC. Certificate of Incorporation is conclusive evidence.	Not compulsory. Unregistered Partnership Firm will not have the ability to sue.	Compulsory registration required with the ROC
Name	Name of a public company to end with the word "limited" and a private company with the words "private limited"	No guidelines.	Name to end with "LLP" "Limited Liability Partnership"
Capital contribution	Private company should have a minimum paid up capital of ₹1 lakh and ₹5 lakhs for a public company	Not specified	Not specified
Legal entity status	Is a separate legal entity	Not a separate legal entity	Is a separate legal entity
Liability	Limited to the extent of unpaid capital.	Unlimited, can extend to the personal assets of the partners	Limited to the extent of the contribution to the LLP.
No. of shareholders / Partners	Minimum of 2. In a private company, maximum of 200 shareholders	2- 50 partners	Minimum of 2. No maximum.
Foreign Nationals as shareholder / Partner	Foreign nationals can be shareholders.	Foreign nationals cannot form partnership firm.	Foreign nationals can be partners.
Meetings	Quarterly Board of Directors meeting, annual shareholding meeting is mandatory	Not required	Not required.

Annual Return	Annual Accounts and Annual Return to be filed with ROC	No returns to be filed with the Registrar of Firms	Annual statement of accounts and solvency & Annual Return has to be filed with ROC
Audit	Compulsory, irrespective of share capital and turnover	Compulsory	Required, if the contribution is above `25 lakhs or if annual turnover is above `40 lakhs.
How do the bankers view	High creditworthiness, due to stringent compliances and disclosures required	Creditworthiness depends on goodwill and credit worthiness of the partners	Perception is higher compared to that of a partnership but lesser than a company.
Dissolution	Voluntary or by Order of National Company Law Tribunal	By agreement of the partners, insolvency or by Court Order	Voluntary or by Order of National Company Law Tribunal

2. *Co-operative Societies*

A co-operative organisation is "an association of persons, usually of limited means, who have voluntarily joined together to achieve a common economic end, through the formation of a democratically controlled business organisation, making equitable contributions to the capital required and accepting a fair share of risks and benefits of the undertaking".

*98*A cooperative society is a voluntary group of people who come together for the benefit of all members. Their main goal is to safeguard their economic interests and avoid exploitation by middlemen who are focused on making bigger profits. Co-operatives are registered under Co-operative Societies Act, 1912 or under State Cooperative Act.

Features of Co-operative Societies

Co-operative societies have the following features:

1. ***Voluntary Associations***: Co-operative societies are voluntary associations of members. People with common interests (producers or consumers) come together and bring the capital and skills. They may leave the societies any time they want.

2. ***Organisation***: The affairs of co-operatives are organised by elected members who frame policies for their activities. All members of the co-operative have one vote irrespective of the number of shares held by them. Thus, people with more financial resources cannot dictate terms for those who are financially weak.
3. ***Membership***: Anybody can join the co-operative society. There is no limit on the maximum number of members.
4. ***Capital***: The co-operatives raise funds from members by issuing shares. However, the amount raised is not sufficient to meet their financial needs. They supplement the financial resources by raising loans from Central and State Co-operative Banks. Government also provides grants to co-operative societies.
5. ***Motive***: The co-operatives work mainly for their needs and promotion of common interests. Though profit is not their goal, some profit is earned to meet their expenses and investments.
6. ***Return***: As the purpose of co-operatives is to promote interests of its members, the return to shareholders is usually low.
7. ***Distribution of Profits***: Profits of co-operatives are not wholly distributed to members as dividends. A part of profits is transferred to reserves, a part is used for the welfare of society and remaining is paid as dividends at a fixed rate. Surplus, if any, is distributed to members as bonus in proportion to the volume of business transacted by them.

   In case of consumer co-operatives, bonus is paid in proportion to purchases made by the members and in producers' co-operatives, it is paid in proportion to sales made by them.
8. ***Entity***: Co-operative store has entity distinct from their members. It can own separate property, sue, and be sued by third parties and transact business in its own name.
9. ***Control***: Co-operative stores are under the control of Co-operative Societies Act, 1912 or under the State Co-operative Societies Act.

Merits of Co-operative Societies

Co-operative societies have the following merits:

1. ***Limited Liability***: The liability of members is limited to the amount of capital contributed by them. Members are not accountable for the debts of cooperative societies.

2. ***Finance***: They do not have huge financial requirements. Capital contributed by members and reserves meet their requirements (for growth and expansion) to a large extent. If need be, they can raise loans from Central and State co-operative banks.
3. ***Sharing of Profits***: Profits are shared according to volume of business transacted by members. This motivates them to work hard to earn more.
4. ***Secrecy***: The accounts need not be disclosed to public. Secrecy is maintained amongst members.
5. ***Formation***: A minimum of 10 adult members can voluntarily form a cooperative society. Very few legal formalities are required for its registration.
6. ***Low Operating Costs***: Members operate the stores themselves. There are no middlemen in selling the goods to consumers. There are no expenses on advertising and selling. The operating cost is low resulting in low prices of goods.
7. ***Management***: These societies are managed by consumers themselves. Each member has one vote irrespective of the capital contributed by him. Policies and procedures are also framed by the consumers. This results in effective management of cooperative societies.
8. ***No Bad Debts***: Sales are made in cash. The stores, therefore, do not have the risk of bad debts.
9. ***Services***: As these societies are governed by social objectives, they check concentration of economic power in the hands of a few and develop the habit of thrift and moral values amongst the members.
10. ***Assistance by Government***: Government helps these societies by providing loans at concessional rates.
11. ***Separate Legal Entity***: As cooperative societies enjoy a status separate from their members, they are not affected by death, illness or lunacy of the members. They are stable forms of organisation.
12. ***Social Appeal***: A part of their profits is used for social cause. Another part is transferred to reserves. Remaining profits are distributed in proportion to business done by members rather than capital contributed by them. These societies, thus, have a social appeal.

Limitations of Co-operative Societies

Co-operative societies suffer from the following limitations:

1. ***Limited Capital***: As those who form these societies have limited financial strength, the societies operate at small or middle scale.
2. ***Restriction on Transfer of Interest***: Transfer of interest is restricted by law. A member who wants to withdraw has to surrender his share to the society. He cannot transfer it to the third person.
3. ***Lack of Interest***: Even though the societies work for the benefit of consumers, they often, lack interest and initiative to form cooperatives. They prefer to buy from retailers than form cooperatives.
4. ***Management***: These societies are managed by consumers who lack managerial ability to run these stores. Professionally qualified managers cannot be afforded as they expect high salaries.
5. ***Lack of Motivation***: These stores work purely on honorary basis. The efforts of members are not followed by incentives. There is, thus, lack of motivation to conduct the affairs of the societies.
6. ***Vested Interests***: As these stores work for the benefit of members and non-members (non-members can also be consumers), members may misuse funds for their personal interests. This defeats the purpose of forming these societies.
7. ***Government Regulation***: Though less than a company, these societies are bound by government rules and regulations. They must get their accounts audited and submit their reports to the Registrar.

Suitability of Co-operative Societies

These are suitable forms of organisations where people with limited financial means want to promote their economic interests. They generally buy and sell goods of general consumption such as food products, stationery items, textiles, etc.

Types of Co-operative Societies

Co-operatives can be of different types depending upon the functions they perform. Some of these are as follows:

1. ***Producers' Co-operatives:*** These co-operatives are formed to collect the inputs and sell outputs in the local markets. Profits are shared by members or reinvested for growth of the co-operatives. The cooperatives procure inputs (raw materials, tools, equipment etc.) for their members and sell outputs in

the market. They help in improving quality of the products and promote brand loyalty of the consumers.

2. ***Marketing Co-operatives*:** These co-operatives sell produce of their members at lucrative prices in the market. Small producers who generally do not have attractive bargaining capacity cannot fetch attractive prices for their products. They become members of marketing co-operatives which sell their products at good prices and provide several marketing facilities like transportation, warehousing, labelling, packaging, grading etc. Sale proceeds are distributed amongst members in proportion to their contribution in the sales pool. Elimination of middlemen and selling the goods directly to consumers fetches attractive prices and profits.
3. ***Credit Co-operatives*:** Members, who may be farmers, artisans or wage earners, with limited financial means form these co-operatives. Their capital contribution and deposits by members and outsiders comprise the financial resources of these co-operatives. The co-operatives use these resources to provide loans on easy terms to the members. Members are, thus, freed from high rates of interests by money lenders. These co-operatives promote the habit of savings amongst the members. They operate in both rural and urban areas.
4. ***Farming Co-operatives*:** These co-operatives are formed in rural areas where farmers own small pieces of land because of their division and sub-division. To enjoy economies of large-scale production, the farmers pool their farms and jointly cultivate it. Members can use modern means of agriculture, better seeds and equipment, better irrigation facilities, better fertilisers and, thus, maximise their output. The combined output is more than output of their individual land holdings.
5. ***Housing Co-operatives*:** In cities, where buying land and constructing houses is becoming costly for middle class families, housing cooperatives help in acquiring residential accommodation at reasonable prices. These cooperatives buy land or houses from the municipal authority, construct houses and provide them to the members at affordable prices. They may also provide land to members who construct houses on their own. They provide land or houses on instalments also. Housing co-operative societies build complexes with common parks, streetlights, car parking and other civic amenities. These societies are gaining wide popularity in cities these days.
6. ***Retailer Co-operatives*:** These are voluntary associations of retailers who form a buying organisation. They do central purchasing, obtain economies of large-scale purchases (trade discount) and sell the goods at prices competitive

with those of large-scale stores (departmental stores or chain stores). Profits are shared by retailers in proportion to their purchases. Non-member retailers can also purchase from these cooperatives, but they cannot share the profits earned by members retailers.

7. ***Consumer Co-operatives*:** These co-operatives are formed by consumers who make direct purchases from producers and sell them at affordable prices to the members. Profits are distributed amongst members in proportion to capital contributed by them. Surplus profits are distributed as bonus in proportion to the volume of business transacted by members, that is, in proportion to purchases made by them.

Questions

I. Long Answer Questions

1. Who is a `Sole Trader'? What are the merits and limitations of sole trader form of business?
2. What are the rights and obligations of partners?
3. Explain the merits and limitations of registration of the partnership firm.
4. Define Limited Liability Partnership. Explain its features and merits.
5. Explain the procedure for registration of a partnership firm. What are the consequences of non-registration of a firm?
6. Distinguish between partnership and Hindu undivided family types of business.
7. State the features of `Partnership' form of business organisation. Explain the consequences of registering the partnership firm.
8. Explain the features and merits of Hindu undivided family.
9. Define partnership and discuss various kinds of partners in a firm.

II. Write short notes on:

(i) Kinds of partners
(ii) Sole trading concern
(iii) Partnership deed
(iv) Sleeping partner
(v) Joint Hindu family business
(vi) Secret partner

❑❑❑

4

Chapter

Social Responsibility

"The price of greatness is responsibility". - *Winston Churchill*

4.1 CORPORATE SOCIAL RESPONSIBILITY

In contemporary socio-economic perspectives, the ongoing engagement between the organisations, society, and the environment results in a range of responsibilities, both internal and external, commonly referred to as social responsibilities. Society is increasingly expecting companies to exhibit social responsibility, recognising them as entities with resources and skills to contribute to problem-solving. Businesses, alongside the government, play a crucial role in addressing social issues. Corporate managers are evolving into transformational leaders, shifting from transactional approaches, and demonstrating a positive commitment to people and their development.

"Corporate social responsibility is basically a concept whereby companies decide voluntarily to contribute to a better society and a cleaner environment."

"Social responsibility is an organisation's obligation to benefit society in ways that transcend the primary business objective of maximising profit."

"Social responsibility refers to the obligation of an organisation to seek actions that protect and improve the welfare of society along with its own interests."

"CSR is about capacity building for sustainable livelihoods. It respects cultural differences and finds the business opportunities in building the skills of employees, the community, and the Government."

Corporate Social Responsibility (CSR) is a central concern for all companies and an integral part of their operations. It revolves around three dimensions of value creation: profit, people, and the planet. Companies actively promote CSR across their entire value-creation chain, assuming responsibility for the social, economic, and ecological consequences of their actions. They engage in dialogues with stakeholders involved in these dimensions. CSR embodies an organisation's commitment to conduct in an economically and environmentally sustainable manner while considering the interests of direct stakeholders.

Corporate social responsibility means that big companies and businesses promise to help with issues they think are important. This might mean giving money to companies that are trying to help the environment, trying to use less energy, doing charity work, speaking up for people's rights, supporting social movements, and other important things. The mission of a socially responsible organisation (SRO) is to influence the development and advocacy of socially responsible business practices. These practices benefit not only the SRO and its employees but extend to the broader community, the economy, and the global environment. SROs aim to reshape the way business is conducted, making a positive impact in both profit and not-for-profit sectors.

4.2 NATURE OF CORPORATE SOCIAL RESPONSIBILITY

1. **Perspective:** CSR encompasses a wide range of interpretations, ranging from mere legal compliance to pure philanthropy. Its benefits extend to employees, suppliers, customers, and the wider community. Adhering to laws is the baseline requirement for companies to operate legitimately. However, CSR goes beyond contractual obligations, reaching from considerations for employees and shareholders to focus on vulnerable segments of society.
2. **Healthy Social Environment**: A healthy social environment is crucial for business growth. The government's role in managing business is transitioning from "governing businesses" to the "business of governance." Businesses must uphold ethical practices everywhere they operate. Sustainable, long-term goals are attainable only in a stable, healthy environment. Challenges related to social responsibility cannot be tackled by companies alone; it requires a collaborative effort involving governments, civil society groups, development institutions, and citizens.
3. **Self-enlightenment**: Companies often accept social responsibility without external persuasion, driven by their own experiences or observations of others. To bridge the gap between intentions and actions, companies must extend their focus beyond short-term benefits and integrate CSR policies at the strategic level. The corporate sector has influence over significant resources and, thus, plays important role in influencing various aspects of social life.

4. **Profit and Service:** Companies must strike balance between profits and responsibilities to the society. Since companies are products of society, it is imperative for them to contribute to its well-being, not just capitalise on it. Nevertheless, financial stability is crucial for companies to effectively fulfil their social objectives. An economically unsustainable enterprise would be unable to meet its social goals.
5. **Goal, Not Philosophy:** Social responsibility aims to address society's expectations for an enhanced standard of living, and is not merely a business philosophy, theory, or attitude serving as a guiding principle for behaviour.
6. **Moral Responsibility:** Transitioning from responsibilities to consumers, workers, shareholders, and the community, the Gandhian concept of trusteeship asserts that companies should be answerable to the public, acting as trustees for both their wealth and people. They are obligated to work for the betterment of society, utilising corporate power for social welfare. Responsibilities extend towards shareholders, workers, consumers, the environment surrounding the company, and the State.
7. **Legal Requirements:** Social responsibilities are integral to the corporate agenda, driven in part by government actions and legislation concerning employment protection, equal opportunities, the Companies Act, consumer laws, product liability, and environmental safeguards. Legal requirements formalise specific aspects of social responsibilities, making them essential components of corporate obligations.
8. **Pervasive Activity:** Individuals at all organisational levels engage in social responsiveness, addressing various segments of society through financial and non-financial initiatives. Some social responsibilities include raising wages, establishing optimal working hours, offering pension and provident fund benefits, providing housing, health, and recreational facilities for workers and their families, and ensuring the education, health, and overall welfare of workers and their families, providing consumer satisfaction by delivering quality goods at fair prices, engaging in ethical advertising, and actively participating in environmental protection.

4.3 LEVELS OF SOCIAL RESPONSIBILITY

R. Joseph Monsen outlines a hierarchy of social responsibilities with four levels:

1. **Obey the Law**: This level involves fulfilling social responsibility by simply adhering to legal requirements.

2. **Fulfil Public Expectations**: Beyond legal compliance, this level extends to meeting public expectations, such as providing job opportunities, delivering quality goods, and controlling pollution.
3. **Anticipate Public Expectations**: Moving higher in the hierarchy, companies not only fulfil societal expectations but also anticipate future needs, devising programmes to address them.
4. **Create Public Expectations**: At the highest level, managers not only respond to existing public demands but also set standards for social responsibility, actively contributing to the betterment of society.

4.4 HISTORICAL PERSPECTIVES OF SOCIAL RESPONSIBILITY

The expectations of society from business have evolved through three phases:

1. **Profit Maximisation**: In the past, businesses primarily focused on serving the interests of owners. Social responsibility was maximising profits within legal boundaries.
2. **Trusteeship Management**: In subsequent years, the concept broadened to include other stakeholders like employees, consumers, and creditors. Social responsibility included providing good working conditions, delivering goods of the right quality and quantity, ensuring timely repayment of loans. Managers were seen as trustees of business property, holding it in trust for the welfare of society.
3. **Quality of Life Management**: In the 1960s, a broader perspective of social responsibility emerged. Business enterprises aimed not only to maximise profits but also contribute to uplifting society. The focus shifted towards enhancing the quality of life in the community.

4.5 PHILOSOPHICAL PERSPECTIVES OF SOCIAL RESPONSIBILITY

Like historical perspectives, there are three phases of philosophical perspectives of social responsibility:

1. **Traditional Philosophy:** Like profit maximisation, this perspective defines social responsibility as producing goods and services at a low cost. Economist *Milton Friedman* strongly supports this philosophy. According to him, business should efficiently use shareholders' funds to provide them a fair return on capital. The primary responsibility of business is to look after the interests of shareholders, while social problems are best addressed by the government rather than business enterprises.

2. **Stakeholder Philosophy:** Comparable to trusteeship management, this perspective broadens the scope of social responsibility to include the interests of various sections of society, such as consumers, government, labour unions, suppliers, etc. It looks after the concerns of stakeholders for the long-term survival of firms.
3. **Affirmative Philosophy:** This philosophy focuses on the broadest spectrum of social responsibility. Managers look after the mutual interests of the firm and stakeholders. They anticipate the needs of society and integrate them with the needs of the organisation. This approach emphasises a comprehensive approach to social responsibility, aiming for a harmonious balance between organisational objectives and social well-being.

4.6 PRINCIPLES OF CORPORATE SOCIAL RESPONSIBILITY

Companies adhere to the following principles of CSR:

1. **Supply Chain Responsibilities:** Social responsibilities should include all stakeholders, regardless of the nature of their relationship (formal or informal), the product or service involved, or the geographic location. This includes suppliers, contractors, alliances, etc. Companies should promote Corporate Social Responsibility practices across their entire chain of operations.
2. **Stakeholder Involvement:** Companies need to communicate with stakeholders; workers, suppliers, local population, consumers, social organisations, and public authorities, to gather feedback on the consequences of company behaviour. This helps to establish mutually agreed-upon agreements regarding company norms, values, rights, and obligations.
3. **Transparency and Reporting:** Companies should prioritise transparency regarding their policies and social conduct. Reporting involves informing stakeholders about their conduct and its impact on others through regular public reports, assessment reports, annual reports and meetings, data, and consultation processes.
4. **Independent Verification:** Companies need to internally oversee their CSR policies, report quality, and management systems. Independent organisations, not connected to the companies, should carry out this verification process, earning the complete trust of shareholders. The results of these verification procedures should be disclosed to the public in a proper and transparent manner.

4.7 ARGUMENTS FOR AND AGAINST CORPORATE SOCIAL RESPONSIBILITY (CSR)

1960s and 1970s, observed a significant shift towards social awareness. Various social concerns, such as civil rights for minorities, equal rights for women, environmental protection, workplace safety, and consumer issues, influenced the business. There was broader understanding of corporate responsibilities beyond profit, giving rise to Corporate Social Responsibility (CSR). It involved addressing social problems that organisations must actively contribute to resolving. This evolving perspective on business emphasises a commitment to ethical practices that benefit society at large. However, there are diverse opinions on the extent of social responsibility that businesses should assume.

Arguments in Favour of CSR

1. ***Protect the Interests of Stakeholders:*** Acknowledging social obligations is not just a moral stand but also a strategic move for the long-term survival of businesses. Although there may be initial costs, treating social responsibility as an investment pays off in long-term profitability. This shift in perspective recognises the significance of harmonious relationships between businesses and their stakeholders.
2. ***Avoid Government Regulation:*** Government exerts influence on organisations through regulations that prescribe their actions and limitations. Diverse agencies regulate business operations – for instance, the Central Pollution Control Board addresses environmental pollution, the Securities and Exchange Board of India safeguards investors' rights, and the Employees State Insurance Corporation promotes employee health. Non-compliance with these regulations leads to penalties for organisations.
3. ***Self-enlightenment:*** Contrary to the notion that laws dictate social responsibility, firms voluntarily embrace social responsibility. It is an inherent aspect of their operations, driven by a sense of ethical duty. Businesses take a proactive role in contributing positively to society, emphasising their independent commitment to fulfilling social expectations beyond legal requirements.
4. ***Professionalisation:*** Adapting to social expectations is integral to sustaining a positive and responsible business image. A successful business aligns its actions with prevailing social responsibilities. With increasing professionalism, managers adhere to ethical codes set by recognised bodies that binds them to social values and the broader society. The key consideration is not whether to fulfil social responsibilities but determining the extent of such responsibilities.

CASE FOR SOCIAL RESPONSIBILITY

Perception Reasons

- Business partners, suppliers and customers favour doing business with reputable organisations.
- A good image attracts potential employees, especially in competitive hiring modes.
- Government and public groups may be more accommodating or open on community impact
- issues.
- Donors and volunteers are more willing to contribute if the not-for-profit supports the same values they do.

Business Reasons

- Philanthropic programmes can open new markets.
- Strong employee support services reduce absenteeism and turnover and improve employees' productivity.
- Community involvement helps a strong corporate culture which results in innovation, higher quality and more commitment.
- Future competitiveness and success depend upon the health of the committees in which the business operates.
- Well-defined ethics programmes can protect against legal exposure, fines, and sanctions.
- Environmental management increases efficiency in materials and energy use, thus, lowering costs.
- • Monitoring social responsibility can prevent fraud and organisational wrongdoing.

Altruistic Reasons

- "It is the right thing to do."
- "We have an obligation to share our success."
- "We have a responsibility to give something back to the community."

Arguments Against CSR

1. ***Business is an Economic Activity:*** Those against social responsibility argue that businesses must focus on the economic viability of their operations. The primary responsibility for social welfare lies with the government, not businesses.
2. ***Quantify Social Benefits:*** Defining social responsibility and determining the extent of business involvement in it, along with allocating resources to uphold social values, involves subjective considerations. Deciding whose interests take precedence—whether shareholders over suppliers or vice versa—adds complexity to the concept of social responsibility.
3. ***Cost-benefit Analysis:*** In evaluating social benefit programmes, if initial costs outweigh the benefits, it underscores the need for a balanced approach to social responsibility that aligns with the overall well-being of the business and society.
4. ***Transfer of Social Costs:*** Costs associated with social programmes may pass on to consumers by increasing the prices of goods and services. Alternatively, if companies opt to maintain prices, the impact of social costs may be reflected in the form of lower wages for employees or reduced dividends for shareholders.
5. ***Sub-optimum Utilisation of Resources:*** Utilising scarce resources for social goals can be counterproductive, as it goes against the primary purpose of business. Striking a balance between social responsibility and efficient resource utilisation is crucial for sustainable business practices.

4.8 DIMENSIONS OF CSR

The dimensions of CSR deal with quality of social life. Business is responsible to the following groups:

1. Shareholders
2. Employees
3. Customers
4. Community
5. Organisations
6. Government

1. Shareholders

Shareholders invest capital in a business with specific expectations.

i. Ensure fair and regular dividends to compensate shareholders for their investment.

ii. Increase in the value of the investment, reflected in a progressively higher dividend pay-out each successive year.

iii. Safeguard the interests of equity shareholders by maintaining adequate assets to fulfil their claims in the event of winding up.

iv. Provide accurate financial information in annual reports, ensuring shareholders are informed about the security of their investment.

2. Employees

Businesses are obligated to fulfil the following responsibilities towards their employees:

i. Ensure suitable working conditions, such as adequate lighting, ventilation, and sanitation facilities, to create a healthy work environment.

ii. Provide financial benefits like pension, provident fund, medical, and recreation to meet the diverse needs of employees and enhance job satisfaction.

iii. Allow employees to participate in decision-making processes, encourage valuable and constructive contributions.

iv. Conduct training programmes to update employees' knowledge and offer incentives to boost individual productivity.

v. Acknowledge the rights of workers to form trade unions and negotiate for fair wages and working conditions.

vi. Adhere to labour laws related to wages, dispute resolution, bonus payment, gratuity, compensation, and protection of workers' rights.

vii. Provide job security to employees, promoting satisfaction and overall productivity.

3. Customers

Companies have several responsibilities to their customers:

i. Deliver goods that meet the right standards in terms of quality, price, quantity, and availability that ensures customer satisfaction and loyalty.

ii. Furnish customers with comprehensive information regarding the use and quality of goods. This enables them to make informed decision-making.

iii. Offer after-sales services such as installation, repair, and warranty to improve its corporate image.

iv. Refrain from malpractices like hoarding and black marketing and ensure a consistent and steady supply of goods.

v. Adhere to established health and safety standards to ensure the well-being of consumers.

4. Community

Businesses have responsibility to safeguard the interests of the community by addressing various aspects:

i. Adhere to pollution standards, ensuring a healthy environment for the community.
ii. Contribute funds for development of art and culture within the community.
iii. Support the government in urban and rural planning for overall well-being of the nation.
iv. Endorse health care programmes that contribute to healthier society, benefiting both workers and the organisations.
v. Provide employment opportunities to enhance the community's economic well-being.
vi. Optimally utilise the resources to maximise output while minimising costs.
vii. Conduct social programmes like career counselling sessions and knowledge enhancement workshops to contribute to community's growth.
viii. Address social issues such as untouchability, poverty, and racism.
ix. Adhere to socially acceptable codes of conduct and avoid unfair practices like hoarding, speculation, and adulteration.

5. Organisations

Companies bear responsibilities toward each other in specific ways:

i. Avoid cut-throat competition in the interest of healthy competition that promotes mutual interests of the organisations.
ii. Collaborate by sharing scarce resources for overall corporate efficiency and sustainability.

6. Government

Companies uphold responsibilities to the government in the following ways:

i. Honestly submit their returns and pay taxes enabling the government to support and promote business interests.
ii. Comply with legislative measures, including income-tax law, company law, labour laws, and other laws to support the government's regulatory framework.

iii. Enhance the nation's global standing and strengthen foreign exchange reserves, contributing to broader national goals.

4.9 SOCIAL RESPONSIVENESS AND SOCIAL AUDIT

Social responsiveness is "the development of organisational decision processes whereby managers anticipate, respond to, and manage areas of social responsibility."

Important elements of social responsiveness are:

i. Social goals need to be carefully planned and integrated into the overall planning process of a firm.

ii. Evaluate the needs of society and analyse how other companies are addressing these needs, serving as a benchmark for responsible business practices.

iii. Ensure transparency about the company's social goals, through disclosure in annual reports.

iv. Conduct cost-benefit analysis for addressing social problems and implement the most effective approach for optimal outcomes. This ensures clear understanding of the economic aspects of social responsibility.

Measurement of Social Responsiveness

As social programmes are integral to the overall planning process, their effectiveness should align with planned goals. A specific management tool that serves this purpose is social audit.

Social audit is "a systematic study and evaluation of the social, rather than the economic performance of an organisation." It involves formal analysis of the organisation's social performance that contributes to promotion of social values and identifies areas where there is need to enhance social culture.

Merits of Social Audit

1. It determines the extent to which companies have accomplished their social goals.
2. Cost-benefit analysis for social programmes helps in evaluation of their overall impact.
3. It helps companies identify potential areas where socially productive programmes can be implemented, contributing to a better society.
4. Recognised as an important tool for measuring social responsibility, social audit findings are incorporated into companies' annual reports, ensuring transparency and accountability in their social performance.

Problems in Social Audit

I. Problems faced by Social Auditor of his Own Making

Social welfare programmes extend beyond mere assessment of inputs and outputs. Social auditor needs to maintain a positive approach when evaluating these programmes. For instance, if the auditor designs a programme for food and nutrition but rejects it because it does not align with WHO specifications, he may be able to justify why targets of the programme are not achieved. This holistic approach ensures a comprehensive evaluation of social welfare programmes, emphasising their transformative impact on society.

II. Problems beyond the Control of Social Auditor

1. Social welfare programmes often address problems by examining the interconnected levels of symptoms and causes. These issues typically show at three distinct levels:
   i. **Level I:** At the first level, symptoms are identified, such as health problems. The underlying cause might be traced as absence of sanitation facilities.
   ii. **Level II:** Causes identified at the first level transform into symptoms at the second level. For instance, lack of sanitation facilities, initially a cause, becomes a symptom at this level, with the root cause being the low income of the people.
   iii. **Level III:** The causes identified at the second level become symptoms at the third level. For example, poor educational facilities may serve as a cause for low income, highlighting the interconnected nature of social problems across these three levels.
2. When focusing on a specific area like rural health, social auditors should broaden their approach to address various interconnected social issues simultaneously. For instance, while targeting rural health improvement, the auditor should also aim to enhance rural education, sanitation, drinking water, housing, nutrition, pollution, agriculture, trade, and industry. This comprehensive approach ensures a more holistic and effective strategy for overall rural upliftment.
3. Insufficient information is a challenge in evaluating social welfare programmes. Relying solely on past accounts and reports may hinder effectiveness of the audit. An effective social welfare programme should be built on internal evaluation mechanisms and contemporary statistical methodologies.

4. Assessing the impact of social programmes is not immediate. For instance, the effects of initiatives like disease immunisation or rural education take time to show results. It involves a specific gestation period before the impact can be accurately assessed. This needs long-term perspective when evaluating the success of social welfare efforts.

Questions

I. Long Answer Questions

1. Explain the meaning, nature, and scope of social responsibility.
2. What do you mean by social responsibility? State the historical and philosophical perspectives of social responsibility.
3. Discuss the arguments for and against social responsibilities of business.
4. State the stakeholders to whom business organisations are socially responsible.
5. "A tool available for measuring the firm's social responsiveness is social audit." Explain.

II. Write short notes on:

(i) Social responsibility

(ii) Social audit

III. Multiple Choice Questions

1. Social audit measures:
   (*i*) Social responsiveness
   (*ii*) Economic responsiveness
2. Focus on profit maximisation at the cost of social responsibility is:
   (*i*) Amoral management
   (*ii*) Immoral management
   (*iii*) Moral management
3. Social responsibility is not supported by:
   (*i*) Milton Friedman
   (*ii*) Keith Davis

Answers

1. (i) 2. (ii) 3. (i)

IV. Case Study

(I) Access to Healthcare: Pfizer

When disaster strikes, emergency assistance in healthcare is crucial. To aid in these circumstances, Pfizer has a three-pronged approach; product donations, grants and solutions to access.

Grants have been provided to countries such as Haiti in the aftermath of Hurricane Matthew and the global refugee crisis in Europe and the Middle East. This money is provided in cooperation with NGOs to reach as many people as possible.

During the COVID-19 pandemic, through its Global Medical Grants programme, Pfizer provided $5 million to help improve the recognition, diagnosis, treatment and management of patients. In addition, grants were made available to clinics, medical centers and hospitals to improve the management and outcome of COVID-19 patients.

Source: https://digitalmarketinginstitute.com/blog/corporate-16-brands-doing-corporate-social-responsibility-successfully

Questions

1. How important is it for a company to assume social responsibilities?
2. Pfizer has made efforts to look after which sections of society?
3. How do you relate corporate social responsibility with long-run sustainability of a company?

(II) XYZ Co. Ltd. is a socially responsible company. Its objectives, plans and policies are made keeping in mind the interests of various stakeholders. It wants to launch a new social programme but cannot afford its costs given its current profit level. The other two options are:

(i) increase in prices, or

(ii) decrease in wages.

Either of the two options is against the concept of social responsibility. The company, therefore, decides to drop the programme.

Questions

1. What course of action do you suggest for the company?
2. Can the company maintain balance between the interests of various stakeholders? If so, how?

❑❑❑

5

Chapter

Responsible Business and Ethical Conduct and Values

5.1 RESPONSIBLE BUSINESS AND ETHICAL CONDUCT

In today's rapidly evolving business landscape, the importance of responsible business practices and ethical conduct cannot be overstated. Companies are increasingly recognising that their success is not solely measured by financial performance, but also by their impact on society and the environment. This holistic approach to business is driven by commitment to ethical values, which guide decision-making and foster a culture of integrity. At the heart of responsible business is the concept of corporate social responsibility (CSR). CSR is the idea that businesses have a duty to contribute positively to society beyond their economic contributions. This includes practices such as reducing environmental footprints, engaging in fair labour practices, and contributing to community development. Companies that embrace CSR understand that their operations have far-reaching impacts and that they have a responsibility to manage these impacts in a way that benefits the society.

Ethical conduct in business involves adhering to moral principles and standards of behaviour that are considered right and just. This includes honesty, fairness, transparency, and respect for stakeholders. Ethical businesses ensure that their practices are aligned with both the letter and the spirit of the law, going beyond mere compliance to embrace ethical norms. By doing so, they build trust with customers, employees, investors, and the broader community. One of the key elements of ethical conduct is *transparency*. Transparent businesses openly share information about their operations, decisions, and performance. This fosters accountability and allows stakeholders to make informed decisions. Transparency also helps to build credibility and trust, as stakeholders can see that the business is committed to ethical practices and is not hiding any negative aspects of its operations.

Another important aspect of ethical conduct is *fairness*. Businesses must ensure that they treat all stakeholders, including employees, customers, suppliers, and the community, with fairness and respect. This means providing fair wages, safe working conditions, and opportunities for growth and development. It also means dealing fairly with customers by providing honest information about products and services and handling complaints and issues promptly and effectively. *Respect* for stakeholders is also a fundamental value in ethical business conduct. This involves recognising and valuing the contributions and interests of all parties affected by the business. It means listening to stakeholders' concerns and addressing them in a manner that is considerate and respectful. By doing so, businesses can build strong, positive relationships with their stakeholders, which can lead to long-term success.

Responsible business practices and ethical conduct provide numerous benefits.

They can enhance a company's reputation, making it more attractive to customers, investors, and potential employees. Companies known for their ethical practices are often seen as leaders in their industries, setting standards for others to follow.

Ethical businesses are better equipped to manage risks and avoid scandals that can arise from unethical behaviour.

Responsible business practices can lead to increased employee satisfaction and loyalty. When employees feel that their employer is committed to ethical values and social responsibility, they are more likely to be engaged and motivated. This can result in higher productivity and lower turnover rates, ultimately benefiting the company's bottom line.

Ethical conduct can drive innovation. Companies that prioritise ethical values are often more open to new ideas and approaches that can improve their operations and contribute to societal well-being. This can lead to the development of new products, services, and business models that address social and environmental challenges.

Thus, responsible business practices and ethical conduct are essential for long-term success in today's business environment. By embracing ethical values, companies can build trust with stakeholders, enhance their reputation, and create a positive impact on society. Businesses are better positioned to thrive in a world where the expectations for corporate behaviour are continually rising.

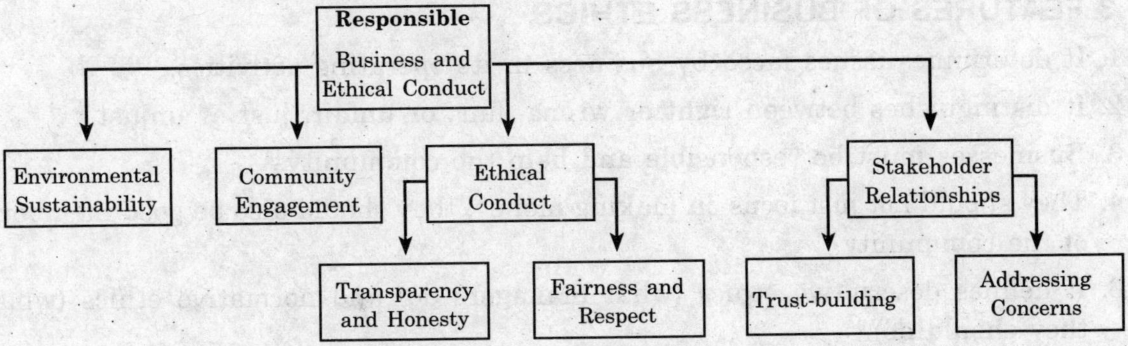

5.2 ETHICS

"Ethics deals with the study of laws of morality and rules of conduct. It determines the rightness or wrongness of actions. It defines the ultimate ends that man should admire and ideals that he wishes to seek in life. Ethics is the science of judging specifically human ends and the relationship of means to those ends. In some way, it is also the art of controlling means so that they will serve specifically human ends." — *Garret*

'Ethics' is derived from the Greek word 'ethos' which means character. It distinguishes between good and bad, right, or wrong. It is governed by a set of principles or code of conduct. Though ethics varies with individual perception, it is generally determined by socially accepted norms. There is no defined set of rules that defines what actions are right or wrong, what is virtue and what is vice, and what determines moral obligation of a person.

1. Ethical behaviour varies from person to person. What is ethical for one may be unethical for others.
2. Though depending on individual perception, ethics relates to behaviour within the confines of socially accepted norms.
3. Ethics is involved in all business and non-business activities.
4. Ethics is not related to law. What is ethical may be illegal or vice versa.

'Management Ethics' is social responsiveness of a company. It is "the discipline dealing with what is good and bad, or right and wrong, or with moral duty and obligation. It is a standard of behaviour that guides individual managers in their works". Business ethics applies ethical principles to business activities.

"It is the set of moral principles that governs the actions of an individual or a group."

5.3 FEATURES OF BUSINESS ETHICS

1. It determines issues faced by business in its operating activities.
2. It distinguishes between right or wrong, fair, or unfair, just or unjust.
3. Businesses must be responsible and help the community.
4. They should not just focus on making money; they should also be good members of the community.
6. It defines descriptive ethics (what managers do) and normative ethics (what they should do).
7. It is broader than the law. Some things may be good but against the law, or legal but not right.

5.4 NEED FOR BUSINESS ETHICS

1. Doing the right thing in business, like paying fair wages and keeping workplaces safe, helps a company last a long time. Even if some unfair things make quick money, being ethical protects a business in the long run. Meeting ethical duties is key for lasting success of business.
2. Business exists in the community and must take care of the community's interests to do things that are right for everyone.
3. Doing the right things helps the business compete with others.
4. Laws make sure that business acts ethically. They encourage businesses to do what is right.

   For instance, if customers or workers face unfair treatment, they can complain under the Consumer Protection Act or Labour Laws.

5.5 GUIDELINES FOR ETHICAL BEHAVIOUR

The following guidelines are prescribed by *James O'Toole* for ethical behaviour:

1. **Obey the Law:** Obeying legal practices conforms to ethical values.
2. **Tell the Truth:** Disclosing fair accounting results and telling the truth reflects ethical behaviour.
3. **Respect for People:** Ethics requires managers to respect people that represent all stakeholders.
4. **The Golden Rule:** The golden business principle is 'Treat others as you would want to be treated'. This will always result in ethical behaviour.

5. **Above All, Do No Harm:** Even if it is not against the law, managers should stay away from bad practices. For instance, they should avoid using chemicals that cause pollution, even if it is not illegal.
6. **Practice Participation:** Not Paternalism: Managers should include the needs of stakeholders in business decisions and let them be part of the choices.
7. **Act when you have Responsibility:** Actions must be responsibly taken for the benefit of the organisation and stakeholders.

5.6 ETHICAL ACTIVITIES

The following ethical activities are observed by managers *(Barry Posner* and *Warren Schmidt)*:

1. The foremost goal of managers is to make their organisations effective.
2. Profit maximisation and stakeholders' interests were not the central goals of the managers studied.
3. Attending to customers was seen as important.
4. Integrity was the characteristic most highly rated by managers at all levels.
5. Pressure to conform to organisational standards was seen as high.
6. Spouses are important in helping their mates grapple with ethical dilemmas.
7. Most managers seek the advice of others in handling ethical dilemmas.

5.7 TYPES OF MANAGEMENT ETHICS

Three types of management ethics or standards of conduct are as follows (Archie *B. Carroll):*

1. **Immoral Management:** Immoral management means not following ethical rules. Managers focus on making the most money, even if it means breaking the law or not caring about employees.
2. **Moral Management:** Moral management is about making the most profit while still doing what is right. Managers stick to ethical values and principles, following professional and legal rules. The guiding principle is: "Is this action, decision, or behaviour fair to us and all parties involved?"
3. **Amoral Management:** Amoral management falls between moral and immoral ethics. Managers think about ethics when necessary. There are two types of amoral management:

1. ***Intentional***: Managers purposely avoid making ethical business decisions. They think ethics are only for non-business activities.
2. ***Unintentional:*** Managers do not intentionally skip ethical practices. Sometimes, they make decisions without thinking about the moral side of things.

5.8 APPROACHES TO MANAGEMENT ETHICS

There are following approaches to management ethics:

1. **Utilitarian Approach:** Managers look at how decisions affect people. It is about the action itself, not why it is done. They balance the good and bad outcomes, and if the good is more than the bad, the action is performed. For example, managers consider pollution standards and the impact of pollution under this approach.
2. **Moral Rights Approach:** This approach focuses on the basic rights people have; the right to speak, the right to be safe, and the right to express feelings. In business, managers share information in a way that looks out for people's well-being. When reporting in annual reports, they consider the nature, timing, and truthfulness of the information.
3. **Social Justice Approach:** This believes that business actions should be fair and equal for everyone. Employees should not be treated unfairly because of their caste, religion, race, or gender. It is fine to treat people differently based on their abilities. For example, all employees with the same skills should be treated the same, but it is fair to treat efficient employees differently from inefficient ones.

5.9 DEVELOPMENT OF ETHICS

Study of ethics has developed as a science of moral reasoning in the following phases:

1. **Greek Ethics :** It advocated that ethics deals with duties of a person as a good citizen of the nation. A good or ethical man is the one who performs his duties as a good citizen. Famous advocates of this view are Socrates, Plato and Aristotle.
2. **Medieval Ethics :** This is the period when Christianity spread in Europe. It spread the thoughts that ethics is not just a part of politics (as said in the Greek philosophy). It does not deal with duties of a person. Rather, it deals with increasing inner aspect of one's morality.

3. **Modern Ethics :** This era of ethics believes in performing actions whose results bring good to us and to others.

   It deals with determining rightness of the acts. It tells about what individuals or institutions ought to do. Moral theories that advocate modern ethics deal with two components;

   (a) ***Theory of Value or Theory of Good:*** It decides about what is good or valuable, though it does not make this explicit. It focuses on properties that we want to be realised in our actions. These properties may be compliance with law of nature, human freedom, social solidarity or a combination of one or more of them.

   (b) ***Theory of the Right :*** It does not tell about which properties are valuable but tells about what individuals and institutions should do by responding to vauable properties.

   Based on the above, there are two kinds of moral theories;

- Consequentialist or teleological theories.
- Non-consequentialist or non-teleological/deontological theories.

While teleogy is the ethics of ends and consequences, deonotology is the ethics of duty and obligations.

1. **Consequentiality or Teleological Theories :** Teleological ethics deals with consequentialism. It is associated with utilitarianism, ethical egoism and other goal-based approaches to consequentialism. These theories emphasise on goals and ends in determining moral quality of conduct and character. It refers to the tightness of actions or moral values of character. It uses ends and goals to justify virtues and actions. "Teleogical theories hold that rightness or wrongness of action is always determined by its tendency to produce certain consequences which are intrinsically good or bad." They assert that right actions are those that have the best consequences. They give priority to 'good' over 'right'. According to them, all actions that maximise the good are right actions. What is good is independent of what is right.

   Teleological theories provide different views on what is good. According to egoistic theories, good is the good of the person who is acting. According to universalistic theories, good is the good of all those who are affected by an action. Utilitarianism or universalistic is the best known teleological theory. Jeremy Bentham, John Stuart Mill and Henry Sidgwick were the famous utilitarianists who asserted that actions should be judged on the basis of the amount of pleasure they produce on all those who are affected by those actions. They should bring good to all and not just those who perform those actions.

Features of Teleological Theories

Teleological theories have the following features:

1. It gives priority to what is 'good' over what is 'right'. Good is the purpose or goal of human actions. Human actions should bring greatest happiness for greatest number of people.
2. All actions that contribute to 'good' are moral actions. An action that brings happiness for the greatest number of people is a right action.
3. Results or consequences determine the rightness or wrongness of moral actions. One of the important teleological theories is that of consequentialism.

Consequentialism - Meaning

It is a theory of ethics (teleological theory) that defines rightness or wrongness of an action by the goodness or badness of its results. It states that end results of all our actions should be good. Ends should justify the means. If the result of an action is good or right for individual's long-term self-interest and also for the greatest number of people in society, that action should be considered right. Right actions are those that have good effect on our health, reputation, economic and social well-being, environment etc. and also on the well-being of others.

Consequentialism, thus, focuses on the best consequences of our actions for all concerned. It holds that what makes an action right or wrong is its consequences only. This theory became popular in the 18th century.

Forms of Consequentialism (Consequential Theories)

There are two forms of consequentialism:

(a) Theory of Ethical Egoism : In this form of consequentialism, the desired end is the long-term self-interest of the individual. It claims that while making a moral decision one should consider the long-term self-interest of the decision. Short-term self-interest, if any, should be sacrificed for the sake of long-term self-interest. If long-term self-interest can be achieved by performing an action, that action should be performed. *Thomas Hobbes* and *Ayn Rand* are associated with this thinking. The ethical egoist maintains that an action is right in as much as it maximises one's own good, and wrong in so far as it detracts from one's self-interest. As with other consequentialists, the ethical egoist believes that consequences alone make an action right or wrong, good or bad. What distinguishes the egoist from other conseqeuntialists is that the egoists measure only consequences to themselves, i.e., their own self-interest, and not to anyone else. An action is morally right if the consequences of that action are more favourable than unfavourable, only to the agent performing that action.

(b) Utilitarianism : In this from of consequentialism, the desired end is not long-term self-interest of the individual but greatest happiness to the greatest number. Any action that brings greatest happiness to the greatest number of people is a desirable action and should be performed. Advocates of this thinking are Jeremy Bentham and John Stuart Mill.

2. Deontological Theories: Deontology is a theory of ethics advocated by philosophers such as Kant, Ross and John Rawls. This theory considers actions to be right or wrong regardless of their consequences. Actions that have moral values are right, whether or not they are good. If telling lies is morally wrong, it remains wrong even if it brings happiness to some people. Actions are, thus, right or wrong depending on whether they are morally right or wrong, irrespective of their consequences. What is 'right' has priority over what is 'good'. Deontology is derived from the Greek word 'deon', which means obligation or duty It stresses on what is obligatory and what one ought to do, whether or not it is good to do so. Speaking truth may not bring good to some but, one must speak the truth as it is the moral duty of each one of us to speak the truth. There are two approaches to deontology:

(a) Act Deontology : It claims that obligation and moral duties cannot be generalised. It does not follow rules for performing specific actions. Actions are performed according to circumstances. For example, 'In this situation, I must not break my promise' is an obligation that represents act deontology.

(b) Rule Deontology : It claims that obligations and moral duties can be generalised. Moral duties or values consist of general rules and not actions according to circumstances. For example, 'we must always keep our promises' is an obligation that represents rule deontology. These values, actions or duties are fundamental and do not depend upon circumstances of particular situations. Actions are performed according to rules and not circumstances.

Kant, Ross and Rawls are the prominent deontological thinkers. *Kant* says that result and consequences should not guide our actions. Our actions should follow the moral law. If breaking a promise or telling a lie is wrong, that action is immoral. According to *Ross*, we should all follow our moral duties regardless of their consequences. One moral principle can be sacrificed only for another moral principle.

John Rawls says that fairness is prior to goodness. Fairness of society's rules is more important than consequences of their rules

Differences Between Deontological and Teleological Theories

The following table highlights the major points of difference between deontological and teleological theories:

	Deontological Theories	Teleological Theories
1.	Rightness or wrongness of an action is determined by its morality and not its consequences.	Rightness or wrongness of an action is determined by its consequences.
2.	Prominent thinkers are Kant, Ross and Rawls.	Prominent thinkers are Bentham and J.S. Mill.
3.	They give priority to 'right' over 'good'	They give priority to 'good' over 'right'.
4.	Right action may not necessarily maximise the good.	Right action is that which maximises the good.
5.	Right actions may or may not bring happiness.	Right actions bring happiness to individuals performing the action (egoist theory) or happiness to greatest number of people (utilitarianism).
6	They are the theories of ethics that deal with duty and obligation.	They are the theories of ethics that dealt with goals and end results of actions.

5.10 ETHICAL DECISION MAKING

Ethical decision-making involves the following steps:

- **Step 1 :** Define the problem PLUS
- **Step 2 :** Identify alternatives
- **Step 3 :** Evaluate the alternatives PLUS
- **Step 4 :** Make the decision
- **Step 5 :** Implement the decision
- **Step 6 :** Evaluate the decision PLUS

Until now we have been discussing a generic decision model that is followed in management training programmes. But our concern is not just decision making; it is ethical decision-making.

The ethical component of the decision-making process takes the form of a set of "filters". Their purpose is to separate the sought after elements from their environment.

At key steps in the process, the decision maker can stop and run his considerations though these filters and separate the ethical aspects from the remainder of the decisions. This ensures that the ethical issues involved in the decision can be given consideration.

In their academic form, the language for these filters is too complex and academic for most employees.

To make it easy to understand and apply these ethics filters, the word PLUS has been adapted.

- **P = Policies**

  Is it consistent with the organisation's policies, procedures and guidelines ?

- **L = Legal**

  Is it acceptable under the applicable laws and regulations ?

- **U = Universal**

  Does it conform to the universal principles values the organisation has adopted?

- **S = Self**

  Does it satisfy the manager's personal definition of right, good and fair ?

PLUS presumes effective communication with all employees so there is a common understanding of :

- The organisation's policies and procedures as they apply to the situation.
- The applicable laws and regulations.
- The agreed to set of "universal" values-in this case Empathy, Patience, Integrity. Courage.
- The individual's sense of right, fair and good arising from their personal values set.

PLUS also presumes a formal mechanism, provided by the organisation, to allow employees access to a definitive interpretation of the policies, laws and universal values when their own knowledge of these PLUS factors is insufficient for them to make the decision with a high level of confidence.

The PLUS filters work as an integral part of steps 1, 3 and 6 of the decision-making process. The decision maker applies the four PLUS filters to determine if the ethical component(s) of the decision are being satisfied.

- **Step 1 :** Define the problem (PLUS surfaces the ethical issues)

  Does the existing situation violate any of the PLUS considerations ?
- **Step 2 :** Identify available alternative solutions to the problem
- **Step 3 :** Evaluate the identified alternatives (PLUS assesses their ethical impact)

  Will the alternative 'I am considering' resolve the PLUS violations ?

  Will the alternative 'being considered' create any new PLUS considerations ?

  Are the ethical trade-offs acceptable ?
- **Step 4 :** Make the decision
- **Step 5 :** Implement the decision
- **Step 6 :** Evaluate the decision (PLUS sorts out new ethical issues)

  Are there any new PLUS considerations to be addressed ?

The user should realise that the PLUS filters do not guarantee an ethical decision. They merely ensure that the ethical components of the situation will be sorted out so that they might be considered.

While PLUS suggests a process for assessing the ethical impact of a decision, ultimately whether or not the decision meets the ethical standards of the organisation or the individual decision maker is a matter of personal responsibility. After all, ethics is about choices.

5.11 VALUES

Values are a set of principles that people cherish as stable life goals formed from life experiences. Quality of life is a product of physical, social, environmental, mental, and spiritual health and wholeness. Values enhance the quality of individual and collective life, involve personal and community discipline and sacrifice of immediate gratification needs. They refer to intrinsic worth or goodness, influence decisions, perceptions, and behaviours.

They represent a person's belief about what is right or wrong and lay standards against which individual behaviour is judged. They determine the overall personality of an individual and the organisation he is working for, shape how they interact both professionally and personally. They define who individuals are and why they choose certain jobs. For example, someone driven by achievement may pursue entrepreneurship.

"Values are global beliefs that guide actions and judgements across a variety of situations."

–Milton Rockeach

5.12 FEATURES OF VALUES

1. Human values are social and ethical norms common to all cultures, societies, and religions. They are the guiding force to take specific decisions in specific societal issues. They are, however, dynamic and change with changing times.
2. Values represent synthesis of social progress, justice, and spiritual growth. They guide actions and judgments across a variety of situations.
3. They are a set of principles that enhance the quality of individual and collective life. They are concerned with the internal development of the person, purifying mind, and heart. They cultivate love, understanding, and provide a standard of morality.
4. They are comprehensive standards rooted deep in the very conditions of human existence, refer to intrinsic worth or goodness that eliminate misery, avoid conflict, and enhance quality of life.
5. They are manifested in thoughts, speech and actions of every human being and serve the process of 'becoming' in the sense that they transform the level of consciousness to purer, higher levels.
6. The value system is formed by a hierarchy of values. It contains judgmental elements as they help people in deciding what is right or desirable. Everyone does not hold the same values.
7. They have both content and intensity attributes. Content tells which conduct is important and intensity specifies how important it is.

5.13 IMPORTANCE OF VALUES

Values are enduring beliefs about what is right or desirable. It is hard to change and guide the behaviour daily. They are crucial in management as they shape ethical conduct and provide direction, integrate human impulses and desires consistently, creating norms for behaviour. They influence judgments about what is good or bad, desirable, or undesirable. Values affect motivation, perception, attitudes, and behaviour. In organisations, they foster harmony and help achieve goals collectively. As individuals evolve, their values may shift, reflecting changing priorities like valuing family over career success. Understanding values is vital in studying organisational behaviour as they underpin attitudes and motivation.

5.14 INNATE (BASIC) VS. ACQUIRED VALUES

Values can be innate, meaning they are inherent or inborn qualities such as love, peace, and honesty, or acquired, shaped by external influences like culture and environment. Innate values are rigid and fixed, while acquired values are flexible and changeable. Innate qualities, like cognitive aptitude, tend to remain constant throughout life and can predict long-term job performance. Acquired values, such as cultural customs and habits, indicate what a candidate brings to a job when they join.

5.15 VALUES AND BELIEFS

Beliefs and values significantly influence decision-making, affecting perceptions of others and how others perceive individuals. Beliefs are convictions people hold to be true without necessarily having any evidence, shape thoughts, behaviours, and attitudes. They originate from life experiences, spiritual learnings, and culture. They are often based on what is seen, heard, read, and experienced during upbringing, with many rooted in religious or cultural backgrounds. Belief can include that all people are created equal, and everyone must be treated with equal respect, regardless of differences like gender, race, religion, age, education, or status. Conversely, some may believe that not all people are created equal.

- Beliefs are concepts, that people consider true.
- They influence attitudes and opinions.
- They are based on experiences, observations, and reflections.
- They serve as the foundation for values and behaviours.

Values are derived from the underlying beliefs. Commitment to beliefs can transform them into values. Strong beliefs can become values, but not all values become beliefs. Values dictate judgments of what is "good" or "bad" within a community, culture, or society. These values are unwritten rules that set behavioural standards in daily life. Values are socially accepted desires and goals that people learn and internalise through upbringing, education, or societal influence. They represent subjective preferences, standards, and aspirations, focusing on what is right, good, or desirable like honesty, perseverance, loyalty, faithfulness, conservation of the environment, etc. For instance, believing in the inherent goodness of people likely results in values centered around kindness and selflessness. Believing that contributing to society will make a better world corresponds with the value of creativity. Believing that friendship and connections are important corresponds with the value of loyalty.

- Values reflect ideas that people consider important.
- They shape human behaviour, communication, and interactions.

- They provide standards for competence and morality.
- They are broad principles that apply across different situations and contexts.
- They tend to be long lasting and resistant to change.

Beliefs and values are similar in the following ways:

- Both beliefs and values are influenced by the external environment.
- Both affect behaviour and shape experiences of the world.
- Both offer a shared sense of identity and community.
- Beliefs and values can change over time.

Beliefs are different from values in the following ways:

Beliefs	Values
They are assumptions about the world.	They attribute worth of the objects and behaviours.
They originate from life experiences, spiritual learnings, and culture.	They are influenced by beliefs.
They affect morals and values.	They reflect morals through behaviour, character, and personality.

5.16 TYPES OF VALUES

One of the most established surveys to assess individual values is the Rokeach Value Survey.

Rokeach divided values into two types:

1. Terminal Values 2. Instrumental Values

1. Terminal Values

Terminal values are the ultimate goals individuals strive to achieve in their lifetime. They represent the end-states of existence and signify the highest values in a person's value system. These values are shared by groups and are crucial for shaping individuals' lives. Examples include happiness, self-respect, recognition, inner harmony, prosperity, and professional excellence.

2. Instrumental Values

Instrumental values are the behaviours individuals adopt to achieve their ultimate goals, the terminal values. They represent acceptable means of achieving goals and focus on traits like honesty, sincerity, and ambition. Instrumental values reflect preferred ways individuals choose to live, guiding personal development and success. Examples include self-awareness, a comfortable life, and motivation for achievement in work-related behaviour.

Rokeach Value Survey lists 18 terminal and 18 instrumental values as given below:

Terminal Values	Instrumental Values
• A world at peace (free of war and conflict) • Family security (taking care of loved ones) • Freedom (independence, free choice) • Equality (brotherhood, equal opportunity for all) • Self-respect (self-esteem) • Happiness (contentedness) • Wisdom (a mature understanding of life) • National security (protection from attack) • True friendship (close companionship) • Salvation (saved eternal life) • A sense of accomplishment (a lasting contribution) • A world of beauty (beauty of nature and the arts) • A comfortable life (a prosperous life) • An exciting life (a stimulating active life) • Social recognition (respect, admiration) • Mature love (sexual and spiritual intimacy) • Inner harmony (freedom from inner conflict) • Pleasure (an enjoyable leisurely life)	• Cheerful (light-hearted, joyful) • Love (affectionate, tender) • Honest (sincere, truthful) • Self-control (restrained, self-discipline) • Capable (competent, effective) • Ambitious (hard-working, aspiring) • Polite (courteous, well mannered) • Imaginative (daring, creative) • Independent (self-reliant, self-sufficient) • Intellectual (intelligent, reflective) • Broad-minded (open-minded) • Logical (consistent, rational) • Courageous (standing up for your beliefs) • Obedient (dutiful, respectful) • Helpful (working for the welfare of others) • Responsible (dependable, reliable) • Clean (neat, tidy) • Forgiving (willing to pardon others)

Terminal values are the ultimate goals individuals aim to achieve in their lifetime, while instrumental values are the behaviours or modes of conduct used to attain these goals. Terminal values represent the core objectives, and the values people aspire to embody, while instrumental values are rooted in human personalities and character traits. They deal with views on acceptable means of achieving terminal values and focus more on personal traits and character.

5.17 FACTORS AFFECTING VALUES

These factors explain the sources of the value system. Factors in value formation are as follows:

1. **Institutions:** Various institutions like family, religious institution, schools, state, cultural and social institutions develop values that help in deciding what is right and wrong; whom to be rewarded for good behaviour and whom to be punished for bad behaviour.
   i. *The family* serves as the most influential force in an individual's acquisition of societal norms and values. Children absorb certain values from their family during their formative years, which they carry with them indefinitely. The methods employed by parents in nurturing, educating, and guiding their children instill values within them.
   ii. Being part of *society* exposes people to its values and different groups within it. Society shapes an individual's value system by developing basic manners and discipline through schooling, interaction with peers, friends, and teachers in educational institutions. Various other societal groups like religious, economic, and political entities to which an individual is affiliated also impact their value system.
   iii. *Religious institutions* develop strength and a set of values and traditions that shape an individual's behaviour and decision-making. Religious values help in distinguishing between right and wrong.
2. **Organisational Values:** Organisation is an important instrument in developing a value system. Values vary from organisation to organisation. Individuals prefer to work in organisations whose values system matches their value system. If their value systems do not match, they leave the organisation or adjust to the values of the organisation.
3. **Peers and Colleagues:** There is a close association of an individual with his peer group. In the process of interaction, an individual develops attitudes, beliefs, and values from his group members. He follows group norms and style of the group members.
4. **Life Experiences:** Life experiences play a crucial role in shaping an individual's values. One learns significantly from personal experiences and from the experiences of others.

5. **Cultural Factors:** Cultural factors influence an individual's values, including norms, beliefs, and behaviour patterns accepted by society or organisation. Whether someone is cooperative, friendly, or helpful, willing to take risks, save money for the future, and care for loved ones is influenced by their cultural background.
6. **Situational Factors:** Situations are unforeseen and an individual changes his values as the situation demands. For example, an individual who faces the threat of losing a job may commit unethical acts to save his job.
7. **Personal Factors:** Personal attributes such as ability, intelligence, education determine an individual's values. For example, if one is intelligent, it may result in faster understanding of values.

5.18 VALUES AND BEHAVIOUR

Values are instilled in minds from childhood. Children learn about good, bad, right, and wrong from parents, educational institutions, and social groups. These values become integral to personality as individuals mature and are passed on to future generations to foster a healthy society.

In the business world, every person whose behaviour is value-based shapes the culture of the organisation. How good an organisation is depending upon how good the people are managing it. Values in individuals develop a value-based organisation, society, nation, and the world as a whole. Values are the shared beliefs about what is good or bad, desirable, or undesirable in a culture. They are crucial for understanding attitudes and motivation in the workplace, setting standards for competence and morality, and guiding behaviour. Values strongly influence employee conduct, affecting their passion for work, team dynamics, and synergy. For instance, an employee valuing honesty, hard work, and discipline is likely to exhibit these traits and be an efficient worker and positive role model. Conflicts may arise when employees realise their colleagues do not share their values, leading to tensions, such as hard-working employees face clash with those seen as lazy or unproductive.

In an organisational setting, values affect behaviour of an individual as follows:

1. Decisions made by a person to solve problems are influenced by their value system.
2. Employee interactions, cooperation, and competition are shaped by their values.
3. An employee's adherence to ethical or unethical behaviour depends on their values.

4. Employee retention in organisations is longer when their values align with organisational values.

Values develop a sound organisation culture that promotes the image of the organisation in the society. Values in individuals develop a value-based orgnisation. Value based behaviour can be abserved in the following spheres :

1. Finance and Accounting

Values in this area cover :

- Creative accounting, earnings management, financial analysis.
- Avoid insider trading, securities fraud, forex scams.

Executive Compensation : Making excessive payments to corporate CEO's.

Bribery, Kickbacks, Facilitation Payments : While these may be in the (short-term) interests of the company and its shareholders, these practices are anti-competitive and offend against the values of society.

2. Values of Human Resource Management

The values of human resource management (HRM) cover issues arising around the employer-employee relationships, such as the rights and duties between employer and employee. These include :

- Discrimination issues included discrimination on the basic of age, gender, race, religion, disabilities, etc.
- Issues affecting the privacy of the employee, workplace observation, drug testing.
- Issues affecting the privacy of the employer, whistle-blowing (Whistle blowing means disclosing the wrong doing and misconduct of the company to the public).
- Issues relating to fairness of the employment contract and the balance of power between employer and employee.
- Occupational safety and health.

3. Sales and Marketing

Values reflected in the behaviour of marketers take care of the following :

- *Pricing :* price fixing, price discrimination, price skimming.
- *Anti-competitive Practices :* these include issues such as manipulation of loyalty and supply chains.
- *Content of Advertisements :* attack ads, sex in advertising.
- *Children and Marketing :* marketing in schools
- Black markets, grey markets.

4. Production

This area of business values and ethics deals with the duties of a company to ensure that products and production processes do not cause harm to the society. The issues that concern value based managerial behaviour cover the following :

- Not ot make defective, and inherently dangerous products and services.
- Ethical relations between the company and the environment pollution, environmental ethics.
- Ethical problems arising out of new technologies: genetically modified food, mobile phone radiation and health.
- Product testing ethics: animal rights and animal testing, use of economically disadvantaged group (such as students) as test objects.

5. Intellectual Property, Knowledge and Skills

Knowledge and skills are valuable. However, it is not known who has the greater right to an idea; the company who trained the employee or the employees themselves? The country in which the plant grew, or the company which discovered and developed the plant's medicinal potential ? This gives rise to disputes over ownership. Value based managers take care of the following.

- Patent infringement, copyright infringement, trademark infringement.
- *Misuse of the Intellectual Property System to Stifle Competition :* patent misuse, copyright misuse.
- *Employee raiding :* the practice of attracting key employees away from a competitor to take unfair advantage of their knowledge.
- The practice of employing all the talented people in a specific field, regardless of need, in order to prevent any competitors employing them.

6. International Business

Mengers' behaviour in the area of international business reflects the following values.

- Search for universal values as a basis for international commercial behaviour.
- Comparison of business ethical traditions in different countries.
- Ethical issues arising out of international business transactions, e.g. the fair trade movement; transfer pricing.
- Issues such as globalisation.

- Varying global standards, e.g. the use of child labour.
- The way in which multinationals take advantage of international differences, such as outsourcing production (e.g. clothes) and services (e.g. call centres) to low-wage countries.

Questions

I. Long Answer Questions

1. Discuss the concept and types of values. How do values shape human behaviour?
2. Explain the basic characteristics of values.
3. Explain the values which you feel is the most important in your life. Why do you think so?
4. How do values shape the human behaviour ?
5. Expalin different sources of values.
6. Expalin terminal and instrumental values of a dynamic business firm. How does value system develop in an organisation ?
7. Define ethics and explain its features ?
8. Expalin the different phases of development of ethics ?
9. Discuss the need and various determinants of business ethics ?
10. What is the need for business ethics ? Explain the approaches to management ethics.
11. Expalin the meaning and importance of values. How are values different from ethics ?

II. Write short notes on:

(i) Values and business behaviour.

(ii) Terminal and instrumental values.

(iii) Values and ethics.

(iv) Values and beliefs.

III. Multiple Choice Questions

1. To decide whether an action is wrong or right is:

   (*i*) Social responsibility (*ii*) Ethics

2. Ethics that justifies managers' actions on society at large is:

   (*i*) Utilitarian approach (*ii*) Moral rights approach

   (*iii*) Social justice approach

3. The values that are the ultimate goals individuals strive to achieve in their lifetime are:

   (i) Instrumental Values (ii) Terminal Values

Answers

1. (ii) 2. (iii) 3. (ii)

IV. Case Study

Values refer to the institutional standards of behaviour that strengthen commitment to the Vision, and guide strategy formulation and purposive action. The core values of the company are shaped around the belief that enterprises exist to serve society. In terms of this belief, profit is a means rather than an end in itself, a compensation to owners of capital linked to the effectiveness of contribution to society and the essential ingredient to sustain such enlarged societal contribution. Thus, the company has embraced an extended role of trusteeship that reaches beyond the assets reflected in the balance sheet to encompass societal assets. An unwavering commitment to integrity, ethical conduct, teamwork, and abiding concern for stakeholders are at the heart of the company's value system. The defining trait of ITC however, is its deeply 'Indian' character that aligns corporate strategy to national priorities. Such a character flows from the Indianness of its soul rather than the origin of its capital. As a premier 'Indian' enterprise, ITC consciously engages across the value chains towards maximising benefit for the Indian society. Such a combination of values determines choice of corporate strategy, orients such strategy in favour of Indian value chains wherever feasible, and engages the organisation willingly in confronting the larger societal challenges of inclusive and sustainable growth. The company's abiding commitment to society provides depth of moral content and infuses energy across the enterprise, thus elevating collective corporate effort to the mission for the ultimate benefit of all stakeholders, including the shareholders.

Questions

1. How has developing the value system in this organisation helped it in achieving its objectives?
2. What values in business management can prosper its image in the market?

❑❑❑

06

Chapter

Joint Stock Company

6.1 INTRODUCTION

Company is a corporate body, formed after it is registered under the Companies Act. It is a voluntary association of members who contribute capital divided into small units known as shares. Members who buy shares are known as shareholders and collectively, the capital contributed by them is known as share capital. Huge amount of funds can be collected as members have limited liability. In the event of losses, the maximum amount they lose is their capital contribution. A company enjoys a status, distinct from its members. It has a name of its own and can enter into contracts in its own name. It operates through its seal. A seal is company's signature. It has a perpetual life. Incoming and outgoing of members does not affect the existence of a company. It is the creation of law and can be dissolved only by law.

6.2 FEATURES OF A COMPANY

A joint stock company has the following features:

1. **Incorporated Association:** A company comes into existence through compliance with the provisions of the Companies Act. It must be registered under the Companies Act.
2. **Separate Legal Entity:** A company has entity separate from its members. It can own property in its name which cannot be singly or jointly claimed by its members. It can enter into contracts in its own name and can legally sue or be sued by third parties.
3. **Artificial Person:** Though company is a person in the eyes of law, it is only an artificial person. It cannot act like a natural person. It depends upon natural persons such as directors, managers, shareholders etc. for its functioning.

4. **Limited Liability:** The liability of members is limited to the unpaid value of shares held by them. If X holds 100 shares of ₹10 each on which ₹6 has been paid, he cannot be called upon to pay more than ₹4 per share for meeting the debts of the company. They cannot be held liable for the debts of the company. However, in case of companies limited by guarantee or unlimited companies, shareholders contribute the guaranteed amount or an amount sufficient to fully repay company's debts.
5. **Separate Property:** Company, being a separate person, can own separate property. It can use and dispose its property the way it wants. No member has any right in the company's property.
6. **Share Transferability:** Shares of a public company are freely transferable. Shareholders can transfer their shares whenever they want.
7. **Perpetual Succession:** A company continues to exist unless it is wound up. It is not affected by incoming and outgoing members. Death, insolvency or lunacy of members does not affect its existence.
8. **Common Seal:** A company works through natural human beings like directors, managers, employees etc. These individuals are not liable for the contracts of the company; therefore, they do not sign agreements in their names. A company acts through its own signature. A company's signature is its common seal.
9. **Distinction between Management and Ownership:** Company's owners are its members who contribute capital and form a voluntary association, registered under law. The affairs of the company are not conducted by the owners. The owners elect their representatives, known as directors, who look after the affairs of the company on their behalf.
10. **Capital:** Huge amount of capital can be raised by companies to expand their operations.

6.3 MERITS OF A COMPANY

Company form of organisation has the following merits:

1. **Limited Liability:** All members of the company have limited liability. They are not accountable for its debts except to the extent of unpaid value on shares. In case of companies limited by guarantee, members are liable to contribute the guaranteed amount. Only unlimited companies have members with unlimited liability. Limited liability attracts people to invest in the share capital.
2. **Capital Resources:** A company can gather large amounts of capital. Its capital is divided into shares of nominal value. People with limited money can buy

shares and contribute to the company's capital. This ability to raise capital allows the company to undertake large projects, grow, and diversify into new areas.

3. **Perpetual Succession:** A company's entity is separate and distinct from its members. It is not affected by members joining or leaving. Therefore, it is a stable form of organisation and continues until it winds up its affairs.
4. **Area of Operations:** Company can have wide area of operations because of its large size, perpetual succession and financial strength.
5. **Transferability of Shares:** Members can freely transfer shares to others through stock market operations. There is no legal restriction on transfer of shares.
6. **Management:** A company's ownership is separate from its management. With large-scale operations, its managers are professionally qualified to make quick and efficient decisions in a dynamic environment. This ensures optimal use of resources.
7. **Public Confidence:** A company's accounts are audited and disclosed in the annual reports. The public can see the financial position (Profit and Loss Account and Balance Sheet) and make investment decisions based on its financial strength. This raises public confidence and helps the company enter deeper into the market.
8. **Democratic Management:** Management is in the hands of directors elected by the shareholders. These directors have rights, duties, and powers given by the Companies Act. They work in the interest of shareholders and other stakeholders.
9. **Social Responsibilities:** As large organisations with substantial financial resources, they spend part of their funds on social welfare. They donate to educational and charitable institutions, and run counselling and healthcare programs, among other activities.

6.4 LIMITATIONS OF A COMPANY

Company form of organisation suffers from the following limitations:

1. **Formation:** Forming a company requires a lot of time and money. Legal steps, such as preparing documents (memorandum and articles of association) and filing them with the Registrar, must be followed. The process is both lengthy and expensive.

2. **Government Interference:** There is too much government interference in running a company. Its formation, daily operations, and winding up are controlled by rules in the Companies Act. The company's accounts must be audited and disclosed in the annual reports.
3. **Secrecy:** As accounts have to be disclosed to the shareholders, secrecy of accounts cannot be maintained.
4. **Delayed Decisions:** Decisions taken by directors, are approved by top executives and communicated to organisational members. This involves lot of time.
5. **Lack of Interest:** Management is vested in the hands of directors. Directors are not owners of the company. They are not personally involved in management of the company.
6. **Oligarchic Management:** Shareholders, as owners of the company, receive meeting notices but often do not attend. Even when they do attend, they usually know little about the company's affairs and remain silent. As a result, a few directors control the management and may make decisions that benefit themselves more than the shareholders. Oligarchy means rule by a few.
7. **Speculation:** There is enough opportunity for share price speculation. Directors have inside knowledge about the company's operations. They can use this information for personal gain by speculating in shares (insider trading). They can buy large quantities of shares when they expect prices to rise and sell them when they expect prices to fall. This harms innocent shareholders. Shareholders lose trust in companies whose shares are manipulated using insider information. They may sell their shares, reducing the market value. This can lead to a financial crisis for the company.

INSIDER TRADING

Insider trading refers to the use of significant facts that have not yet been made public and are likely to affect the prices of company's securities in the stock market. It can be done by using one's official position in a company for personal gains. It is a concept where a person has privilege to obtain company's internal information and uses it for his/her personal advantage. It may include information relating to policies, future, instances of decisions having financial implications or stock price sensitive information. Its main motive is to gain more personally.

8. **Conflicting Interests:** A company interacts with many groups, including shareholders, directors, creditors, workers, suppliers, and the government. Inside the company, there are various departments such as production, personnel,

finance, and marketing. Coordinating the different interests of these groups and departments can be challenging.

6.5 SUITABILITY OF COMPANY FORM OF ORGANISATION

A company is well-suited for large-scale activities spread across wide geographical areas. It typically undertakes projects needing substantial capital and offering high returns. Companies engage in production and manufacturing activities such as fertilisers, chemicals, steel, pharmaceuticals, as well as construction projects like dams, roads, and bridges.

6.6 CODE OF BUSINESS ETHICS

Code of business ethics is essential for a company shaping behaviour, decisions, and a culture of integrity. It not only helps solve ethical issues but also emphasises the organisation's commitment to responsible and sustainable business practices.

Code of business ethics is a practical tool to set the values, principles, and standards that guide the behaviour of employees, management, and other stakeholders in the organisation. It is a formal statement showing the organisation's commitment to ethical conduct and social responsibility. This usually covers codes for professional conduct, handling conflicts of interest, rules for confidential activities, and expectations for legal and regulatory compliance.

Code of business ethics is more than a document. It gives business the ability to work in modern commercial environment with integrity and equitability and ensures sustainable success and benefits to society. The commitment to ethical principles and their application at every level of the organisation brings trust, loyalty, and long-term prosperity.

Principles of Business Ethics

1. ***Integrity and Honesty***: Truthfulness and transparency are vital in all business dealings. Integrity ensures that an organisation consistently sticks to its values, which helps build trust and authenticity with its stakeholders.
2. ***Accountability***: Taking responsibility for one's actions and their effects on the organisation and society is crucial. Accountability empowers workers to act ethically and be responsible for their decisions, leading to a culture of ethical behaviour.
3. ***Respect***: Valuing and respecting the rights and dignity of all individuals is important. Respect fosters an inclusive work environment where every person feels like an integral part of the team.

4. ***Fairness***: Ensuring equal treatment and opportunities for all stakeholders is essential. It means carrying out impartial decisions without bias or favouritism, and ensuring all business practices are just and fair to everyone involved.
5. ***Compliance with Laws and Regulations***: Operating within both legal requirements and the organisation's internal policies is crucial. Compliance ensures that the organisation avoids legal risks and provides assurance that its operations are lawful.
6. ***Confidentiality***: Protecting sensitive data and maintaining its privacy is crucial. If not upheld, trust can be damaged, organisational information may be leaked, and stakeholders' personal data could be compromised.

Components of Business Code of Ethics

1. ***Mission and Vision Statement :*** This affirms what the organisation stands for and its future goals. It sets the "why" for the ethical code by relating it to the overall organisational mission and vision.
2. ***Core Values***: Core values reflect the main principles that shape a company's culture and ethics. These fundamental beliefs guide behaviour and decision-making within the organisation and include principles like honesty, respect, teamwork, and innovation. This creates a strong, positive work environment and ensures everyone works towards the same objectives.
3. ***Behavioural Standards***: Clear examples of acceptable and unacceptable behaviour ensure employees know what actions align with company standards, making it easier for them to meet expectations and maintain a positive work environment. For example, treating colleagues with respect is acceptable, while harassment is not.
4. ***Compliance and Reporting***: Clearly outlining how to report breaches of ethics and ensure compliance is crucial. Active compliance and reporting mechanisms ensure that noncompliance and unethical behaviour are detected and corrected quickly. This maintains a trustworthy and ethical workplace.
5. ***Training and Communication***: Periodic training and effective communication assure that that the code and its meaning are known at every level of employees. It continuously updates the employees in case changes are made in the code.
6. ***Enforcement and Disciplinary Measures***: An enforcement and disciplinary policy ensure that all breaches are treated explicitly, fairly, and consistently. It outlines what will happen in case the code is breached.

Benefits of Code of Business Ethics

1. ***Reputation of Management***: It builds up the organisation's image through commitment to ethical practices. An organisation that has good ethical reputation usually attracts customers, investors, and top-level talent, thus, becoming successful in the long run.
2. ***Risk Mitigation***: It reduces the exposure to legal issues and financial penalties related to wrongdoing.
3. ***Employee Morale***: This creates a conducive work environment in which employees are respected and valued. High morale gives more productivity and lesser turnover, and the labour force stays motivated.
4. ***Customer Trust***: It builds trust among customers and other stakeholders, thus, building long-term business relationships. It is important for brand loyalty and retention of customers.
5. ***Operational Efficiency***: It encourages consistency and clarity in the processes of decision-making. Clear ethical guidelines help in streamlining operations by prescribing a framework of quick and confident ethical decisions.

Applying the Business Code of Ethics

1. ***Leadership Commitment***: Top leadership has to vocally commit and demonstrate ethics. Their commitment ensures proper tone at the top, which is taken by all others, across the hierarchy, with due seriousness toward ethics.
2. ***Employee Engagement***: It is important to engage employees in developing and periodically reviewing the code. Engaged employees are more likely to follow a pre-set code when they have a sense of ownership and participation in its setting.
3. ***Regular Training***: Through training at regular intervals, the employees will remain continuously informed of all the codes and be equipped to face ethics challenges.
4. ***Monitoring and Evaluation***: Developing mechanisms for monitoring compliance and evaluating the effectiveness of the code help in periodical assessments that can identify deficiencies in a system for redress and ensure that the code remains relevant and effective.
5. ***Open Communication Channels***: Open channels of communication and frequent feedback about ethical concerns help develop a transparent culture where employees feel secure when reporting any kind of unethical behaviour, without any fear of retaliation.

- The employees of Google adhere to the Code of Conduct, which ensures that they keep Google honest, while making sure that they will not abuse their users or the community's trust.
- Google motivates its employees to stay away from situations where the personal interest can conflict with the interests of the company.
- Each employee is to behave in a way that reflects credit upon the Company.
- Keep confidential Google's confidential information and not reveal it without authorised permission.
- Employees must comply with all laws.
- Company resources should be used responsibly by the employees and only for purposes authorised during business.
- Raise concerns about suspected unethical behaviour or breaches of the Code through normal established reporting channels.

6.7 TYPES OF COMPANIES

Companies can be classified as follows:

I. Classification on the basis of Incorporation

1. Chartered companies
2. Statutory companies
3. Registered companies

II. Classification on the basis of Liability

1. Companies limited by shares
2. Companies limited by guarantee
3. Unlimited companies

III. Classification on the basis of Control

1. Holding companies
2. Subsidiary companies

IV. Classification on the basis of Ownership

1. Government companies
2. Non-government companies
3. Foreign companies

V. Classification on the basis of Number of Members

1. Private companies
2. Public companies

I. Classification on the basis of Incorporation

On the basis of incorporation, companies can be classified as follows:

1. ***Chartered Companies*:** A company formed under charter of the country is known as chartered company. The rules and regulations governing such companies are given in the charter and not in the Companies Act. Such companies do not exist in India.
2. ***Statutory Companies*:** Statutory companies are governed by a special Act under which they are formed, like Unit Trust of India is formed under Unit Trust of India Act and Life Insurance Corporation of India is formed under Life Insurance Corporation Act. Provisions of Companies Act apply to these companies provided they are not inconsistent with the provisions of the Act under which they are formed.
3. ***Registered Companies*:** A company which is registered under the Companies Act is known as a registered company. Rules regarding its formation, day-to-day operations and winding up are governed by the Companies Act. Reliance Industries, Jaypee Industries, etc. are incorporated as registered companies. Registered companies can be public or private companies.

II. Classification on the Basis of Liability

On the basis of liability, companies can be classified as follows:

1. ***Companies Limited by Shares*:** These are the companies whose shareholders cannot be called upon to pay anything more than unpaid amount on shares held by them; either during life of the company or at the time of its winding up.

   For example, X shareholder holds 100 shares of face value of ₹10 each on which he has paid up ₹7. The company cannot call upon to pay anything more than ₹300 (100 × 3) if assets fall short of its liability.
2. ***Companies Limited by Guarantee*:** Members guarantee to contribute a specified sum towards the assets in the event of its winding up. The amount

that each member guarantees to contribute is specified in the memorandum of association.

A company limited by guarantee may be with or without share capital. In case of a company limited by guarantee with share capital, shareholders are liable to contribute the unpaid amount on shares held by them anytime the company asks them to pay and the guaranteed amount during winding up.

3. ***Unlimited Companies***: In these companies, shareholders have no limit on their liability. Their personal assets can be used to pay the debts. Company being a separate legal entity, such claims cannot be made by creditors directly on shareholders. The claim can be made by official liquidator at the time of winding up.

   Unlimited companies may be with or without share capital. If they are with capital, the amount of share capital with which a company is to be registered is specified in its Articles of Association. It also states the number of members with which the company is registered.

III. Classification on the Basis of Control

On the basis of control, companies can be classified as follows:

1. ***Holding Companies***: A holding company is the one that
   - (i) controls the composition of Board of Directors of another company,
   - (ii) holds more than 50% of nominal value of equity share capital of another company,
   - (iii) is a holding company of another company which is holding company of another company. For example, if company A is holding company of company B which is a holding company of company C, A becomes holding company of C company also.
2. ***Subsidiary Companies***: A subsidiary company is the one whose
   - (i) board of directors is controlled by another company (it means that holding company has power to appoint or remove all or majority of directors of the subsidiary company).

(ii) More than 50% of the nominal equity capital is held by another company and who is subsidiary of a company which itself is a subsidiary of another company. If company C is a subsidiary of company B which is a subsidiary of company A, company C is also a subsidiary of company A.

IV. Classification on the Basis of Ownership

On the basis of ownership, companies can be classified as follows:

1. ***Government Companies***: These are the companies in which not less than 51% of the paid-up share capital is held by the Central Government, or State Government or Governments, or partly by Central Government and partly by one or more State Governments. A subsidiary of a government company is also a government company.
2. ***Non-Government Companies***: Companies which are not government companies are non-government companies.
3. ***Foreign Companies***: These companies are incorporated outside India but have a place of business in India. Maintaining an office, a store house, godown or other premises where business is conducted in India amounts to having a place of business in India.

V. Classification on the Basis of Number of Members

On the basis of number of members, companies can be classified as follows:

1. ***Private Companies***: A private company has a minimum paid up capital of one lakh rupees or such higher paid up capital as may be prescribed and that by its articles—
   (i) restricts the right to transfer its share, if any;
   (ii) limits the number of members to 200; not including persons who are or were in the employment of the company;
   (iii) prohibits any invitation to public to subscribe for any shares in or debentures of the company; and
   (iv) prohibits any invitation or acceptance of deposits from persons other than members, directors or their relatives.
2. ***Public Companies***: A company which is not a private company is a public company. Rules do not prescribe any minimum paid-up capital. It is also a

private company which is a subsidiary of a company that is not a private company, that is, a private company which is a subsidiary of a public company is a public company.

Private and a Public Company

	Features	Private Company	Public Company
1.	Minimum number of members	2	7
2.	Maximum number of members	200	No limit
3.	Shares transferability	Shares cannot be transferred.	Shares are freely transferable
4.	Prospectus	Cannot issue a prospectus.	It can invite public to subscribe for shares or debentures through prospectus.
5.	Minimum number of directors	2	3
6.	Maximum number of directors	15 but can be raised by special resolution passed by shareholders	15 but can be raised by special resolution passed by shareholders
7.	Retirement of directors	Directors do not retire by rotation.	2/3rd of directors are rotational out of which out of which 1/3rd must retire by rotation at each annual general meeting.
8.	Quorum	2 unless otherwise provided by the articles of association.	5 if number of members on the date of meeting is less than equal to 1,000. 15 if number of members on the date of meeting is between 1,000 and 5,000. 30 if number of members on the date of meeting is more than 5,000.
9.	Managerial remuneration	No restriction on managerial remuneration.	Total managerial remuneration cannot exceed 11% of the net profits

10.	Public deposits	It cannot accept deposits from public. Deposits can be accepted from shareholders, directors and their relatives.	It can accept deposits from the public.
15.	Name	Name must end with the word 'Pvt.'	Name must end with the word 'Ltd.'in case of company with limited liability and 'unlimited' 'in case of company with unlimited liability.

Privileges of a Private Company

A private company (provided it is not a subsidiary of public company) does not involve public money. It is exempt from public accountability. It, therefore, enjoys several privileges and exemptions from provisions of the Companies Act. Some of the privileges are as follows:

1. It can start operations with only 2 members as against 7 in case of a public company.
2. It can allot shares without issuing a prospectus.
3. In case of further issue of capital, it need not first offer shares to existing shareholders.
4. It has two directors as against three in case of a public company.
5. Quorum for general meeting is two as against five in case of public company.
6. It can provide financial assistance to anyone to subscribe to its shares or shares of its holding company.
7. Its managerial remuneration can exceed 11% of net profits.
8. Its profit and loss account is filed with the Registrar but is not made open to public. Therefore, the public cannot inspect its profit and loss account.
9. It may, by its Articles of Association, provide special disqualifications for appointment of its directors.
10. A person can be a director in 20 companies at a time (including private and public companies). In a public company, a person cannot be a director in more than 10 companies.

Questions

I. Long Answer Questions

1. Bring out differences between public and private company.
2. Define joint stock company. Write merits and limitations of Joint Stock Company.
3. Discuss different kinds of company.
4. Define "Joint Stock Company". Explain why Joint Stock Company form of organisation is popular.
5. What is a private company? How does it differ from a public company?
6. What are the privileges and exemptions available to a private company.

II. Write short notes on:

(i) Private company
(ii) Foreign company
(iii) Holding company

❑❑❑

07

Chapter

Formation of a Company

7.1 INTRODUCTION

Formation brings a company into existence through compliance with legal procedures. The stages in the formation of a company consist of the following steps:

1. Promotion
2. Incorporation
3. Floatation
4. Commencement

A private company is formed after obtaining the certificate of incorporation. It need not obtain the certificate of commencement. A public company comes into existence after obtaining the certificate of commencement.

7.2 PROMOTION

The promotion stage is the foundational phase in the creation of a company, involving several critical steps designed to evaluate and prepare for the establishment of a new business.

1. **Idea Conception:** This initial step revolves around the generation of a business idea. It begins with identifying a market need or an opportunity that a new company could address. The creativity and vision of the founders define what the company will offer—a product, service, or combination of both.
2. **Feasibility Study:** Once the idea is formulated, it undergoes a detailed investigation to test its viability. This involves conducting market research to understand potential demand, competition, target demographics, and other market dynamics. Financial feasibility is also assessed through preliminary financial models to estimate costs, revenues, and profitability. The goal is to ensure that the idea can be turned into a sustainable business model.

3. **Resource Assembly:** If the feasibility study yields positive results, the next step is to gather the necessary resources to turn the idea into reality. This includes securing financial resources, such as initial capital investment, and funding sources like loans or investor capital. Human resources are also crucial, which involves identifying key personnel who will drive the company's efforts, including experts in product development, marketing, and operations.
4. **Groundwork for Launch:** With resources in place, the promoters focus on detailed planning and preparation for the launch. This includes creating a business plan that outlines the strategy for market entry, growth objectives, and operational plans. Legal and administrative groundwork is also laid during this phase, ensuring that all regulatory requirements are met, and the company is positioned to operate smoothly.

Throughout the promotion stage, the emphasis is on meticulous planning and preparation. Each step is crucial to ensure that the business idea not only has the potential to succeed but is ready to be transformed into a functional and competitive enterprise.

Promotion is the "discovery of business opportunities and the subsequent organisation of funds, property and managerial ability into a business concern to make profits therefrom".

— *C.W. Gerstenberg*

Process of Promotion

Promotion is the final step in turning a business idea into a real company ready to compete in the market. This stage moves the business from planning to operation, where it starts interacting with customers and making money. Promotion is crucial because it methodically transforms a business idea into a working company, prepared to handle market challenges. The process of promoting a company involves a series of strategic steps designed to transition a business idea into reality.

1. *Explore Business Opportunities*

- **Idea conception:** The promoter identifies a potential market need or opportunity and conceives a business idea tailored to address it.
- **Feasibility analysis:** This involves evaluating the conceived idea to assess its viability in the current market. It includes market research, competitor analysis, and financial projections to ensure the idea can generate sustainable profits.

2. *Assemble Resources*

- **Human resources:** The promoter recruits key personnel with the expertise necessary to develop the product and manage the business. This includes technical experts, marketing professionals, and operational managers.

- **Material resources:** It involves securing the physical materials necessary to produce goods or deliver services. This could involve sourcing raw materials, technology, or any specialised equipment.
- **Managerial talent:** It involves engaging skilled managers who can oversee various functions within the company, from operations to finance, ensuring efficient business processes.

3. Provide Finance

- **Capital sourcing:** It identifies and secures sources of capital through investments, loans, or equity financing to fund the initial operations and long-term growth of the company.
- **Budget allocation:** It distributes the acquired finances strategically across different areas of the business to ensure optimal utilisation of resources.
- **Financial planning:** It develops a financial plan that details the inflow and outflow of money, forecasts financial needs, and prepares for potential risks.

4. Legal and Administrative Setup

- **Legal compliance:** It ensures that the business meets all legal requirements, including registrations, licenses, and permits, crucial for operating the business.
- **Corporate governance:** It establishes a framework for how the company is controlled and operated, ensuring that it meets the highest standards of corporate governance.

5. Strategic Planning and Execution

- **Business strategy:** It drafts strategies that define the company's path to market entry, growth, and competitive positioning.
- **Operational planning:** It sets operational processes and logistics that will enable the production of goods or delivery of services.

6. Marketing and Public Relations

- **Brand development:** It creates brand identity that connects with target customers and differentiates the company from competitors.
- **Marketing strategy:** It develops and implements a marketing plan to effectively promote the company's offerings and gain market reputation.

Elements of Promotion

The elements of promotion encompass essential steps in forming and launching a business venture, ensuring its strategic alignment with market needs and operational capabilities. This structured approach to promotion ensures that each critical aspect of the business idea is carefully planned and evaluated, laying a strong foundation for successful business operations.

1. *Discovery*

- **New enterprise formation:** Conceiving an idea to exploit technological opportunities or to introduce new products.
- **Expansion of existing enterprise:** Envisioning expansion to capitalise on economies of scale or existing economic opportunities.
- **Combination of enterprises:** Considering mergers or alliances to reduce costs or competition.

2. *Investigation*

- **Market research:** Conducting extensive market analysis to validate the demand, competition, and potential barriers.
- **Feasibility study:** Assessing the financial and operational feasibility of the conceived idea.
- **Risk analysis:** Identifying and evaluating potential risks associated with the business idea.

3. *Assembly*

- **Resource gathering:** Mobilising financial, human, and material resources necessary for the venture.
- **Strategic planning:** Developing strategies for management, operations, and market entry.
- **Legal setup:** Ensuring all legalities are addressed, including registrations and compliance with regulations.

4. *Financing*

- **Capital acquisition:** Securing necessary capital through loans, investments, or equity financing.
- **Financial structuring:** Planning the financial architecture of the enterprise to support growth and sustainability.
- **Budget management:** Allocating and managing financial resources to ensure efficient use and financial health.

PROMOTER

Promoter is an individual, association, partnership or a company that carries out the process of promotion. They are the persons who originate the idea of forming a company, arrange the resources, hold the resources together, supervise the steps to form the company, get together the subscribers to memorandum of association, get the memorandum and articles of association prepared, printed, executed and registered, make arrangements with brokers, bankers and legal advisors, arrange for underwriters, make preliminary contracts with sellers, prepare and circulate prospectus etc.

Promoters are not necessarily those engaged in the initial formation of a company. All those who assist promoters in carrying out the functions of promoters are also promoters unless they do so in the capacity of professional experts. An accountant who values the proposed company's assets, for example, is not a promoter as he only exercises his professional expertise. If the same accountant arranges with people who will provide funds to the proposed company, he will be a promoter.

According to Sec. 2(69) of the Companies Act, 2013, Promotor means a person:

1. who has been named as such in a prospectus or is identified by the company in the annual return; or
2. who has control over the affairs of the company, directly or indirectly whether as a shareholder, director, or otherwise; or
3. under whose advice, directions, or instructions the Board of Directors of the company is accustomed to act:

Provided that nothing in sub-clause (c) shall apply to a person who is acting merely in a professional capacity.

Functions of Promoters

Promoters carry out the following functions:

1. They originate or conceive the idea of forming a company.
2. They make arrangements with people who have funds to convert the idea into reality
3. They seek the opinion and guidance of experts and legal advisors to test the economic and legal significance of the proposed project.
4. They satisfy consumer needs by producing the desired goods and services.
5. They benefit the society by providing them employment opportunities in the proposed concern.

6. They increase social welfare by reducing unhealthy competition and uneconomic costs.. This is done by combining the enterprises through mergers, joint ventures etc.
7. They get together subscribers to the memorandum.
8. They get the memorandum and articles of associations prepared and registered.
9. They arrange with bankers, brokers, and legal advisors.
10. They appoints first directors.
11. They settle the terms of preliminary contracts with vendors.
12. They arrange with underwriters to secure the issue of share capital.
13. They arrange for preparing, advertising and circulating prospectus and provide the necessary capital for the proposed company.
14. They acquire the business or property which the company has to manage.

After performing these functions, the promoters hand over the control of the company to the directors whereby their duties come to an end. Thus, the day directors take over the business of a company, the duties of promoters cease to exist.

Promoters are usually the persons who are also the directors of the company being formed. They are also the persons who convert their sole proprietary business into company form of organisation and secure controlling interest in the management of the company.

Qualities of a Promoter

In order to carry out the process of promotion, promoters should have the following qualities:

1. Imagination and far sightedness
2. Moral conviction to give support to the ideas.
3. Ability to organise various resources.
4. Initiative and innovative capabilities.
5. Ability to motivate and induce people to utilise the assembled resources to achieve the desired purpose.
6. Confident to transform the idea into action.
7. Persistent and honest with belief in the capacity and capability of self and others

Legal Position of a Promoter

Under the Companies Act 2013, the role of a promoter is extensively regulated to ensure transparency and accountability in the company formation process. The legal position, fiduciary duties, and liabilities of promoters are as under.

Fiduciary Duties and Obligations

1. ***Fiduciary Relationship:*** From the moment they undertake the creation of a company, promoters are considered to be in a fiduciary relationship with the company and its prospective shareholders. This relationship imposes a duty to act with utmost good faith and in the best interests of the company.
2. ***Disclosure of Personal Interest:*** Promoters are required to disclose any personal interest they have in business transactions or contracts proposed with the company. This disclosure must be made to an independent board of directors or directly to the shareholders in a general meeting, depending on the governance structure established.
3. ***Prohibition of Secret Profits:*** It is unlawful for promoters to make secret profits from transactions involving the company without full disclosure and approval from the company. If promoters obtain assets and sell them to the company at a profit without proper disclosure and consent, they are deemed to have made secret profits.
4. ***Transparent Dealings:*** Promoters must ensure all transactions are conducted transparently and fairly to avoid any conflicts of interest.
5. ***Duty of Care:*** Promoters must perform their functions with all due care and diligence, ensuring proper execution of legal formalities and exercising necessary due diligence before entering contracts on behalf of the company.

Legal Responsibilities and Liabilities of a Promoter

The Companies Act 2013 emphasises a robust framework for the regulation of promoters, ensuring that the foundations of new companies are built on principles of integrity, fairness, and accountability. This regulatory environment is designed to foster trust among investors and to facilitate a healthy corporate culture from the outset.

1. ***Accuracy of Prospectus:*** Promoters are legally accountable for the veracity and completeness of the information in the prospectus. Any misstatement or omission can lead to legal action from investors or regulatory bodies.

2. ***Liability for Misstatements:*** If misstatements in the prospectus lead investors to make decisions that result in losses, promoters can be held liable for those losses.
3. ***Criminal Liability:*** In cases of fraud or deceit during the formation or management of the company, promoters may face criminal charges, which could include fines or imprisonment.
4. ***Compensation for Losses:*** Promoters may be required to compensate the company or its members for any loss suffered due to fraudulent acts or breaches of duty.
5. ***Regulatory Scrutiny and Penalties:*** Promoters must comply with all regulatory requirements during the formation of the company. Failure to do so can result in penalties from regulatory bodies, including the Securities and Exchange Board of India (SEBI).
6. ***Return of Gains from Unfair Practices:*** If found guilty of making secret profits or engaging in unfair practices, promoters might be compelled to return those gains to the company.
7. ***Duty to Avoid Conflict of Interest:*** Promoters should avoid any situation where their interests conflict with their duties to the company. They must prioritise the company's interests in all their actions during its formation.
8. ***Breach of Duty:*** Promoters can be held liable for breaching their fiduciary duty, such as failing to disclose a conflict of interest. Promoters are personally liable for any contracts entered into on behalf of the company before incorporation unless the company adopts such contracts after incorporation.

Remuneration of a Promoter

Promoters play a vital role in the formation and initial setup of a company, and their remuneration reflects their contributions. The forms of remuneration can include monetary payments, shares, and reimbursement of expenses, governed by the company's policies and legal frameworks such as the Companies Act, 2013, and SEBI regulations. Ensuring fair and transparent compensation practices for promoters is essential to align their interests with the long-term success of the company and safeguard stakeholders' interests.

Modes of Remuneration

1. ***Payment in Cash:*** Promoters may receive direct cash payments for their services in setting up the company. This payment is usually agreed upon before

the company is incorporated and can be part of the initial expenses borne by the company.

2. ***Shares:*** Promoters can be compensated with shares in the company. This serves both as a reward and an incentive for the promoters to work towards the company's success. The allocation of shares ties the promoters' interests to the long-term growth of the company.
3. ***Reimbursement of Expenses:*** Promoters are often reimbursed for the expenses they incur during the formation of the company. This includes costs related to market research, feasibility studies, legal fees, registration fees, and other initial setup costs.

Factors Influencing Remuneration

1. ***Nature of Services Provided:*** The complexity and scope of the services provided by the promoter can influence the amount and form of remuneration. Extensive involvement in legal, financial, and strategic aspects of company formation may warrant higher compensation.
2. ***Initial Capital Raised:*** If promoters are instrumental in securing significant capital, their remuneration may reflect their efforts and success in this area.
3. ***Terms of Agreement:*** The terms of the agreement between the promoters and the company's founders or initial board members play a crucial role. This agreement typically outlines the specific remuneration details and conditions.

7.3 REGISTRATION/INCORPORATION

Registration incorporates a company as an entity, separate and distinct from owners. It results in the formation of legal body corporate. To form a company, promoters get together seven members in case of a public limited company and two in case of a private company to act as signatories to memorandum of association.

According to Companies Act, 2013, a company may be formed for any lawful purpose by:

a. seven or more persons, where the company to be formed is to be a public company;

b. two or more persons, where the company to be formed is to be a private company; or

c. one person, where the company to be formed is to be One Person Company, that is to say, a private company.

by subscribing their names or his name to the memorandum of association and complying with the requirements of this Act in respect of registration.

Incorporation is the legal process of forming a company or corporation. The process involves drafting and filing various documents with the Registrar of Companies (RoC) and complying with the provisions of the Companies Act, 2013. Once incorporated, the company becomes a separate legal entity from its owners, capable of conducting business, owning assets, incurring liabilities, and entering into contracts.

Procedure for Registration

Promoters follow the following steps for registration of a company:

1. **Availability of Name:** When establishing a company under the Companies Act, 2013, the initial step involves selecting an appropriate name. This name must be approved by the Registrar of Companies (RoC) to ensure it adheres to specific regulatory standards as set by the Central Government. Promoters must conduct preliminary search for the availability of their proposed company name via the Registrar of Companies.

Criteria for Name Approval

- **Distinctiveness:** The proposed name should not be identical or bear a close resemblance to any existing company name or trademark that is already registered or under application as per the Trade Marks Act.
- **Compliance with Government Guidelines:** The name should not be considered undesirable by the Central Government. Names that could imply governmental affiliation without authorisation or those that are offensive or misleading, are typically deemed undesirable.

Application for Name Approval

- **Submission to RoC:** Promoters must apply to the Registrar of Companies in the State where the company is intended to be registered. This application should articulate the chosen name and confirm its compliance with the stipulations of the Companies Act.
- **Documentation:** Alongside the application, promoters should include a statement of compliance, confirming that the proposed name adheres to all legal requirements and guidelines.

Examination by RoC

- **Review Process:** Upon receipt of the application, the Registrar of Companies will review the proposed name to ensure it meets all regulatory requirements and does not conflict with existing names or trademarks.

- **Notification of Approval:** If the proposed name is found to be compliant and available, the RoC will notify the promoters of the approval. This confirmation is crucial for moving forward with further registration processes.

Registration of Name: Once approval is received, promoters are advised to officially register the company name by the specified date provided by the RoC. This registration secures the name and allows promoters to proceed with drafting the Memorandum and Articles of Association.

This procedure ensures that the company name is legally compliant and helps to establish its brand identity in the market.

To fully understand the nuanced process of company registration under the Companies Act, 2013 in India, it's essential to delve into the detailed procedures involved in preparing, signing, and filing the Memorandum of Association (MoA) and Articles of Association (AoA). These documents not only establish the company's legal identity but also outline the governance structure and operational guidelines it will follow. Here's a detailed breakdown of each step:

2. Preparation of Memorandum of Association and Articles of Association

Memorandum of Association

The Memorandum of Association serves as the cornerstone of the company, defining its scope and limitations. The important clauses are:

- **Name Clause:** This specifies the unique name of the company, chosen to avoid legal conflicts or confusion with pre-existing names or trademarks.
- **Registered Office Clause:** It indicates the exact location of the company's initial registered office, establishing its primary place of business and jurisdiction for legal purposes.
- **Object Clause:** It lists the objectives for which the company is established. It must be comprehensive to encompass all intended activities, thereby providing the company with the flexibility to expand or modify its business scope without needing frequent amendments.
- **Liability Clause:** It details whether the liability of members is limited by shares or guarantee. This clause affects decisions related to financial risk-taking and investment.
- **Capital Clause:** It outlines the amount of capital the company will be registered with, specifying the division into shares. This clause is essential for potential investors and for regulatory compliance regarding share allocation and ownership.

- **Subscription Clause:** It lists the initial subscribers who agree to purchase and pay for the company's shares, signifying their commitment as founding members.

Articles of Association

The Articles of Association provides detailed regulations on the company's internal governance:

- **Directors:** It provides guidelines on the election, duties, powers, and remuneration of directors. This section also addresses the board's composition, meetings, and decision-making processes.
- **Shareholders:** It explains procedures for share issuance, transfers, and shareholder rights. This includes how dividends are declared, shareholder meetings are conducted, and voting rights are exercised.
- **Financial controls:** It includes the management of finances, audit requirements, and fiscal reporting to ensure transparency and accountability.
- **Operational rules:** It provides detailed procedures for the day-to-day management, including administrative duties and delegation of authority.
- **Conflict resolution:** It provides mechanism for handling internal disputes and guidelines for disciplinary procedures to maintain order and corporate governance.

3. **Printing and Signing of Memorandum of Association and Articles of Association:** These documents must be physically printed and professionally bound to ensure durability and accessibility. Each page is to be consecutively numbered, and every subscriber must sign the Memorandum of Association and Articles of Association in the presence of at least one witness, who must attest the signatures and add their personal information, ensuring the authenticity of the signatories.
4. **Identifying Directors and Shareholders:** Determine the individuals who will be the directors and shareholders of the company. Each type of company has specific requirements:
   - ***Private Limited Company:*** Minimum of 2 directors and 2 shareholders.
   - ***Public Limited Company:*** Minimum of 3 directors and 7 shareholders.
   - ***OPC:*** One director and one shareholder (same person).
5. **Digital Signature Certificate (DSC):** Obtain a Digital Signature Certificate for all proposed directors. The DSC is used to sign electronic documents submitted

to the MCA. It can be obtained from authorised certifying authorities like eMudhra, Sify, or NSDL.

6. **Director Identification Number (DIN):** Apply for a Director Identification Number for all proposed directors if they do not already have one. DIN is a unique identification number required for anyone intending to be a director in a company, issued by the MCA.
7. **Filing of Documents:** For the company to be legally registered, the following must be submitted to the Registrar of Companies (RoC):
    - Memorandum of Association and Articles of Association duly signed by all subscribers.
    - Declaration by a company secretary, lawyer, or certified accountant affirming that all legal requirements are met.
    - Full personal and professional details of the directors and subscribers, including any other directorships held and their consent to act as directors.
    - Provisional address until the permanent address is established.
8. **Grant of Certificate of Registration:** If the Registrar is satisfied with respect to the documents filed, payment of registration and filing fees and conformity to other legal requirements, he will enter the name in the Register of Companies and issue a 'Certificate of Incorporation'. With effect from the date mentioned in this certificate, the company will be incorporated as a body corporate and subscribers to the memorandum and other members are given the right to carry out the functions of an incorporated company.

Contents of the Certificate of Incorporation

The Certificate of Incorporation includes several key details:

1. **Corporate Identity Number (CIN)**
    - The Corporate Identity Number is a unique identification number assigned to each company registered in India.
    - The company must use the CIN provided in the Certificate of Incorporation for all subsequent filings with the RoC and other regulatory bodies. This includes annual returns, financial statements, and other statutory documents.
2. **Company's Name**
    - This is the legally registered name of the company as approved by the Ministry of Corporate Affairs (MCA).

- The company's name is used in all business dealings, contracts, and legal matters. It ensures that the company is recognised under this name for all its operations.

3. Date of Incorporation

- This is the date on which the company is officially registered and incorporated by the RoC.
- The incorporation date marks the beginning of the company's legal existence. It is also used for determining compliance deadlines for various filings and statutory requirements.

4. Registered Office Address

- This is the official address where the company's records are maintained and official communications are sent.
- The registered office address is critical for legal and compliance purposes. It must be a physical location within India where the company can be contacted and where important documents can be delivered.

Legal Implications of the Certificate

- The Certificate of Incorporation is conclusive evidence of the company's lawful registration. Any irregularity, consequently found to have been committed before registration but detected after the issue of certificate of registration shall not be valid, safeguarding the entity's legal status and ongoing operations.
- This process ensures the company is fully prepared to operate within the legal framework, fostering trust among shareholders, customers, and regulatory bodies.

Validity of certificate of incorporation ensures the following:

1. Perpetual Existence

- Once issued, the Certificate of Incorporation grants the company a perpetual existence. This means the company continues to exist until it is legally dissolved or wound up.
- The company can operate indefinitely, beyond the lifetimes of its shareholders and directors, providing stability and continuity in business operations.

2. Indefinite Validity

- The Certificate of Incorporation does not have an expiration date. It remains valid as long as the company adheres to regulatory compliance and maintains its status with the Registrar of Companies.

3. Compliance Requirements

- The company must file annual returns and financial statements with the RoC.
- Regular filing of income tax returns, GST returns, and other applicable tax filings.
- Conducting regular board meetings and annual general meetings (AGMs) as stipulated by the Companies Act, 2013.
- Keeping accurate and up-to-date statutory registers, such as the register of members, register of directors, and register of charges.

4. Consequences of Non-Compliance

- Non-compliance with regulatory requirements can result in penalties and fines imposed by the RoC and other regulatory authorities.
- Persistent non-compliance may lead to the company being struck off the register by the RoC, which effectively means the company is dissolved and ceases to exist.
- The company and its directors may face legal action for failing to comply with statutory obligations.

5. Revocation of Certificate

- The Certificate of Incorporation can be revoked if it is found that it was obtained fraudulently or if the company engages in illegal activities. The revocation is done through legal proceedings and is a rare occurrence.

6. Voluntary Dissolution

- The company may choose to dissolve voluntarily by passing a special resolution and following the procedure for winding up as per the Companies Act, 2013.
- Involves settling debts, distributing assets among shareholders, and filing the necessary documents with the RoC to officially close the company.

Online Registration of a New Company

The registration process is conducted online through the MCA portal, involving the following steps and forms:

1. **Digital Signature Certificate (DSC):** Digital signatures are needed to file forms on the MCA portal. All proposed directors and subscribers of the Memorandum of Association (MoA) and Articles of Association (AoA) must have a DSC to sign the documents. DSC can be obtained from government-recognised certifying authorities.

2. **Director Identification Number (DIN):** The Director Identification Number (DIN) is a unique number for anyone who wants to be a director in a company. It is an 8-digit unique ID given to all directors, both new and existing. It is mandatory, and no one can become a director without a DIN. All proposed directors must provide their DIN, name, and address proof in the company registration form. They can get a DIN while filing the SPICe+ form, the company registration form.

   SPICe+ is a web-based form that allows to get a DIN for up to three directors. If the company has more than three directors, it can start with three directors and add more after incorporation. The new directors can get their DIN by filing the DIR-3 form, as only proposed directors can apply for DIN through SPICe+.

3. **Registration on the MCA Portal:** To apply for company registration, it needs to fill out and submit the SPICe+ (Simplified Proforma for Incorporating Company electronically Plus) form on the MCA portal. The company's director must first register on the MCA portal. After registering, the director can log in to access services like filing e-forms and viewing public documents.

   The company must reserve its name by submitting two proposed names in Part-A of the SPICe+ form. This step is crucial because if the name is similar to an existing company, LLP, trademark, or contains prohibited words under the Companies (Incorporation Rules) 2014, the SPICe+ form will be rejected.

   If the SPICe+ form is rejected due to the company name, the applicant must re-file another SPICe+ form with a new name and pay the fee again. Once the name in Part-A is approved, it will be reserved for 20 days. Within this period, the company must complete and submit Part-B of the SPICe+ form online. The applicant needs to provide details of the company and directors, attach required documents and DSC, check the form, and submit it.

4. **Certificate of Incorporation:** Once the registration application is filled out and submitted with the required documents, the Registrar of Companies will review it. After verifying the application, the Registrar will issue the Certificate of Incorporation.

   The Certificate of Incorporation includes the PAN and TAN assigned by the Income Tax Department. An email with the Certificate of Incorporation, PAN, and TAN attached will also be sent to the applicant.

Documents Required for Company Registration

The general documents required for registering a Company are as follows:

Documents for Directors and Shareholders

- Proof of identification for all directors and shareholders. Any one of the following can be submitted:
  - PAN card
  - Aadhar card
  - Driving license
  - Passport
- Proof of address for all directors and shareholders. Any one of the following can be submitted:
  - Latest telephone bill (not older than 2 months)
  - Latest electricity bill (not older than 2 months)
  - Bank account statement with address
- DIN and DSC for all directors

Documents for the Company

- Proof of the company's registered office. Any one of the following can be submitted:
  - Tenancy/rental agreement between the landlord and company/LLP
  - Letter or NOC from the landlord permitting use of the office/premises as the company/LLP's registered office.
  - Sale deed of the company office premises in the name of the company/LLP
  - Memorandum of Association outlining the company's objectives and the liability of its members
  - Articles of Association detailing the by-laws for company operations

Forms to Be Filled for Incorporating a Company

Several forms are required for the incorporation of a company:

1. **SPICe+ (INC-32):** The main form for company incorporation, covering name reservation, incorporation, DIN allotment, and various registrations.
2. **e-MoA (INC-33):** Electronic Memorandum of Association.
3. **e-AoA (INC-34):** Electronic Articles of Association.
4. **AGILE-PRO-S (INC-35):** For obtaining GSTIN, EPFO, ESIC, and professional tax registration.

5. **INC-9:** Declaration by subscribers and first directors, auto-generated during the SPICe+ process.

Once these forms are approved by the Ministry of corporate Affairs, the applicant will receive an e-mail for the same. The status of the forms will get changed to 'Approved' and a Corporate Identity Number (CIN) is generated. Thus, a new company gets formed through the online process.

7.4 FLOATATION/CAPITAL SUBSCRIPTION

Under this stage, capital is raised by the company.

Private company having share capital is prohibited by its Article to invite public to subscribe to its securities. Thus, it need not pass through capital subscription stage. It can offer securities privately to a selected group of people through 'private placement'.

Public company with share capital invites public to subscribe to its securities through issue of prospectus. SEBI regulates issue of securities to the public through rules and regulations that regulate the securities market. As per SEBI regulations, the following procedure is followed for raising capital:

- Directors file a copy of prospectus with the Registrar.
- Prospectus is circulated in public to invite them to subscribe to shares of the company.
- Applications are received from the public to subscribe for shares through Company's bankers.
- At least 90% subscription must be received (minimum subscription) within 30 days from the date of issue of prospectus so that Directors can proceed with allotment.
- Once the formal resolution of allotment is passed:
    - allotment letters are posted.
    - return of allotment is filed with the Registrar.
    - share certificates are issued in exchange of allotment letters.
- If minimum subscription is not received within 30 days from the date of issue of prospectus or such other period as may be specified by SEBI, application money shall be refunded to the applicants within such time and manner as may be prescribed.

7.5 COMMENCEMENT

Commencement of business is a critical step for newly incorporated companies under the Companies Act, 2013. This requirement ensures that companies are operational and engaged in business activities soon after incorporation. Failure to comply with these requirements can lead to significant penalties and legal consequences.

Under Section 10A of the Companies Act, 2013, the following steps must be taken for a company to commence business:

1. **Filing a Declaration:** The company must file a declaration with the Registrar of Companies (RoC) within 180 days from the date of incorporation stating that every subscriber to the memorandum has paid the value of the shares agreed to be taken by them. This declaration is submitted in Form INC-20A.

   The declaration confirms that the company has received the subscription money from its shareholders and that it has verified the registered office address.

2. **Verification of Registered Office:** The company must also file a verification of its registered office with the RoC within 30 days of incorporation using Form INC-22, if this was not provided during the incorporation process.

Consequences of Non-Compliance

Failure to comply with the requirements for commencement of business can result in penalties and legal actions, including:

1. Penalties for the Company and Directors

- **Company Penalty:** The company may be liable to pay a penalty of ₹50,000 if it fails to file the declaration within the specified period.
- **Director Penalty:** Every officer who is in default, such as the directors, may also be liable to pay a penalty of ₹1,000 for each day of default, subject to a maximum of ₹1,00,000.

2. Restrictions on Business Activities

- **Prohibition on Borrowing:** Until the declaration is filed, the company is not permitted to commence business activities or borrow money. This means the company cannot enter into any business transactions or take loans until it complies with Section 10A requirements.

3. Striking off by RoC

- **Registrar's Power:** The Registrar of Companies has the power to initiate the process of striking off the name of the company from the register if the company does not comply with the requirements of filing the declaration for commencement of business within the stipulated time.

- **Dissolution of Company:** This can lead to the company being dissolved, and it would no longer legally exist. The striking-off process is initiated if the RoC believes that the company is not carrying on any business or operation.

Compliance with the commencement of business requirements is crucial for newly incorporated companies under the Companies Act, 2013. Filing the necessary declarations and verifying the registered office address within the stipulated time frames ensures the company can legally start its business operations and avoid severe penalties or dissolution. Adhering to these steps not only establishes the company's legal standing but also promotes operational readiness and credibility with stakeholders.

Questions

1. Long Answer Questions

1. Explain the procedure for formation of a company.
2. What do you mean by promotion? Explain the elements and process of promotion.
3. Define 'promoter'. What are the functions performed by promoters?
4. Discuss the roles and responsibilities of promoters during the company formation process, as outlined in the Companies Act, 2013.
5. Define promoter. Discuss the characteristics of promoters.
6. Discuss the steps in formation of a company.
7. What are the different stages in the promotion of a company?
8. What do you understand by promotion? Describe various stages in promotion of a Joint Stock Company.
9. What do you mean by 'Incorporation'? Discuss the procedure for incorporation of a Joint Stock Company.

II. Write short notes on:

(i) Promoters.
(ii) Procedure to get Certificate of Commencement of Business.
(iii) Importance of minimum subscription.

❑❑❑

08

Chapter

Documents for Formation of a Company

8.1 DOCUMENTS TO BE FILED WITH REGISTRAR OF COMPANIES

Documents to be filed with Registrar of Companies for formation of a company are:

I. Memorandum of Association

II. Articles of Association

III. Prospectus

8.2 MEMORANDUM OF ASSOCIATION

It is a legal document required to incorporate a company. It provides the company's foundation. It defines the company's constitution and outlines its objectives, powers, and limitations. Among its clauses, it lists the company's objectives, defining the scope of its operations. It not only sets but also limits the company's powers, restricting their exercise. Any action taken by the company outside the 'objects clause' of the Memorandum of Association is ultra vires and not binding. Shareholders know where their money will be invested. It also helps outsiders (creditors, suppliers, etc.) understand the company's range of activities.

Significance of Memorandum of Association

1. Legal Identity

- ***Distinct Entity***: The Memorandum of Association gives the company its legal identity, separate from its shareholders and directors. It grants the company the authority of a separate legal person.
- ***Ownership and Liability***: Depending on the business, a company can own property, incur debts, and enter into contracts independently. This limits

liability for companies, protecting the personal assets of shareholders and directors from being used to settle company debts, encouraging entrepreneurial risk-taking.

2. Scope of Operations

- ***Specified Activities***: The Memorandum of Association specifies the goals and activities the company is permitted to undertake. This constraint keeps the company from involving in ultra vires (beyond the powers) activities.
- ***Operational Clarity***: It clearly defines the activities of the business, providing clarity and focus, and enables the management to align strategies and operations with the company's objectives.

3. Credibility

- ***Trust and Transparency***: A well-drafted Memorandum of Association strengthens the trust of investors, creditors, and other stakeholders in the company. It showcases transparency regarding what the company is set to do and what it is not.
- ***Funding and Creditworthiness***: With clear objectives and a well-defined scope of operations, it becomes easier for the company to attract funding or credit, giving investors and creditors comfort knowing the company has a stable core strategy.

4. Regulatory Compliance

- ***Legal Framework***: The Memorandum of Association forms the basis of the company's legal framework, governing its conduct and establishing it according to various laws and regulations.
- ***Accountability***: The Memorandum of Association is a tool of accountability for regulatory authorities, who can monitor the company's operations and penalise non-compliance. Adherence to the Memorandum of Association is crucial, as breaches can have legal implications.

5. Shareholder Assurance

- ***Safeguarding Interests***: The Memorandum of Association assures shareholders that the company will not operate outside of what is documented. This protection safeguards their investments, ensuring the company remains aligned with its core objectives.
- ***Reduction of Risks***: By preventing unauthorised activities, the Memorandum of Association mitigates the risk of mismanagement or deviation from the company's strategic goals, increasing shareholder trust and security.

6. Corporate Governance

- ***Structural Clarity***: The Memorandum of Association explicitly defines the company's structure, including the roles and responsibilities of directors and other key officers, fostering good corporate governance.
- ***Decision-making Framework***: The Memorandum of Association sets the limits of the company's goals and operational boundaries, providing a framework for decision-making that ensures the company's actions are consistent with its values and strategies.

In summary, the Memorandum of Association is an essential document that certifies a company's legal existence to serve its stated purpose, enhances its credibility, ensures legal compliance, assures shareholders, and optimises corporate governance. This inclusive and transparent approach significantly contributes to trust and stability among all involved parties.

Contents (Clauses) of Memorandum of Association

Memorandum of Association contains the following clauses:

1. Name Clause
2. Registered Office Clause
3. Objects Clause
4. Liability Clause
5. Capital Clause
6. Association or Subscription Clause

1. ***Name Clause***: The company is a separate legal entity, having an identity of its own. It must, therefore, have a name that it must-
   i. affix along with the address of its registered office outside each of its offices and places of business in a conspicuous position, easily legible letters and local language of the area concerned,
   ii. engrave on its official seal,
   iii. mention along with the address of its registered office on all business letters, notices, bills etc.

Guidelines for Choosing a Name

Some of the guidelines issued by the Ministry of Company Affairs are mentioned below:

i. Name should not be identical with the name by which some other company is already registered.
ii. It should not closely resemble the generally accepted abbreviations such as WHO, SAIL, GAIL etc.
iii. It should not convey any contact with the Government, like National, Union etc.
iv. It should not convey any contact with persons of high esteem.
v. It should not use the name of a registered trademark.
vi. It should end with the word 'limited' in case of companies limited by shares or guarantee or 'private limited' in case of private companies.
vii. It should not attract the provisions of Emblems and Names (prevention of improper use) Act, 1950.

2. ***Registered Office Clause***: It indicates the name of the State in which the company's registered office is situated. The registered office establishes the company's domicile. Statutory books and registers such as register of members, debenture-holders etc. are kept at its registered office. All communications and correspondence are maintained at the registered office. Notice of the registered office must be given to the Registrar of Companies within 30 days of its incorporation.

3. ***Objects Clause***: It defines the objects of the company for which it is established and defines the scope of its activities beyond which any act will be void and ultra vires. The objects clause is divided into two parts:
   - **Main Objects:** The primary objectives that define the core business activities.
   - **Ancillary Objects:** Additional activities that support the main objectives.

   The objects clause provides useful information to all those who deal with the company.

4. ***Liability Clause***: It states the liability of the members of the company.

   i. For companies with limited liability, it states whether liability is limited by shares or guarantee. In case of liability limited by shares, members cannot be called upon to pay anything more than the unpaid amount on shares held by them. In case of liability limited by guarantee, the liability clause states the amount which each member has undertaken to contribute towards the assets of the company in the event of winding up.

ii. For companies with unlimited liability, the liability clause is not given in the Memorandum of Association. Absence of this clause refers to unlimited liability of the company.

5. ***Capital Clause***: It states the total amount of share capital with which the company is registered, its division into units (shares) of fixed denomination and the value of each share. It states the limit of capital (authorised share capital) beyond which the company cannot issue shares unless it alters its Memorandum of Association to that effect.

6. ***Association or Subscription Clause***: It contains the names, addresses and occupations of the subscribers who form the company. It indicates the number of shares that each subscriber agrees to take. The subscribers (at least 7 in case of public company and 2 in case of private company) sign the Memorandum of Association in the presence of at least one witness who will attest their signatures. Each subscriber must take at least one share and pay for the shares as any other member.

Changing Clauses of the Memorandum of Association

A general procedure for alteration of a company's Memorandum of Association is as follows:

1. ***Board Resolution***: The Board of Directors must pass a resolution proposing the change to the Memorandum of Association. This involves drafting the proposed alteration and justifying the need for it.
2. ***Special Resolution***: A special resolution must be passed by the shareholders in a general meeting. This typically requires a special majority (usually 75%) of votes in favour of the change. Shareholders must be given proper notice of the meeting and the proposed changes.
3. ***Filing with Regulatory Authorities***: After the special resolution is passed, the company must file the necessary documents with the relevant regulatory authority (such as the Registrar of Companies). These usually include the special resolution, the amended Memorandum of Association, and any other required forms or declarations.
4. ***Approval from Regulatory Authorities***: The regulatory authority reviews the documents and, if satisfied, registers the changes. The company may receive a certificate of amendment, confirming the alteration.

5. ***Notification to Stakeholders*:** Once approved, the company should inform all stakeholders (employees, creditors, etc.) about the changes to the Memorandum of Association.

8.3 ARTICLES OF ASSOCIATION

The Articles of Association are the byelaws of the company that explain its rules and regulations and the way its internal affairs will be conducted. They define the rights/ powers of the company and its management. They also maintain contact between the company and its members and amongst members themselves Matters related to administration of a company, such as provisions for making calls, transfer of shares, appointment, powers and duties of auditors etc. are governed by its Articles of Association.

Articles of Association is a document subordinate to Memorandum of Association. Memorandum of Association defines the powers of the company and Articles of Association defines the rules and regulations of the company within the powers conferred upon it by the Memorandum of Association. Memorandum defines the scope of operational area and Articles defines the rules framed by the company to achieve the objectives within the limits defined by Memorandum of Association.

All those who deal with the company assume that the provisions of Articles of Association have been observed by the officers of the company. They are not bound to enquire into the regularity of company's internal proceedings. This is known as the doctrine of indoor management.

Forms of Articles of Association

The forms for Articles of Association (Articles of Association) in tables F, G, H, I, and J for different types of companies have been mentioned under Schedule I of the Companies Act, 2013. Articles of Association must be in the respective form.

- Table F- Articles of Association of a company limited by shares
- Table G- Articles of Association of a company limited by guarantee and having a share capital
- Table H- Articles of Association of a company limited by guarantee and not having a share capital
- Table I- Articles of Association of an unlimited company and having a share capital
- Table J- Articles of Association of an unlimited company and not having a share capital

The company has three alternatives:

1. It may adopt a Table in full.
2. It may wholly exclude the Table and set out its own Articles of Association in full.
3. It may frame its own Articles of Association. and adopt part of the Table.

Unless the Articles of Association of a public company expressly exclude any or all provisions of relevant Table, that Table shall automatically apply to it. [Section 5(8)]

In case of any company, which is registered after the commencement of this Act, in so far as the registered articles of such company do not exclude or modify the regulations contained in the model articles applicable to such company, those regulations shall, so far as applicable, be the regulations of that company in the same manner and to the extent as if they were contained in the duly registered articles of the company.

Contents of Articles of Association

The Articles of Association is a comprehensive document that covers all aspects of the internal governance and operational framework of a company, ensuring clarity, consistency, and legal compliance in its operations.

Definitions and Interpretations

- Definitions of key terms used in the document.
- Rules for interpreting the terms and provisions within the Articles of Association.

Share Capital and Variation of Rights

- Details about the company's share capital.
- Types of shares and rights attached to each type.
- Procedures for altering share capital and varying shareholders' rights.

Share Certificates

- Issuance and form of share certificates.
- Replacement of lost or damaged certificates.

Transfer of Shares

- Procedures for transferring shares.
- Restrictions on share transfers.

Alteration of Capital

- Procedures for increasing, consolidating, subdividing, or cancelling shares.

General Meetings

- Rules for convening and conducting annual general meetings (AGMs) and extraordinary general meetings (EGMs).
- Notice periods, quorum requirements, and voting procedures.

Proceedings at General Meetings

- Procedures for conducting meetings.
- Rules for passing resolutions, including ordinary and special resolutions.

Votes of Members

- Voting rights of shareholders.
- Methods of voting (e.g., show of hands, poll).

Directors

- Appointment, removal, and remuneration of directors.
- Powers and duties of directors.
- Procedures for board meetings.

Powers and Duties of Directors

- Specific powers granted to directors.
- Duties and responsibilities of directors in managing the company's affairs.

Proceedings of Directors

- Rules for board meetings, including quorum and voting requirements.
- Procedures for passing board resolutions.

Borrowing Powers

- Limits on the company's ability to borrow funds.
- Conditions and procedures for borrowing.

Secretary

- Appointment and duties of the company secretary.

Dividends and Reserves

- Policies for declaring and distributing dividends.
- Creation and management of reserves.

Accounts and Audit

- Maintenance and inspection of accounting records.
- Preparation and approval of financial statements.
- Appointment and duties of auditors.

Notices

- Methods for giving notice to shareholders and directors.
- Time frames and validity of notices.

Winding Up

- Procedures for winding up the company.
- Distribution of assets upon liquidation.

Amendments to the Articles

- Procedures for amending the Articles of Association.
- Requirements for shareholder approval of amendments.

Miscellaneous

- Any other provisions deemed necessary for the company's governance.

Alteration of Articles of Association

A company can alter its Articles of Association by passing a special resolution (A special resolution is the one where 3/4th of the majority vote in favour of the matter being discussed) The document Articles of Association, is subordinate to Memorandum of Association and, therefore, cannot exceed the powers given by the Memorandum of Association. It should not be in conflict with the provisions of Memorandum of Association It should also not be inconsistent with the provisions of the Companies Act. The altered Articles of Association should not contain anything illegal or something that is opposed to public policy. The alteration must be for the benefit of the company.

Memorandum of Association and Articles of Association - A Comparison

The Memorandum of Association and Articles of Association are two critical documents in the formation and operation of a company. They serve different purposes and contain distinct information.

1. ***Complementary Documents***: The Memorandum of Association and Articles of Association work together to provide a comprehensive framework for the governance and operation of a company. While the Memorandum of Association outlines the fundamental principles and the external aspects of the company, the Articles of Association focuses on the internal management and operational rules.
2. ***Foundation and Function***: The Memorandum of Association serves as the foundation of the company, defining its purpose, scope, and relationship with the outside world, including shareholders and creditors. The Articles of Association functions within the boundaries set by the Memorandum of Association, detailing the company's internal governance and management processes.
3. ***Legal Requirement***: Both documents are legally required for the incorporation of a company. The Memorandum of Association is typically filed first, as it establishes the company's existence and core objectives. The Articles of Association is then filed to set out the rules for managing the company.

Aspect	Memorandum of Association	Articles of Association
Purpose	Defines the company's constitution and its fundamental relationship with the outside world.	Provides the rules and regulations for the internal management of the company.
Content	Includes the company's name, registered office, objectives, liability of members, capital structure, and subscriber details.	Includes rules about the conduct of meetings, appointment of directors, voting rights, financial management, and other internal processes.
Scope	Outlines the broad and fundamental aspects of the company, including its powers and objectives.	Focuses on detailed, day-to-day governance and management procedures within the company.
Alteration	Difficult to alter. Changes usually require special resolutions and approval from regulatory authorities.	Easier to amend compared to the Memorandum of Association. Changes can typically be made with shareholder approval.

Legal Position	Acts as the company's charter. It is a primary document that binds the company.	Acts as the company's bylaws. It is a subordinate document to the Memorandum of Association.
Relationship with External Parties	Governs the company's relationship with external parties, such as shareholders, creditors, and the public.	Governs the relationship between the company's internal stakeholders, such as directors and shareholders.
Registration	Must be filed with the Registrar of Companies during incorporation.	Must also be filed with the Registrar of Companies, usually alongside or after the Memorandum of Association.
Legal Effect	Binding on the company and its members. External parties can rely on it.	Binding primarily on the company and its members. Does not directly affect external parties.
Visibility and Public Access	Public document accessible by anyone interested in the company's basic details and objectives.	Typically available to shareholders and members, with less accessibility to the general public.

8.4. PROSPECTUS

A public company incorporated under the Companies Act, 2013, can raise investments from the general public through various methods. Since the company gathers funds from the public, it must be accountable to them. To protect investors' interests, the Companies Act, 2013, requires the company to file a prospectus with the Registrar before raising funds.

A prospectus is a document that a company issues to invite the public to deposit money or buy its securities. It contains essential information about the company and its securities for potential investors. According to Section 2(70) of the Companies Act, 2013, a prospectus is any document described or issued as a prospectus. It includes a red herring prospectus (Section 32), a shelf prospectus (Section 31), or any notice, circular, advertisement, or other document that invites the public to subscribe to or purchase any securities of a corporate body.

A prospectus is a document that gives all the key information about a company when it seeks investment from the public. It serves as an invitation for people to buy the company's securities. People who want to invest can offer to buy shares at a price within a specified range. The company then decides how to allocate these shares to the investors.

Whenever a company wants to raise money from the public, it must inform them about its financial status and the reason for needing the investment. The prospectus is the first document that the company uses to share its financial details and other important information.

According to Section 28(2) of the Companies Act, 2013, any document used to make an offer for sale to the public is considered a prospectus. It is important to note that this document must be issued to the general public, not just a specific group of people. For example, if a newspaper ad offers certain shares for sale, it is also considered a prospectus.

Features of a Prospectus

1. Comprehensive Information

- **Detailed business description:** The prospectus provides an extensive overview of the company's business activities, including its products, services, market position, and competitive landscape.
- **Financial health:** It includes historical and current financial statements such as balance sheets, income statements, and cash flow statements to demonstrate the company's financial status and performance.
- **Securities details:** It provides detailed specifics about the securities being offered, including the type of securities (e.g., equity shares, bonds), the number of securities, the offer price, and the terms of the offer.

2. Legal Requirement

- **Regulatory compliance**: Companies must issue a prospectus to comply with securities regulations and laws when raising capital from the public. This requirement ensures that the company meets all legal standards for transparency and investor protection.
- **Investor protection**: The legal requirement for a prospectus is designed to protect investors by ensuring they have access to all necessary information before making an investment decision.

3. Transparency

- **Full disclosure**: The prospectus ensures transparency by providing potential investors with all relevant and material information needed to make an informed decision.

- **Material facts**: It includes all material facts about the company and the securities being offered, reducing the risk of misinformation or fraudulent activities.

Types of Prospectus

1. Shelf prospectus
2. Red Herring prospectus
3. Abridged prospectus
4. Deemed Prospectus

1. **Shelf Prospectus:** Drafting a prospectus requires many details and disclosures for investors. When a company intends to make multiple public offers in one financial year, it becomes hard to create a new prospectus each time. However, important changes in the company's financial status need to be communicated to investors. To balance these needs, the law introduces the concept of a shelf prospectus.

   Section 31 of the Companies Act, 2013, explains that a "shelf prospectus" is a prospectus used for one or more issues of securities over a certain period without needing a new prospectus each time. This single prospectus covers all the offers within a specified period. The Securities Exchange Board of India (SEBI) can specify which classes of listed companies can file a shelf prospectus. The shelf prospectus is valid for up to one year from the date of the first offer. Companies must follow strict disclosure rules when issuing a shelf prospectus. While filing a shelf prospectus, a company must also file an information memorandum with the Registrar within three months before the second or any subsequent offer under the shelf prospectus. This document includes:

   i. New charges created.

   ii. Changes in the financial position since the last offer of securities.

   iii. Any other prescribed changes.

2. **Red Herring Prospectus:** While big companies issue prospectus for funding, mid-size and small companies also need investments and make public offers. To protect their rights and help them access finance, the law includes the concept of a red herring prospectus.

   According to Section 32 of the Companies Act, 2013, a "red herring prospectus" is a prospectus that does not include complete details about the amount or price of the securities. Instead, it provides a price range, allowing the company to assess the value of its securities and achieve the required minimum subscription, which might not be possible if all details were provided upfront.

A red herring prospectus follows the same regulations as a regular prospectus. It must be filed with the Registrar of Companies at least three days before the public issue. Additionally, after the securities are fully subscribed, the company must file the complete details of the issue with the Registrar and the SEBI.

The Red-Herring Prospectus is crucial for both the company and investors. It provides a preliminary look into the company's offerings, ensuring that the final prospectus is well-informed and aligned with market expectations, thereby facilitating a smoother and more successful offering process.

Characteristics of Red-Herring Prospectus

i. **Preliminary Information:** This document provides extensive details about the company and the offering but does not include the final offer price or the total number of shares being offered. It serves as the initial disclosure to prospective investors.

ii. **Indicative:** The Red-Herring Prospectus gives potential investors an overview of the financials, operations, products/services, and market size of the company. This helps in evaluating the commercial and financial sustainability of the investment opportunity.

iii. **Non-binding:** The information in a Red-Herring Prospectus is non-binding. Data can be updated with feedback and current market conditions before the final prospectus is released.

iv. **Marketability:** It acts as a marketing tool to generate interest ahead of the forthcoming offer, creating a potential investor funnel.

v. **Regulatory compliance:** The document adheres to the requisite regulatory requirements for disclosures, lending credibility and transparency to the offering.

vi. **Feedback mechanism:** It allows the company to receive feedback from prospective investors, enabling necessary adjustments to the final offering terms.

Importance of Red-Herring Prospectus

i. **Market testing:** The primary intention of issuing a Red-Herring Prospectus is to assess whether there is enough demand from investors to buy. This helps the company gauge interest and gather initial feedback from the market, which can be used to refine and finalize the terms of the offer.

ii. **Informing investors:** It provides potential investors with enough preliminary information to quickly understand the deal. This early disclosure helps investors decide whether to invest further time in due diligence.

iii. **Creating interest:** It generates excitement and interest among potential investors and other financial markets, potentially leading to a more successful IPO.

iv. **Building investor confidence:** By providing detailed information about the company and its offerings, the Red-Herring Prospectus helps build confidence among potential investors.

v. **Compliance assurance:** It ensures that all legal requirements are met before the final prospectus is published, thereby reducing legal risks.

vii. **Assessing market conditions:** It allows the company to understand current market conditions and investor sentiment, which can be crucial for setting the final offer price.

viii. **Strategic planning:** It helps the company in strategic planning by identifying key areas of interest and concern among investors, enabling them to address these issues in the final prospectus.

3. **Abridged Prospectus:** To cut cost of issuing a prospectus that may run into hundreds of pages, also making it challenging for retail investors to understand detailed prospectus because of their limited financial knowledge and resources, an abridged prospectus accompanies the application form in case of public offer.

   Section 2(1) of the Companies Act, 2013, defines an abridged prospectus as a summary containing the key features of an issue. SEBI specifies which features to include. Section 33 of the Act requires that an abridged prospectus be attached to the application form for purchasing securities. However, this requirement can be waived if the application form is for:

   i. A genuine invitation to someone to enter into an underwriting agreement for the securities, or

   ii. Securities not offered to the public.

   If a company fails to comply with these abridged prospectus rules, Section 33(3) states it may face a penalty of up to Rs. 50,000 for each default.

4. **Deemed Prospectus:** When a company wants to issue its securities through an intermediary, the document with the details of these securities is called a deemed prospectus. Section 25(1) of the Companies Act, 2013, governs deemed

prospectuses. This document is considered a prospectus for the company whose securities are being offered to the public.

The prospectus, including variations like the statement in lieu of prospectus and the red-herring prospectus, is essential for maintaining transparency and trust in the investment process. These documents ensure that investors have access to all necessary information to make informed decisions, thereby fostering a fair and efficient market. They play a critical role in protecting investors and ensuring that companies comply with legal and regulatory standards when raising capital. By providing comprehensive and accurate information, the prospectus helps to build investor confidence and supports the integrity of the financial markets.

Contents of Prospectus

1. Company Information

- **Business Overview**: A detailed description of the company's business, including its history, mission, vision, products, services, and market position.
- **Corporate Structure**: Information about the company's organisation structure, including details of its subsidiaries, affiliates, and key business units.

2. Financial Statements

- **Balance Sheets**: Details of the company's assets, liabilities, and shareholders' equity, providing a snapshot of the company's financial position at a specific point in time.
- **Income Statements**: Information on the company's revenues, expenses, and profits over a specific period, showing the company's financial performance and profitability.
- **Cash Flow Statements**: Data on the company's cash inflows and outflows, demonstrating its liquidity, cash management, and financial health.

3. Risk Factors

- **Market Risks**: Potential risks related to market conditions, competition, economic factors, and regulatory changes that could impact the company's business.
- **Operational Risks**: Risks associated with the company's operations, including production challenges, supply chain disruptions, and management issues.
- **Financial Risks**: Risks related to the company's financial stability, such as high debt levels, cash flow issues, and exposure to financial markets.

4. Use of Proceeds

- **Purpose of Funds**: An explanation of how the funds raised from the offering will be used, such as for business expansion, debt repayment, research and development, or other corporate purposes.
- **Allocation**: A detailed breakdown of the allocation of funds to different projects or purposes, providing transparency on the company's planned use of the capital raised.

5. Management

- **Leadership Team**: Information about the company's management team, including their backgrounds, qualifications, experience, and roles within the company.
- **Corporate Governance**: Details about the company's governance structure, including information on the board of directors, executive compensation, and corporate policies.

6. Terms of the Offering

- **Securities Details**: Specifics about the securities being offered, including the type (e.g., shares, bonds), quantity, offering price, and terms.
- **Offering Period**: Information about the timeline of the offering, including the opening and closing dates for subscriptions.
- **Subscription Details**: Instructions on how investors can subscribe to the offering, the payment terms, and the process for allocating securities.

Statutory Requirements as to the Issue of a Prospectus

The following statutory requirements as to the issue of a prospectus must be complied with:

1. A prospectus issued by a company shall be dated and that **date** shall, unless the contrary is proved be taken as the date of publication of the prospectus. The date of publication of prospectus is the date that appears on the prospectus. The date of issue is the date of its filing with the Registrar. Date of issue can be different from date of its publication.
2. The prospectus shall be issued if it has been delivered to the Registrar for **registration** on or before the date of issue. It has to be signed by all the persons named therein as directors or proposed directors.
3. The prospectus delivered for registration must be **accompanied with the following documents**:

(a) consent of expert in writing to the issue of prospectus with the statement included therein.

(b) a copy of every contract required to be specified in the prospectus.

(c) adjustments made in the financial statements signed by the persons making their report on it (adjustments made by auditors, accountants, etc. in their reports relating to financial statements, profit and loss, assets and liabilities etc.)

(d) consent in writing of auditors, attorney, legal advisor, solicitor, banker or broker, to act in that capacity.

4. The fact that **prospectus has been delivered for registration with the Registrar must appear on the face of prospectus**.

   The prospectus should be issued within 90 days of the day when it is delivered to the Registrar. If it is issued after 90 days, it will be considered to be an issue which has not been registered with the Registrar.

   Failure to comply with the above provisions (registration and issue of prospectus) will attract fine which may extend up to Rupees three lakh.

Statement in Lieu of Prospectus

A public company having share capital shall file with the Registrar a statement known as Statement in lieu of Prospectus, if:

(i) it does not issue a prospectus because it raises capital from private sources without public invitation to subscribe for shares or debentures, or

(ii) it has issued a prospectus but has failed to allot shares because the issue has been under subscribed.

The public company is required to submit this statement with the Registrar of Companies at least 3 days before the allotment of shares. This document contains all the information found in a prospectus and is signed by all current or future directors of the public company. Without filing this statement, the company cannot issue any shares or debentures. This statement should be signed by every person listed as a director or proposed director of the company or by their authorised agent in writing. When a private company transforms into a public company, it must provide the Registrar with a statement in lieu of prospectus.

Contents of Statement in Lieu of Prospectus

- Company Name.

- The company's share capital is divided into ordinary shares and the value of one share.
- Description of the planned activities and prospectus.
- Names, addresses, roles and responsibilities of proposed or appointed directors, officers, appointed lawyers and company secretaries.
- Rules for selecting and compensating these corporate representatives.
- Voting rights during company meetings.
- Quantity and value of shares and debentures intended to be issued.
- Names, jobs and addresses of those selling goods bought or offered for sale by the company.
- Amount to be paid in cash, stocks or bonds to each real estate seller.

Failure to comply with these rules can result in a fine of up to ₹1,000 for the company and every director responsible. Where a statement in lieu of prospectus delivered to the Registrar includes any untrue statement, any person who authorised the delivery of the statement in lieu of prospectus for registration shall be punishable with imprisonment for a term which may extend to 2 years with fine which may extend to ₹5,000 or both, unless he proves that the statement was immaterial or he had reasonable ground to believe, and did upto the time of delivery for registration of the statement in lieu of prospectus believe, that the statement was true.

Differences Between Prospectus and Statement in Lieu of Prospectus

	Prospectus	Statement In Lieu of Prospectus
Purpose	Provides information about a company's securities	Used when a regular prospectus cannot be used
Content	Offers detailed information about the company	Contains less detailed information
Issue	Issued by a newly public company or one offering new securities	Issued by a company already trading
Approval	Requires approval from securities commission	No approval needed
Distribution	Distributed to potential investors	Not widely distributed
Timing	Prepared at the time of or before offering securities	Can be prepared or distributed at any time
Use	Used to gather investment through securities	Used for less formal purposes

Questions

1. Long Answer Questions

1. Explain the meaning, importance and contents of Memorandum of Association.
2. What is Articles of Association? What are its contents?
3. What are the contents of a Prospectus issued by a company?
4. What is a 'Memorandum of Association'? Explain its importance and contents.
5. What is Articles of Association? Explain the differences between Articles of Association and Memorandum of Association.
6. Discuss various documents to be filed at various stages of incorporation of a Joint Stock Company.

II. Write short notes on:

(i) Memorandum of Association
(ii) Articles of Association
(iii) Statement in lieu of Prospectus
(iv) Prospectus

❑❑❑

9 Chapter

Management Concept and Nature

"The best executive is the one who has sense enough to pick good men to do what he wants done, and self-restraint to keep from meddling with them while they do it."

— *Theodore Roosevelt*

9.1 MANAGEMENT

Management is the *process* that *optimises* human, material, and financial resources of the organisation for effective achievement of its *goals*.

- *process* involves a series of actions (functions) performed by managers.
- *optimisation* gets maximum output (goods and services) out of minimum inputs (men, materials, money, machine etc.).
- *goals* are the end results those managers and stakeholders (shareholders, consumers, suppliers, workers etc.) aim to achieve.

"Management is a distinct process consisting of activities of planning, organising, actuating and controlling, performed to determine and accomplish stated objectives with the use of human beings and other resources." –*Terry* and *Franklin*

"Management is the process of designing and maintaining an environment in which individuals, working together in groups, efficiently accomplish selected aims."

–*Koontz* and *Weihrich*

"Management is an art of knowing what is to be done and seeing that it is done in the best possible manner." –*F. W. Taylor*

"Management is to forecast, to plan, to organise, to command, to co-ordinate and control activities of others. –*Henri Fayol*

9.2 FEATURES OF MANAGEMENT

1. **Activity**: Management organises a team to work towards a common goal. Leaders and rules make sure things run smoothly.
2. **Process**: It is a step-by-step plan that helps the organisation reach its goals.
3. **Required for All Organisations**: Every type of organisation, profit or non-profit, business, government, or a club, needs management to work well.
4. **Required at All Levels**: Management is needed at every level of organisation, whether it is the top managers, middle managers, or front lines workers, though every level has different responsibilities.
5. **Goal-oriented**: Management helps a group of people achieve the goals they have agreed upon.
6. **Intangible**: One cannot see or touch management but can see the results when an organisation is well-run compared to one that is not well managed.
7. **Dynamic**: The role of management changes over time. The business world keeps evolving, and managers adapt to new situations.
8. **Discipline**: While management takes ideas from other fields like psychology and sociology, it is a field of study on its own. Managers learn specific skills and knowledge to do their job.
9. **Management and Society**: Management is influenced by values, culture, and beliefs of the society and helps it in ways like creating jobs and preserving its interests.
10. **Group Effort**: Management helps people in working together. They set goals, make plans, and control how things are going.
11. **Global Function**: Management is not limited to one country or culture. It is used globally because companies work across borders.

9.3 IMPORTANCE OF MANAGEMENT

"Management is the specific organ of the modern institution. It is the organ on the performance of which the performance and the survival of the institution depends."

–Peter F. Drucker

A well-managed organisation can effectively utilise its resources (human, physical and financial), achieve its objectives as well as meet society's needs. Effectiveness (doing the right things) and efficiency (doing things right) are the fundamentals to managerial success. As *Drucker* puts it, "effectiveness rather than efficiency is essential to business. The pertinent question is not how to do things right, but how to find the right things to do, and to concentrate resources and efforts on them."

1. **Achieve Goals**: Management guides a company toward its goals. It lays out tasks and makes sure that right people do the right things.
2. **Use Resources Wisely**: Management helps to make the best use of limited resources, people and their skills, materials and machines, and money.
3. **Build Managerial Skills**: Management teaches managers to be problem solvers. They learn to analyse problems and find the best solutions. This also helps them think ahead to prevent problems and make their organisations competitive.
4. **Balance Multiple Goals**: Management helps decide which goals are most important and allocates resources in the order of priority.
5. **Economic and Social Development:** Drucker argues that the level of development in a country is not solely determined by economic factors or the amount of savings and capital investment. Instead, good management practices are the driving force behind economic and social development. The real essence of development lies in the energy and efforts of people, rather than just accumulation of economic wealth. Management plays a crucial role in mobilising human energy towards development. Economic and social progress are the natural outcomes of effective management.
6. **Balance Individual and Organisational Goals**: Management makes sure that personal goals align with the goals of the organisation. Employees work towards organisational goals while achieving their own.
7. **Make Things Work Well**: Efficiency is about doing things correctly, but effectiveness is about doing the right things. Management helps the organisation focus on the right objectives to get things done efficiently.
8. **Deal with Competition**: Management encourages innovation to keep up with rapidly changing technology. It helps adapt to complex changes in the world.
9. **Improve Society**: Management promotes social development by guiding efforts towards societal needs like health, education, and the environment. It also teaches respect for values, traditions, and social culture.

10. **Analyse the Environment**: Management helps organisations analyse their strengths and weaknesses and how they relate to the challenges and opportunities in their surroundings, to minimise risks and make the most of opportunities.

9.4 ASPECTS OF MANAGEMENT

I. Management as an Activity

Management as an activity is the art of getting things done through people. It is about what managers do, not just what they should do. This can be broken down into three categories:

1. ***Interpersonal Roles or Activities:*** Managers interact with different people. They attend meetings and events, welcome visitors, hire and train employees. They communicate with people inside and outside the organisation, like superiors, subordinates, peers, consumers, suppliers, and the government.
2. ***Informational Roles or Activities:*** Managers share information with various people, consumers, creditors, employees, suppliers, and the government. They gather information from different sources and pass it along through meetings, notices, and messages. They also connect with people outside the organisation.
3. ***Decision-making Roles or Activities:*** Managers make decisions to introduce new products, resolve issues of employees, figure out where to allocate resources, and negotiate with groups inside or outside the organisation.

II. Management as a Process

From a practitioner's point of view, management is the process of making plans, organising resources, leading people, and ensuring everything goes as planned to achieve the goals of the organisation. This process is carried out at all levels and involves four main functions:

1. ***Planning:*** Managers set goals and decide how to reach those goals.
2. ***Organising:*** They put everything in order, making sure resources achieve the goals.
3. ***Leading:*** They inspire and guide their team through motivation, leadership, and communication skills.
4. ***Controlling:*** They make sure things go as planned and take actions to fix deviations, if any.

Since management deals with people, it is often described as:

- ***Social Process:*** Management involves working with people to make the best use of human resources, turning ideas into products or services. It satisfies human needs through financial and non-financial rewards.

- ***Continuous Process:*** Organisations constantly need management to keep their resources working together.
- ***Integrating Process:*** Management coordinates activities and resources within an organisation, like production, personnel, marketing, and finance, to get maximum output at minimum cost.

III. Management as Discipline

Management is a special area of study with its own set of ideas and rules that help organisations run smoothly. Even though it borrows ideas from fields like psychology and sociology, it is a full subject on its own.

IV. Management as a Group

From a sociologist's point of view, management is a team effort. Managers at different levels work to set goals and make decisions.

As organisations become complex, they need a group of people with special knowledge to handle the complexities. How well an organisation does, depends on how well the managers perform.

V. Management as an Economic Resource

From the economist's point of view, management is a valuable resource, just like land, labour, and capital. It handles ideas, things, and people to make an organisation successful.

Ideas: Managers come up with ideas that lead to innovations, new markets, customers, technologies, and products in a constantly changing world.

Things: Resources (people, materials, money, and technology) turn ideas into reality. Managing resources means using them effectively to produce things at the lowest cost.

People: All the ideas and things need people to make them happen. Good management means finding the right people, training, and developing them, and keeping them motivated to do their best.

9.5 NATURE OF MANAGEMENT

I. Management as Science

Science develops, tests and experiments with ideas to build a pool of knowledge. By testing ideas, scientists figure out how different things are connected.

1. ***Clarity of Concepts:*** Management can be considered as science because it has well-defined concepts, developed through experiences of managers in various organisations.
2. ***Scientific Methods:*** Management is considered as science because it uses scientific methods for carefully observing things, developing ideas (hypotheses), testing those ideas, and developing theories.
3. ***Clarity of Theory:*** Management can be seen as science because it has developed general principles like unity of command, unity of direction, etc., through careful observation and experiments, applied in different organisations and situations.
4. ***Causal Relationship:*** Like science, management follows a scientific approach in understanding how certain practices lead to specific outcomes. For example, the idea that "having one boss creates loyalty toward superiors" is generally true in many organisations, though it is not always true.
5. ***Systematised Theory of Knowledge:*** Science is not just about having principles or theories; it is also about using those principles in an organised way. Management concepts have been organised into theories and successfully applied in different organisations, which makes it a structured body of knowledge, much like science.
6. ***Universal Application:*** Like scientific principles that work the same way in all situations, countries, and cultures, management principles are often applicable everywhere. For example, the idea that "unity is strength" (Esprit de Corps) is true in every organisation and situation. Thus, we can think of management as a science.

Management is Not an Exact Science

Management is not an exact science like physics or chemistry, which deal with natural phenomena. Instead, it is an applied science, based on information, experience, traditions, and reasoning. It is social science that aims to make people's lives better in specific scenarios. The principles in management are adaptable and flexible, thus, seen as behavioural science or soft science.

II. Management as Art

Art is a way to express feelings, thoughts, and ideas. It is about personal talent and skills to use resources to create expression that does not rely on scientific experiments or testing.

1. ***Artist's Vision:*** An artist has clear idea of what they want to create, just like managers have clear plans and objectives. Managing involves turning disorder into order, sharing the plan with others, and reaching the goal. It brings

together and makes the best use of people's talents. "Management art involves envisioning an orderly whole from chaotic parts, communicating the vision and achieving the goal. It is the 'art of arts' because it organises and uses human talent."

2. ***Knowledge:*** Like artists need to know how to apply what they've learned to create their work; managers use their knowledge and resources effectively to achieve their objectives.
3. ***Communication:*** Like artists communicate well with their team, managers talk to their team about what needs to be done (top-down communication) and listen to their concerns and problems (bottom-up communication).
4. ***Creativity:*** As artists use their imagination, skills, and creativity to make something unique, managers need to be creative to see opportunities and use them to get good results.
5. ***Skilled Performance:*** Just like each artist has their own skills and style, managers use different skills in different situations. They learn from their experience and get good at what they do. Decision-making in management is an artistic process, where personal abilities matter.
6. ***Practice:*** Artists get better through practice, not just following set rules. Management also gets better with practice. Successful business leaders keep learning and improving their skills.

In conclusion, management is an art because it uses skills, knowledge, creativity, judgment, and innovation to understand people and resources to reach the goals of an organisation.

Management - Both Science and Art

Management is both science and art, but it can be hard to say when it is one or the other. As science, it explains theories and principles, and as art, it makes decisions using personal skills.

Science gives knowledge, and art uses that knowledge. Science gives principles, and art uses those principles in real business situations. Science explains the "why" of a situation, while art explains the "how" of solving it. There's no one best way to solve a problem, as every manager uses an approach that suits their experience, knowledge, skills, and creativity.

A successful manager knows how to use management principles in specific situations. The real power in management comes from putting the science of management into action. Success does not come from knowing about management; it comes from using that knowledge in real business situations.

III. Management as Profession

A profession uses special knowledge, learned through formal education and training in a specialised area of study.

1. ***Specialised Knowledge:*** Professionals make decisions based on what they have learned through formal education. Since management is a separate field taught in management schools, it can be considered a 'Profession.'
2. ***Status through Performance:*** Professionals earn their status through performance, and not personal connections. Some people get managerial positions due to personal and political connections. Thus, management is not entirely a profession while it is moving in that direction.
3. ***Code of Ethics:*** Professionals follow a specific set of rules and are committed to serving the best interests of society. Violating these rules can lead to consequences. Although there is a code of ethics established by the All-India Management Association, it is not strictly followed, and there are no clear consequences for not following it. While managers consider the interests of the owners and stakeholders, there is not a universally accepted set of ethics. So, it is not strictly termed as a 'Profession,' though managers do practice ethical behaviours.
4. ***Dedication:*** Professionals work with complete dedication, commitment, and loyalty. Managers also work with dedication and commitment and consistently coordinate resources to align goals of the organisation with individual goals. This makes management a 'Profession.'
5. ***Association:*** Professionals follow the rules of the Association or Council governing their profession, for example, doctors must be registered with the Medical Council of India. With management, it is not mandatory to be a member of the All-India Management Association, so it is not entirely a 'Profession.'
6. ***Professional Qualification:*** To work in a profession, one needs formal qualification and training, like chartered accountants, doctors, and lawyers. While many institutions offer formal education and training in management, many successful managers rely on their experience in managerial roles. Not all successful managers follow a formal code of ethics, so, management may not fully qualify as a 'Profession.'

Thus, management can be seen as a profession when considering its use of general principles, specialised knowledge, and dedication. However, it falls short of being a full-fledged profession when it comes to professional status, a clear code of ethics, and a specific management association. Nevertheless, management is making progress towards becoming a true profession due to:

(i) A growing body of organised knowledge.

(ii) Increasing number of professional institutes offering management courses.

(iii) Greater awareness of ethical practices within business organisations.

(iv) Rising emphasis on principles followed by management experts or consultants.

9.6 MANAGEMENT AND ADMINISTRATION

I. Management and Administration are Different

1. ***Administration is above Management:*** Some American authors, such as Oliver Sheldon, Spriegal, Theo Haimann, and McFarland, believe that administration is a higher-level function where people create policies, plans, and goals. Management is about putting those policies into action.

   According to *Oliver Sheldon*, "Administration is concerned with the determination of corporate policy, the co-ordination of finance, production and distribution, the settlement of the compass of the organisation and the ultimate control of the executive. Management proper is concerned with the execution of policy, within the limits set up by administration and employment of the organisation in the particular objects set before it. Administration determines the organisation; management uses it. Administration defines the goal, management strives towards it."

2. ***Management is above Administration:*** British authors like Breech, Kimball and Kimball, and Richman believe that management is the higher-level job of creating plans and policies and administration is about carrying out those plans and policies.

   According to *Breech*, "Management is a social process entailing responsibility for the effective and economic planning and regulation of the operation of an enterprise in fulfilment of a given purpose or task. Administration is that part of management which is concerned with the installation and carrying out of the procedures by which the programme is laid down and communicated and the progress of activities is regulated and checked against plans".

II. Management and Administration are Same

Authors like *Chester Bernard, George R. Terry, Koontz,* and *O'Donnell* view "management" and "administration" as the same. They believe the difference lies in how these ideas are used.

In their view, both administration and management can be done by the same people at all levels, whether at the top, middle, or bottom of an organisation. People at the top might do more administration, like making policies, while those at lower levels do more management, like putting those policies into action.

Both administration and management involve important tasks like planning, organising, and controlling. One often hears "administration" used in government organisations and "management" in businesses.

9.7 LEVELS OF MANAGEMENT

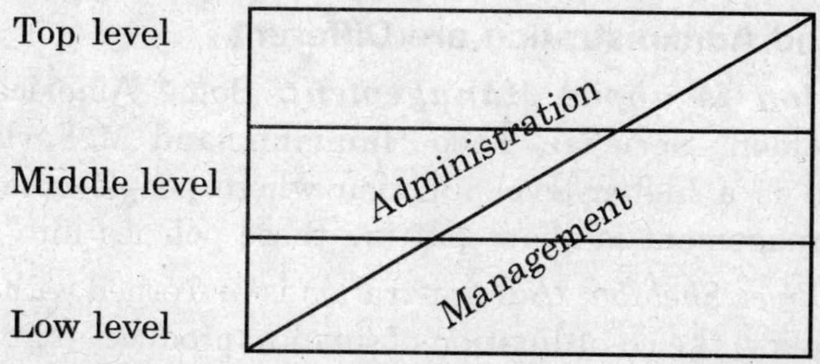

Managers perform planning, organising, staffing, and controlling functions based on the level of responsibility in a company. There are different levels of managers, which creates hierarchy or chain of command in the organisation structure. When a company has more employees, it often needs more levels of management, and when it has fewer employees, it needs fewer levels.

Managers and management can be classified on these levels:

I. Top level Managers or Top Management.

II. Middle level Managers or Middle Management.

III. Lower level Managers or Lower Management work together.

I. Top Management

Top management consists of managers at the highest level, responsible for overall management of the organisation. Managers in this level are generally 'chief executive officers', 'president', 'vice-president', 'general managers', 'managing directors', however, the specific title can change depending on the company. The number of managers in this group is generally the least.

Top managers perform the following functions:

1. ***Set objectives and plans:*** They create goals, plans, and rules for the organisation.

2. ***Manage the work:*** They take care of tasks like planning, organising, finding the right people, giving directions, and making sure everything is going well.
3. ***Choose middle managers:*** They pick people to manage individual departments or teams.
4. ***Coordinate departments:*** They make sure different parts of the organisation work together smoothly.
5. ***Connect inside and outside:*** They link what is happening inside the company with what is going outside in the world.
6. ***Get resources ready:*** They gather the things needed to put plans in action.
7. ***Create departmental budgets:*** They determine how much money each department can use and make rules for how they work.
8. ***Think about everyone's interests:*** They integrate goals of different groups, like the government, customers, suppliers, employees, and owners.

II. Middle Management

Middle management is the bridge between top-level and lower-level managers. The organisation is divided into different departments, and the heads of these departments are middle managers. They have titles like "departmental managers," "plant managers," or "assistant managers," but it can vary by organisation.

They bring plans made by the top managers to action, pass on the rules from the top and the reports from the bottom. They are responsible for the departmental activities and control the work of foremen, inspectors, and supervisors. In big companies, there can be quite a few middle-level managers.

Middle-level managers perform the following *functions*:

1. ***Share top managers' decisions*:** They tell the lower-level managers what managers at the top have decided.
2. ***Set goals and plans*:** They determine the goals, plans, and rules for their departments.
3. ***Manage day-to-day work*:** They make sure that everyday tasks of the company run smoothly.
4. ***Balance demands*:** They balance demands of the superiors with what their team members can do.
5. ***Help with hiring and training*:** They join in the process of finding and training the lower-level managers.

6. ***Coordinate department activities***: They make sure all the divisions of their department are working together well.
7. ***Report to top management***: They send important reports to top managers and judge how well the junior managers are doing.
8. ***Inspire team:*** They encourage their team to work hard and do better.
9. ***Suggest changes***: They share their ideas if they think there should be changes in their departmental rules.

III. Lower Management

These managers are at the lowest level in the management structure. They are the first-line managers or supervisors who connect the middle-level managers and the non-managerial workers.

They supervise the work of regular workers and make sure everything runs smoothly. They directly guide employees to reach the goals, train them and solve issues that come up in their work. They are the "foremen," "supervisors," "office managers," "operating managers," or "superintendents." Usually, a company has the largest number of managers at this level.

Lower-level managers perform the following *functions*:

1. ***Coordinate work***: They make sure that employees use the resources wisely.
2. ***Train employees***: They teach the workers how to do their jobs properly.
3. ***Review employee performance***: They check how well the employees are doing their jobs and share that information with the higher-up managers.
4. ***Plan daily operations***: They determine how everyday work in the company should be done.
5. ***Assign jobs***: They give tasks to the workers and provide training they need.
6. ***Solve worker problems***: If the employees have any issues, they try to solve them.
7. ***Create reports***: They make regular reports about how well the workers are doing.
8. ***Share concerns***: They tell the higher-level managers about problems, ideas, or requests from the employees.

9. ***Ensure safety***: They make sure the tools, machines, and equipment are safe and working well.
10. ***Develop workers***: They help the employees improve and promote corporate image.

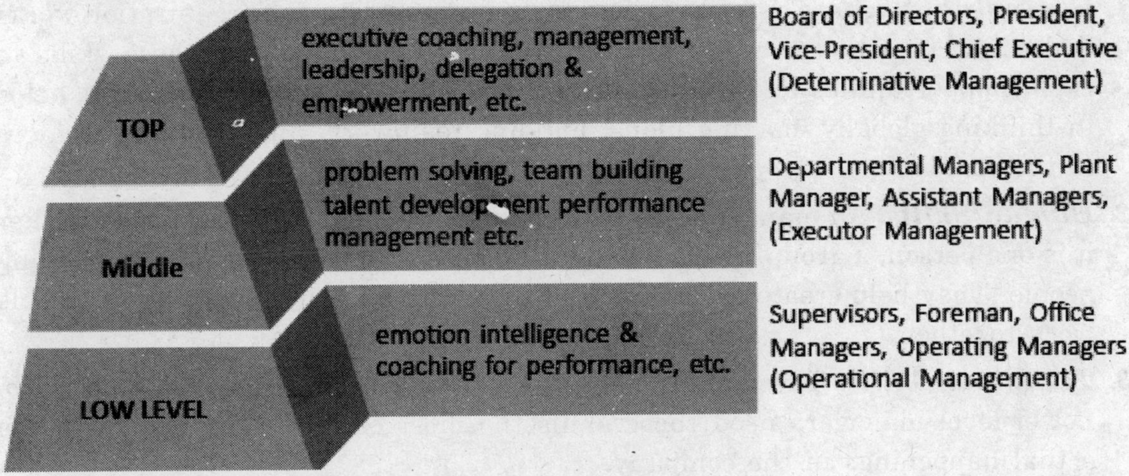

Levels of Management

9.8 MANAGERIAL SKILLS

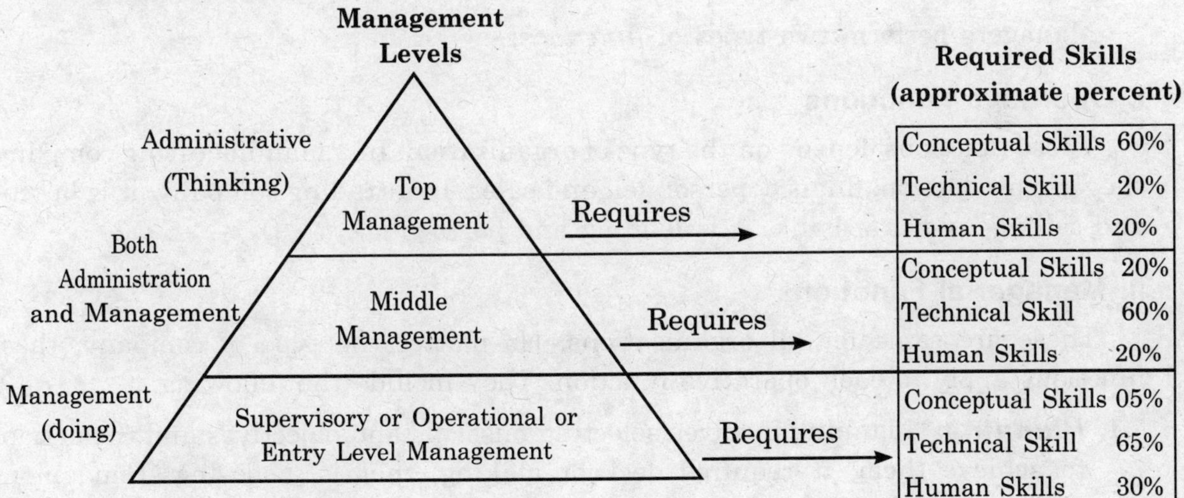

Managerial Skills

As one goes down the hierarchy, the skills change. Lower-level managers focus more on technical skills as they deal with specific job tasks. Higher-level managers use more conceptual skills to coordinate with the outside world. Human skills are same at all levels as managers work with people at all levels.

1. ***Conceptual Skills:*** These skills help to understand how the organisation works and connects with the world outside. Top-level managers use these skills to exploit opportunities and connect them with what the company does. It helps in thinking globally, making plans, building teamwork, and handling changes in the company.
2. ***Human Skills:*** All managers, no matter their level, deal with people—whether it is one person, a group, or a whole team. These skills deal with understanding people. They help create a friendly and cooperative environment where people work together.
3. ***Technical Skills:*** These skills help in knowing how to use tools to do a job. Lower-level managers need these skills the most because they deal with the actual happenings in the company.

9.9 MANAGEMENT FUNCTIONS

Management process gives structure to how management is done, both in theory and practice. This process is based on different functions which managers perform.

Managers perform two types of *functions*:

i. Operative Functions

These functions depend on the type of organisation. In a manufacturing company, they are production, finance, personnel, and sales. In a trading company, it is buying and selling, and in a bank, it is lending and borrowing.

ii. Managerial Functions

These are same for all organisations. No matter the type of company, these functions apply to each operative function. They include the following:

1. ***Planning***: "Planning involves selecting missions and objectives and the actions to achieve them; it requires decision-making, that is, choosing from among alternative future courses of action." –*Koontz* and *Weihrich*

   Planning is deciding about what to achieve and how to get there. It bridges the gap between where we are and where we want to be. Planning answers questions like what needs to be done, when to do it, how to do it, and who should do it.

This applies to all kinds of organisations, whether for-profit businesses or non-profit groups. Planning is needed at every level of management (top, middle, and low), for organisations of all sizes (big or small), and for various goals, whether maximising profits or not.

Top managers spend more time on planning, while lower-level managers put the plans into action. It involves lot of thinking and analysing the environment (both inside and outside the organisation) to make the best use of resources.

2. ***Organising***: "Organisation is the structure and process by which a co-operative group of human beings allocates its tasks among its members, identifies relationships, and integrates its activities towards common objectives."

   – *J.L. Massie*

   It sets up a structure where people work together to achieve their goals.

   (i) **Identifying goals:** What we want to achieve.

   (ii) **Dividing tasks:** Break down the work into different tasks.

   (iii) **Grouping tasks:** Group the tasks together in a way that makes sense.

   (iv) **Assigning tasks:** Each group of tasks is given to a manager who has the authority to make things happen.

   (v) **Coordinating:** Ensure that everyone works together at the same level (horizontally) and up and down the hierarchy (vertically).

3. ***Staffing***: "The staffing function includes the process by which the right person is placed in the right organisational position." – *J.L. Massie*

   It is about finding the right people for the right jobs. It finds out how many people are needed and gets them to fill those positions.

4. ***Directing***: It is "a managerial function that involves the responsibility of managers for communicating to others what their roles are in achieving the company plan."

   "Directing is telling people what to do and seeing that they do it to the best of their ability. It includes making assignments, corresponding procedures, seeing that mistakes are corrected, providing on-the-job instructions and, of course, issuing orders."

   Directing is the action phase. It puts the plans into motion through motivation, communication, leadership and building a strong team spirit.

Motivation is encouraging and inspiring people to do things that help reach the goals.

"Motivation is the state of individual's perspective which represents the strength of his or her propensity to exert effort toward some particular behaviour."
-- *Gibson*

Leadership is the ability to influence the behaviour of people.

It is "influence, that is, the art or process of influencing people so that they will strive willingly and enthusiastically towards the achievement of group goals."

— *Koontz* and *Weihrich*

Communication is exchange of ideas, and information so that the person sending the message and the person receiving it understand it in the same sense.

"Communication is the art of developing and attaining understanding between people. It is the process of exchanging information and feelings between two or more people, and it is essential to effective management."

— *Terry* and *Franklin*

5. ***Controlling***: "Controlling is determining what is being accomplished, that is, evaluating the performance and, if necessary, applying corrective measures so that the performance takes place according to plans."

   It sets standards, measures performance, finds deviations and takes actions to remove them. Monitoring ensures effective implementation of plans. It is a corrective and preventive function, performed at all levels (top, middle and low) of the organisation.

Interdependence of Functions

Managerial functions are inter-related and performed at every level and in all types of organisations, whether business or non-business. They rely on each other. For instance, when a manager is handling staffing, they are also planning, organising, directing, and controlling as part of the staffing function. Similarly, when they are directing, they are also planning, organising, and controlling the direction function.

There is no strict order to follow when using these functions. While planning often comes first in a new organisation, in an established one, one function may precede or succeed another. The importance of these functions varies depending on what the organisation needs at a particular time.

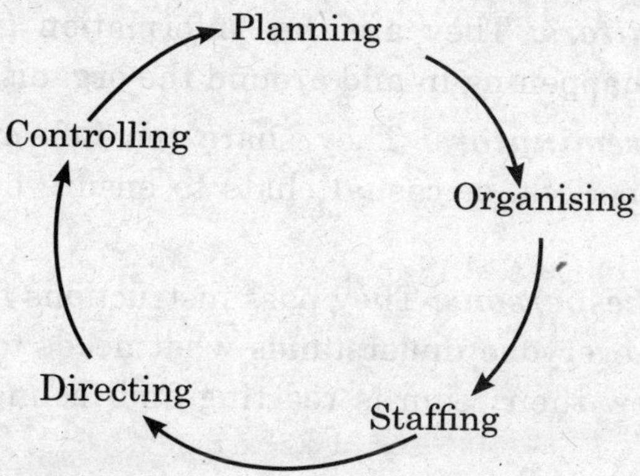

9.10 ROLE OF MANAGERS

In 1973, *Henry Mintzberg* identified 10 basic roles (categorised under three broad headings) of managers. These are:

I. Inter-personal Roles II. Informational Roles III. Decisional Roles

I. Inter-personal Roles

Managers interact with superiors, peers, subordinates, and the outside parties performing the following roles:

1. ***Manager as the Figurehead:*** Manager is the "official face" of the company. He signs important papers, welcomes visitors, attends social events, and recognises employees for their good work. He is the "representative" of the organisation on official occasions.
2. ***Manager as the Leader:*** Manager takes care of the needs of the people, solves problems, sets goals, and makes sure everyone works together to achieve those goals. He acts like a "team captain" who keeps everyone motivated and confident.
3. ***Manager as the Liaison:*** He is the "connection maker" who brings different groups of people within and outside the company together. Inside, they connect superiors, peers, and subordinates. Outside, they connect with society, customers, the government, trade unions, and other external groups.

II. Informational Roles

Managers perform the following roles while they collect information to make business decisions.

1. ***Managers as Monitors:*** They are the "information gatherers." They collect data about what is happening in and around the organisation, to stay informed.
2. ***Managers as Disseminators:*** They share the information with their team through meetings, notices, or casual chats to ensure everyone knows what is happening.
3. ***Managers as Spokespersons:*** They pass instructions from higher-ups to their team, making sure everyone understands what needs to be done. They also let the bosses know how their team is reacting and feeling.

III. Decisional Roles

Managers choose the best alternative to solve organisational problem.

1. ***Managers as Entrepreneurs***: Managers are the creative problem solvers. They come up with new ideas even with limited resources, to keep the business thriving and adapting to what is happening in the world.
2. ***Managers as Disturbance Handlers***: They deal with things that disturb the normal flow of business, like strikes, shortage of materials, complaints from customers etc. They are the "trouble solvers" who make sure things get back on track when there are problems.
3. ***Managers as Resource Allocators***: They decide how to use the resources wisely by distributing them in the right order to achieve the goals efficiently. They act as the "resource manager."
4. ***Managers as Negotiators***: They act as mediators, bringing together the organisation, its employees, and other important groups. They find solutions that benefit both the company and its stakeholders.

9.11 FUNCTIONAL AREAS OF MANAGEMENT

The major functional areas of management are:

I. Production/Operations Management

II. Financial Management

III. Personnel/Human Resource Management

IV. Marketing Management

I. Production/Operations Management

It deals with a "set of components whose function is to transform a set of inputs into some desired output."

"It is the management of productive processes that convert inputs into goods and services."

Operations management involves the following activities:

1. ***Design of the Operations System:*** These are long-term strategic decisions related to product design, process design, location of facilities, layout of facilities and capacity planning.

   i. **Product design:** It decides to produce technologically feasible and marketable products, compatible with organisational goals and design them in terms of cost, quality, and ease of production.

   ii. **Process design***:* It determines the way the product or service is produced.

      a. Which technology shall be used?

      b. Which conversion or transformation process will be used?

      c. What types of equipment shall be used — machines, human labour or computer aided?

      d. How shall the product flow through the production system?

      Various combinations are tried to arrive at the optimum sequence of operations process.

   iii. **Location of facilities:** This decides the place where operations facilities will be located, near the source of raw material or consumers. This decision is affected by fixed costs (cost of land, plant and machinery, construction costs etc.) and variable costs (cost of labour, material, transportation, and distribution costs, etc.)

   iv. **Facilities layout***:* It decides about how to arrange the product and process facilities to produce goods at minimum cost. Product layout means setting up machines in the order needed to make a specific product. Process layout puts similar machines together in one area. For example, in a clothing factory, all cutting machines are grouped in one spot and all stitching and ironing machines in another.

   v. **Capacity planning***:* Capacity means "the maximum theoretical rate of productive or conversion capability for an existing product mix of an organisation's operations." Capacity planning decides the number of products/services to be produced.

2. ***Operations and Control Decision***: Production planning and control involves the following:

i. **Routing:** It determines the path through which operations will be performed.

ii. **Loading:** It decides which machine to use for making things efficiently and managing decisions.

iii. **Scheduling:** It ensures that products are delivered on schedule, so it does not cause delays for other tasks.

iv. **Dispatching:** It decides when head of the operations department gives the go-ahead to start the work.

v. **Expediting:** It makes sure that the work is happening as planned, without unexpected delays.

II. Financial Management

It is "the operational activity of a business that is responsible for obtaining and effectively utilising the funds necessary for efficient operations."

The scope of financial management includes the following:

1. Deciding how big a company should be, how much money it needs, and what kind of assets it should have.
2. Identifying the sources of money to support the company's needs, like loans, investments, or earnings and ensuring their availability at the right time.
3. Deciding how to share the company's profits, whether to reinvest in the business or distribute among the shareholders.

III. Personnel/Human Resource Management

Human resource department performs the following functions:

1. ***Human resource planning*** means finding the right people for a job, both in terms of sources of supply and the number of employees needed. While some are hired from inside the company, some come from outside, like the job market.
2. ***Recruitment*** is about making a job description, and inviting people to apply if they have the right qualifications.
3. ***Selection*** means picking the best person for the job from those who applied.
4. ***Performance appraisal*** checks how well people are doing compared to the goals.
5. ***Training*** helps employees learn and grow in their roles. It can be done on the job or through outside training programmes.
6. ***Rewards*** deal with how much people are paid for their job. Pay varies depending on the skills, knowledge, and abilities required for each job.

7. ***Industrial relations*** keep things peaceful between management and employees.
8. ***Employee communication and participation*** involve telling employees about management decisions and letting them have a say in the decision-making process.
9. ***Personnel records*** match the right person to the right job and help with internal hiring within the organisation.

IV. Marketing Management

Marketing management is "planning, organising, controlling and implementing of marketing programmes, policies, strategies and tactics designed to create and satisfy the demand for the firms' product offerings or services as a means of generating an acceptable profit."

It deals with the following activities:

1. ***Customer Focus***: The main goal is to offer products that satisfy what customers are looking for.
2. ***Product Quality***: This involves how a product looks, what benefits it offers, how it is designed, coloured, and packaged. Making a product that people are proud to own is important.
3. ***Set the Right Price***: Deciding the price of a product is an important marketing decision, influenced by cost, competition, and what customers are willing to pay. The price should allow for the business to grow.
4. ***Promote the Product***: It creates awareness about the product through different methods.
    - **Advertising**: Sharing details about the product through media, like TV and the internet.
    - **Personal selling**: Directly convincing a customer to buy the product.
    - **Sales promotion**: Boosting sales through contests and lotteries, often alongside advertising and personal selling.
5. ***Deliver the Product***: The product needs to get to customers to make sure that the selling process is consistent and effective. This involves deciding how it gets from the seller to the buyer.
    - It could be sold directly from the seller to the buyer.
    - It might go through middlemen like wholesalers or retailers.

Sometimes, more than one way can be used at the same time.

Questions

I. Long Answer Questions

1. "Management is concerned with ideas, things and people". Comment.
2. What are the skills and skill mixtures required of managers at different levels?
3. "Management is the co-ordination of all resources through the process of planning, organising, staffing, directing and controlling, in order to attain stated objectives". Comment on the statement and briefly describe the functions of management.
4. "A manager plans, organises, staffs, directs and controls." Discuss.
5. "Profession means application of specialised knowledge, acquired after attending formal education and training programmes." Discuss in the light of management as a profession.
6. "Management is the art of getting things done through and with people." Comment and explain.
7. Describe the different functional areas of management.
8. Distinguish Management from Administration.
9. Discuss different levels of management in a business enterprise.
10. 'Management is both Art and Science'. Comment.

II. Write short notes on:

(i) Managerial roles.
(ii) Management as profession.
(iii) Administration and management.
(iv) Managerial skills.
(v) Levels of management.
(vi) Administration.

III. Case Study

(I) Hindustan Automobiles

Hindustan automobiles produced spare parts of automobiles. The GM of the company stayed away from his workers and believed in strict compliance to his orders. Authority and responsibility flew strictly in the hierarchical line. The demand for company's products went down and the company come to a close.

Then, Mr. Gupta was appointed as new GM of the company. He scanned the overall working environment of the company, took a round in each and every department of the company, met every worker personally, so much so that he called workers by name and discussed labour-management philosophies with them. Every decision that concerned workers was taken in joint participation by them. Workers could approach him directly in his room without prior appointment. He believed in philosophy - "If you want to get things done through people, you can't be cold and heartless with them." This changed the whole philosophy of management. Workers' morale boosted, production and productivity increased, and profits started rising.

Questions

1. What was Mr. X's perception about management?
2. Did he believe in the concept - "Management is the art of getting things done through and with people."
3. Describe the qualities of Mr. X as a manager.
4. If you were X, would you adopt a similar strategy in your company? Why? If not, what and why?

(II) Success Story of N.R. Narayana Murthy

An Indian IT chief who's really made it big without dropping his ethical precepts by the wayside is Nagawara Ramarao Narayana Murthy, Chairman of Infosys. Born in 1946, Murthy's father was a school teacher in Kolar district, Karnataka, India. A bright student, Murthy went to acquire a degree in Electrical Engineering from Mysore University and later studied Computer Science at the IIT, Kanpur, India.

The Infosys legend began in 1981 when Narayana Murthy dreamt of forming his own company, along with six friends. There was a minor hitch, though-he didn't have any seed money. Luckily, like many Indian women who save secretly without their husband's knowledge, his wife Sudha-then an engineer with Tatas-had saved `10,000. This was Murthy's first big break.

The decade until 1991 was a tough period when the couple lived in a one-room house. The second break came in 1991 when Indian doors to liberalisation were flung open. Murthy grabbed the opportunity with both hands and never looked back ever since. Today, Infosys is the first Indian company to be listed on the US NASDAQ.

While working in France in the 1970s, Murthy was strongly influenced by socialism. The bubble was pricked, however, when he was arrested in Bulgaria on espionage charges. Today, he says: "I'm a capitalist in mind, a socialist at heart." It was this belief in the distribution of wealth that made Infosys one of the first Indian companies to offer employees stock-option plans. Infosys now has 400 employees who are dollar millionaires.

In a poll conducted by Asiaweek, the quiet, soft-spoken man was selected one of the 50 most powerful people in Asia for 2000. And 50 per cent of the respondents in an online poll conducted by The Economic Times voted him the best CEO of India.

He has been the recipient of numerous awards and honors. In 2000, he was awarded the Padma Shri, a civilian award by the Government of India. He was the first recipient of the Indo-French Forum Medal (in the year 2003), awarded by the Indo-French Forum, in recognition of his role in promoting Indo-French ties. He was voted the World Entrepreneur of the Year - 2003 by Ernst & Young. He was one of the two people named as Asia's Businessmen of the Year for 2003 by Fortune magazine. In 2001, he was named by TIME / CNN as one of the twenty-five, most influential global executives, a group selected for their lasting influence in creating new industries and reshaping markets. He was awarded the Max Schmidheiny Liberty 2001 prize (Switzerland), in recognition of his promotion of individual responsibility and liberty. In 1999, Business Week named him one of the nine entrepreneurs of the year and he was also featured in the Business Week's 'The Stars of Asia' (for three successive years -1998, 1999 and 2000). In 1998, the Indian Institute of Technology, Kanpur, one of the premier institutes of higher learning in India, conferred on him the Distinguished Alumnus Award, and in 1996-97, he was awarded the JRD Tata Corporate Leadership Award.

Heading a company with the largest market capitalisation hasn't changed Murthy's life-style much. The man still doesn't know how to drive a car. On Saturdays, his driver's weekly off, the Infosys chief is driven to the bus stop by his wife, from where he boards a company bus to work. Incidentally, Sudha Murthy is now chief of the Infosys Foundation, which channels ` 50 million into charity every year.

Simplicity, humility and maintaining a low profile are the hallmarks of this super-rich Bangalorean. Murthy's unprecedented wealth has catapulted him into the public glare. After the kidnapping of Dr. Rajkumar by forest brigand Veerappan, the Home Ministry sounded the local government about providing Z-category security to Murthy and Premji (Managing Director of Wipro). Both characteristically turned down the offer.

Questions

1. Analyse the case in terms of success due to managerial abilities.
2. How can management principles bring success to an organisation?
3. State the qualities of manager that help in making a business successful.

10 Chapter

Evolution of Management Thought

"Climbing to the top demands strength, whether it is to the top of Mount Everest or to the Top of your career.

To succeed in your mission, you must have single-minded devotion to your goal."

Dr. APJ Abdul Kalam
Former President of India

10.1 INTRODUCTION

The emphasis on management theories gained momentum during the industrial revolution, coinciding with the growth of factories and industrial units. Industrial houses brought together individuals from diverse disciplines, including economists, sociologists, mathematicians, and management practitioners. This collaborative effort led to the innovation of enterprise management methods, which subsequently evolved into management theories.

Management theories serve as a synthesis of ideas from various fields such as science, anthropology, sociology, economics, and philosophy. Modern theories represent an integration of historical thoughts, presenting a comprehensive, contemporary, and meaningful framework for management. "Management thought" refers to the guiding theories and principles for managing people within organisations. These theories offer explanations for the effectiveness of specific practices.

10.2 MANAGEMENT THEORIES

Management theories can be broadly classified into the following schools of thought.

Pre-Scientific Management Theory.

Classical Theory

—Taylor's Scientific Management Theory

—Fayol's Administrative Management Theory

—Weber's Bureaucracy Theory

Behavioural Theory

—Human Relations Theory (or Neo-classical Theory)

—Behavioural Science Theory

Modern Management Theory

—Quantitative Theory

—Systems Theory

—Contingency Theory

—Operational Theory

This chapter discusses the pre-scientific and classical management theories.

10.3 PRE-SCIENTIFIC MANAGEMENT THEORIES

In the 1800s, management theories began to develop as a systematic field of knowledge. Before the formalisation of management theories, there were pre-scientific theories that contributed to the development of management thought. Notable contributions were made by early management thinkers:

1. **Charles Babbage:** A pioneering British thinker in management, *Babbage* laid the groundwork for scientific management. His work shared connections with Adam Smith, an economist, as *Babbage* emphasised work measurement, cost determination, bonus plans, profit sharing, specialisation, and industrial productivity. His insights influenced Taylor's scientific management principles.
2. **James Montgomery:** A textile owner-manager in Scotland, *Montgomery* focused on planning, organising, and controlling. He authored texts on the management of business, contributing valuable perspectives to the field of management.
3. **Robert Owens:** A textile entrepreneur known as the father of personnel management; *Owens* highlighted the significance of people in the workplace. He advocated treating workers as human beings, respecting their values and beliefs. *Owens* believed that satisfying the needs of employees would align their efforts with the organisation's objectives. To improve living conditions, both in the factory and at home, he initiated upgrades to streets, houses, and sanitation facilities. He also introduced social and educational reforms for employees,

endorsing higher wages, participative decision-making, and motivation as factors that could enhance productivity. His ideas on human relations are reflected in the Hawthorne experiments.

4. **Andrew Ure:** An English industrialist, *Ure* focused on the training and moral education of managers to enhance effective management practices.
5. **Charles Dupin:** An industrial educator in France, *Dupin* argued that broader management skills are essential for maximising output. He emphasised the importance of management education over technical education to achieve success in industrial endeavours.

Evaluation of Pre-Scientific Management Theories

These early management theories were closely tied to organisational environments, addressing specific issues in distinct ways. Some theories prioritised production, while others concentrated on human relations. No single theory could universally always apply to all organisations. As the 19th century ended, management evolved into a systematic field of study. Notable contributions during this period include Taylor's scientific management principles.

10.4 CLASSICAL THEORY

Classical theory is the oldest theory of management. As organisations became complex, there arose the need for a systematic approach to management, with primary focus on production. Financial incentives played crucial role in driving organisational output

Features of Classical Theory

1. ***Foundation to Modern Management:*** It encompasses early works on management, laying the groundwork for modern management theory.
2. ***Output Enhancement:*** The theory aims to find methods to increase organisational output.
3. ***Economic Needs of Employees:*** It asserts that employees have strong economic needs that can be satisfied through financial incentives.
4. ***Formal Job Structure:*** The classical theory works on formal job structures to fulfill individual and organisational needs.
5. ***Closed System View:*** It views organisations as closed systems that do not interact extensively with the external environment.

6. ***Universal Management Principles:*** It develops a set of "management principles" deemed universally applicable to all types of organisations, business or non-business.

Merits of Classical Theory

1. Classical theory marks the initiation of management as a distinct field of study.
2. It underscores fundamental management issues, laying the foundation for the later development of management theories.
3. Several principles, such as job specialisation and scientific methods of work, along with functions proposed by classical theory, remain relevant and applicable in contemporary times.
4. The theory furnishes a set of principles derived from experiments and scientific methods that apply to various organisations today.

Limitations of Classical Theory

Classical theory originated when organisations had stable and simple structures, with minimal interaction with the environment. In today's complex and dynamic organisations, the principles of classical theories may not fully align, making them more practical in the past than in the present.

1. The universality of management concepts is not absolute in contemporary organisations. Principles like unity of command may not apply to highly specialised jobs where individuals receive orders from multiple functional heads due to extensive division of work.
2. Employees were traditionally viewed as tools rather than valuable contributors to management objectives, neglecting their social and psychological needs.
3. The focus of classical theory is more on tasks than people, disregarding human behaviour and desires.
4. The theory tends to prioritise monetary rewards over non-monetary ones, which may not always hold true. Non-monetary rewards such as status, power, and recognition can be more influential than money in many cases.
5. Initiative and creativity of employees are often overlooked, and an excessive emphasis on rules can lead people to strictly follow them without understanding their purpose.

Three Main Theories in the Classical School of Thought

I. Taylor's Scientific Management Theory

II. Fayol's Classical Organisation Theory

III. Weber's Bureaucracy Theory

I. Taylor's Scientific Management Theory

Scientific management theory examines work processes with the aim of enhancing economic efficiency, particularly labour productivity. It represents an effort to bring the principles of science into the realm of management. In the early 20th century, the United States faced scarcity of skilled labour, prompting management thinkers to seek ways to enhance labour efficiency and increase productivity. *Frederick W. Taylor*, recognised as the father of Scientific Management, introduced the scientific management theory. *Taylor* observed a lack of scientific approach in many organisations, resulting in resource wastage. Time and work studies were often neglected, and there was no strategic plan regarding the amount of work to be done in a day or how much should be paid.

Frederick W. Taylor

Scientific management was a theory of management that analysed the work flows to improve economic efficiency, specially labour productivity. It was pioneering attempt to apply science to management.

Workers were producing less than their potential due to traditional production methods, relying on a 'hit and trial' approach for work schedules. *Taylor* addressed the following key questions:

1. Could the existing work schedule be reorganised by adding or removing certain operations?
2. Could the sequence of operations be altered?
3. Was there one optimal way of performing the work?

He conducted experiments to find the best way to execute each task by eliminating operations that wasted resources. He aimed to determine the optimum time and motion studies to successfully complete each task.

Taylor's theory is based on experience in three companies:

- Midvale Steel
- Simonds Rolling Machine Company
- Bethlehem Steel

1. **Midvale Steel:** During his time at Midvale, he observed that workers were not operating at their full capacity due to following reasons:
   i. Wages were paid daily, leading workers to come to the factory, but their output remained low.
   ii. Workers were apprehensive that completing tasks quickly might result in job loss or reduction in wages.
   iii. The prevailing method of work was based on the 'Rule of Thumb' or 'Hit and Trial,' lacking a scientific approach.
2. **Simonds Rolling Machine Company:** *Taylor* worked on a project at a company where workers inspected the bicycle ball bearings. The management identified issues such as extended work hours and lack of innovation, leading to low efficiency. *Taylor* conducted a detailed study and timed the movements of the most efficient workers. He motivated and trained the remaining workers to enhance their performance to match that level.

Taylor introduced a 'differential wage rate' system, improving the overall working schedule, including designated rest hours. These changes resulted in significant improvement in quantity and quality of production. The earnings of the workers and the profits of the management saw a notable increase.

3. **Bethlehem Steel:** At Bethlehem Steel, *Taylor* conducted the Pig-iron experiment, where he observed the time and movements of workers engaged in unloading raw materials from incoming railcars and loading finished goods onto outgoing ones. It was noted that a worker could load approximately 12½ tons per day and earn $1.15 daily. Identifying the most efficient worker, Taylor scrutinised his time and motion, introducing changes to the work process. Rest periods and incentive plans were implemented to attain the target output. The goal was set at 47½ tons per day with a wage rate of $1.85 for those meeting the standard. It was observed that workers could achieve this standard, loading nearly 48 tons of goods daily.

Techniques of Scientific Management

Taylor introduced the following techniques to improve productivity:

1. **Separation of Planning and Doing:** In the pre-scientific management era, workers planned and executed their tasks under the supervision of managers. Taylor introduced a change by assigning the planning responsibility to supervisors while workers focused on performing the actual tasks. This division of labour aimed to streamline the workflow and improve work efficiency.

2. **Functional Foremanship:** Taylor introduced the concept of functional foremanship, which involved a departure from the principle of unity of command. Planning and execution were supervised by two sets of supervisors, resulting in a total of eight supervisors overseeing the workers.

   (i) Supervisors concerned with planning in the factory office (planning incharge)

   a. **Instruction Card Clerk:** Issues instructions regarding the use of tools, equipment, and technical details of the work.

   b. **Route Clerk:** Specifies the sequence and route through which the task moves from one machine to another.

   c. **Time and Cost Clerk**: Determines the time and cost at which the work should be performed.

   d. **Disciplinarian:** Ensures discipline by establishing rules for absenteeism, insubordination, and other related matters.

   (ii) Supervisors concerned with execution of work at the shop floor (production incharge)

   a. **Gang Boss**: Manages preliminary operations and determines the physical resources required at the workplace.

   b. **Speed Boss**: Ensures timely completion of work and sets standards for the speed of operations.

   c. **Repair Boss:** Ensures security and maintenance of machines, overseeing activities like regular oiling, check-ups, and repairs.

   d. **Inspector:** Ensures that work is executed according to standards set by the Planning Incharge.

3. **Job Analysis:** The job is analysed on the following parameters:

   i. ***Time Study***: Time study breaks down a job into smaller elements, determining the time required to complete each element. The optimum time to perform the task is identified to establish 'fair day's work,' indicating how much work an individual worker can reasonably accomplish within a specific timeframe. This observed time is set as the standard time for that operation. The same procedure is applied to other operations, and standard time for the entire job is determined.

   ii. ***Motion Study***: Motion study identifies the most efficient way of performing a task. It involves analysis of motions carried out during the job and aims to eliminate unnecessary or wasteful motions that consume additional resources. This identified set of motions becomes the standard for performing the task, ensuring a streamlined and resource-efficient process.

Time and motion studies together determine a fair day's work and best way of performing it.

iii. ***Fatigue Study***: Adequate rest and well-timed rest intervals are important to eliminate fatigue and boost overall work potential. Breaks restore energy and enhance performance. In the perspective of *Frank Gilbreth*, the relationship between motion and fatigue is direct. By eliminating unnecessary motions, fatigue can be minimised. This contributes positively to organisational well-being, influencing productivity, profits, and wages.

iv. ***Method Study:*** It assesses technological viability of the products and develops an operational system optimised for product design, job and process design, selection of capital equipment, facility location, and facility layout. It ensures the most efficient utilisation of production facilities, transportation, storage, and handling facilities to optimise the overall cost of output.

4. **Standardisation of Work:** Standardisation guarantees consistency in operations, where everyone adheres to the same benchmarks for time, cost, and quality. Standard, "a unit of measurement set to serve as a criterion or reference level for performance," applies to products, tools, equipment, work methods, etc. to maximise efficiency of work processes.
5. **Financial Incentives:** Workers primarily have financial needs, and the reward system is tied to performance rather than position. Incentives serve as a connection between remuneration and productivity.
6. **Differential Rate System:** Taylor introduced the 'differential rate system,' where workers receive a higher wage for being more productive and a lower rate for producing less than the standard output. This incentive resulted in wage increases ranging from 30 to 100%.
7. **Scientific Selection and Training:** Scientific selection involves choosing the most suitable individuals for specific roles based on their knowledge, abilities, and experience. This enhances their potential and capabilities through education, training, and motivation.
8. **Task Planning:** Task represents the work that needs to be carried out, turning plans into reality. Task planning involves establishing standards for various aspects:

- ***Skill variety***: The range of skills required to perform the task.

- ***Task identity***: Whether the task involves producing a complete product or only parts of it.
- ***Task significance***: The level of importance associated with the task.
- ***Autonomy***: The degree to which an individual performs the task independently.
- ***Feedback***: Information about successful accomplishment of the task.

9. **Shorter Hours, Rest Pauses:** Long working hours without adequate rest periods can be exhausting, leading to lower performance. Taylor introduced shorter work hours and rest pauses to enhance task efficiency.

Principles of Scientific Management Theory

Taylor believed that the issue lay with management, specifically in setting standards, rather than the workers. To address this, he proposed the following principles:

1. ***Replace Rule of Thumb with Science:*** Work should not be based on experience, trial and error, or the Rule of Thumb. Instead, it should follow a scientific approach, employing time and motion studies. This method breaks down work into smaller units, eliminates unnecessary motions, identifies the best motion, and times it to determine the optimal output per worker per day. Standards for a fair day's work, wages for each operation, and standardisation of operations should be precise rather than based on estimates.
2. ***Harmony, Not Discord in Group Action:*** All members, including employers and employees, should function as a cohesive team. Group actions should be guided by mutual understanding, and disagreements should be resolved through discussions. Workers strive to enhance output, and employers reward productivity with higher wages.
3. ***Co-operation, Not Individualism:*** Individuals should not prioritise personal interests at the expense of organisational interests. They should foster a mindset of mutual thinking and teamwork, emphasising cooperation over individual gains.
4. ***Maximum Output, Not Restricted Output:*** People should not limit production out of fear of job loss. The increase in output should be a collective effort, benefiting both employers (in terms of profits) and employees (in terms of wages).
5. ***Development of Workers to their Full Capacity:*** Workers should strive to reach their full potential through scientific selection, formal education, training, and motivation to contribute their best to organisational output.

Mental Revolution — The Essence of Scientific Management

The principles of scientific management require a "complete mental revolution," demanding a shift in the perspectives of management and workers. Managers take on the responsibilities of planning, organising, leading, and controlling operations, while workers efficiently carry out the assigned tasks.

"... in its essence, scientific management involves a complete mental revolution on the part of the working men engaged in any particular establishment or industry—a complete mental revolution on the part of these men as to their duties toward their work, toward their fellowmen, and toward their employers. And it involves the equal complete mental revolution on the part of those on the managements' side—the foreman, the superintendent, the owner of the business, the Board of directors—a complete mental revolution on their part as to their duties toward their fellow workers in the management, toward their workmen, and toward all of their daily problems. And without this complete mental revolution on both sides scientific management does not exist. That is the essence of scientific management—this great mental revolution."

—*Taylor*

Merits of Scientific Management

1. ***Improved management practices*** gained popularity through scientific methods like work study, incentive plans, and regulated rest hours.
2. ***Efficient allocation of resources*** is achieved by eliminating wasteful time and motions in work processes. It uncovers the true capacity of workers, ensuring a fair day's work for a fair day's wage.
3. ***Scientific approach*** involves scientific selection, education, and development of employees. Problem-solving is methodical with job selection based on specific requirements. Training methods are scientifically designed, ensuring that tasks align with individual skills.
4. ***Work specialisation*** distinguishes planning and execution as separate responsibilities to ensure smooth business operations.
5. ***Mental revolution*** prompts change in the attitude of both employers and employees towards their work.
6. ***Enhanced productivity*** results from better management and efficient allocation of resources, leading to increased profits and wages. This positively impacts the performance of management and workers.

7. ***Harmonious relationships*** develop as management and workers collaborate in the workplace, reducing conflicts and promoting unity of action.
8. ***Improved standards of living*** result from enhanced profits and wages, benefiting both managers and workers.
9. ***Industrial prosperity*** achieved through high productivity, increased profits, and higher wages, contributes to industrial peace, prosperity, and positive corporate image in global markets.
10. Efficient workers are rewarded with higher rates, providing financial gains, and serving as an ***incentive for high production***.
11. ***Job satisfaction*** is promoted through scientific methods, orderly production planning, wage systems, and rest pauses, contributing to satisfaction and boosting overall production.

Limitations of Scientific Management

1. Taylor's approach places **excessive emphasis on the physical and economic needs** of workers while neglecting their social and emotional needs. He regards workers merely as factors of production, overlooking their broader human dimensions.
2. **Labour unions opposed this theory** due to concerns that scientific methods might boost production but lead to job losses. Workers feared that adopting Taylor's methods could result in layoffs, heightening suspicion towards scientific production methods.
3. The emphasis on scientific methods, such as standardisation and task planning, fosters **monotony** as work follows predefined lines of action. This restricts use of creative skills.
4. Differential wage rate, based on standard output, creates **distinctions between efficient and inefficient workers**, resulting in conflicts, resentment, and absenteeism.
5. The theory adopts a **narrow view of management**, primarily focusing on the shop level. It fails to consider management of the entire organisation.
6. The theory is **not suitable for small firms** because they lack the resources to develop scientific methods of production.

It is believed that Taylor was mindful of these considerations. The concept of scientific management aimed to match the right worker with the right job, fostering job satisfaction. Taylor's work on scientific management replaced the 'Rule of Thumb,' introducing order and logic into production planning, costs, wage systems, etc.

II. Henri Fayol's Classical Organisation Theory (Management Process Theory)

While *Taylor* focused on productivity at the shop level, *Fayol* concentrated on general management, addressing the overall administration of the organisation. His work primarily pertained to top-level management, marking the first systematic effort to formalise the administrative approach to management.

Henri Fayol

Henri Fayol developed a general theory of business administration. He was one of the most influential contributors to modern management concepts which propose that management has 5 primary functions:

Planning
Organising
Commanding
Co-ordinating
Controlling

Fayol, who served as junior executive and later director at the French Coal and Iron Company from 1841 to 1925, challenged the prevailing belief that managers are born and cannot be made. He asserted that management is a teachable skill, and managers can be developed through understanding the underlying principles.

Fayol's work on general management continues to shape contemporary business practices, earning him the title of the father of modern management theory. He divided business activities into technical, commercial, financial, security, accounting and managerial activities. While the operating activities were commonly practiced in organisations, there was lack of managerial skills. Therefore, he based his theory on managerial activities of business, classifying the functions of managers as planning, organising, commanding, coordinating and controlling. He identified the qualities of managers as physical, mental and moral with special knowledge and experience that help in understanding human behaviour.

Fayol identified fourteen principles of management, drawing from his practical experience, emphasised their flexibility and non-exhaustive nature, stating that they are generally applicable in various business scenarios but can be adapted as per the specific situation. *Fayol* used the term 'principles' to highlight their adaptable nature, making them indispensable guidelines for effective organisational management.

In his words, "I prefer the word principles in order to avoid any idea of rigidity, as there is nothing rigid or absolute in administrative matters; everything is a question of degree. The same principle is hardly ever applied twice in exactly the same way, because we have to allow for different and changing circumstances, for human beings who are equally different and changeable, and for many other variable elements. The principles, too, are flexible and can be adapted to meet every need; it is just a question of knowing how to use them."

These principles are as follows:

i. **Division of Labour:** It involves breaking down a task into smaller parts. Instead of one person doing the entire job, individuals handle specific portions. This encourages specialisation, enhancing task efficiency.

ii. **Authority and Responsibility:** Authority refers to the right to give orders and the ability to ensure compliance. Managers exercise authority based on their position. Responsibility is the commitment to perform tasks diligently. It involves the obligation to do one's best in carrying out assigned duties. It is crucial to maintain a balance between authority and responsibility as one must have authority proportional to the assigned task.

ii. **Discipline:** It involves adhering to rules and agreements, instilled through effective leadership, guidance, and motivation, good supervision at all levels, clear and fair agreements with employees, recognising accomplishments and addressing non-compliance through penalties.

iv. **Unity of Command:** It signifies a clear structure where each employee reports to one boss. This holds employees accountable to their immediate boss, fostering responsibility. It also helps prevent conflicts and cultivates harmonious relationships between superiors and subordinates.

v. **Unity of Direction:** It means one leader for a specific set of operations ("one head for one plan"). For example, in the finance department, there is a single head overseeing all financial activities. Similarly, the personnel manager establishes policies for recruitment, selection, training, and development across the organisation.

vi. **Subordination of Individual Interest to General Interest:** The organisation is essentially a collective of individuals, each contributing to the overall objectives. Organisational goals take precedence over individual goals. However, effective management involves reaching fair agreements with subordinates to address their individual interests. When employees are content and their needs are met, there is a harmonious balance, ensuring that individual interests do not overshadow the overall organisational welfare.

vii. **Remuneration:** It is essential for organisations to establish a fair remuneration system, ensuring equal pay for equal work so that employers and employees are satisfied with their compensation.

viii. **Centralisation:** Centralisation keeps authority concentrated at the top, while decentralisation occurs when authority and power are delegated to lower levels. More decentralisation enhances importance at the lower levels, while centralisation diminishes it. Organisations strike a balance between centralisation and decentralisation, with smaller organisations tending to be more centralised, and larger organisations favouring decentralisation.

ix. **Scalar Chain:** The chain of command, also referred to as hierarchy of authority, is the line through which instructions move from the top to the bottom of an organisation. All orders are issued top-down, while suggestions and complaints move from bottom to top. While this structure is effective, flow of information through scalar chain can be time-consuming. Information can also move directly between individuals in different departments. When information moves horizontally between people at the same level, it is termed as 'Gangplank.'

x. **Order:** "Right Place, Right Time" emphasises the importance of organising people and materials. This principle ensures that materials are positioned appropriately to facilitate smooth production flow. Jobs are allocated based on individuals' abilities and skills, ensuring that people perform roles that best suit their capabilities. Achieving harmonious alignment of individuals in suitable positions is termed as social order, while maintaining material resources in the right locations is referred to as material order.

xi. **Equity:** Equity ensures that all employees are treated fairly without favouritism. This fosters cordial relationships within the organisation.

xii. **Stability of Tenure:** Stability allows individuals to become familiar with their job environment. Frequent transfers can adversely impact organisational efficiency.

xiii. **Initiative:** It is important for employees to introduce new ideas and approaches, have freedom to initiate plans and contribute to decision-making to enhance the potential for effective collaboration and productivity.

xiv. **Esprit De corps:** "Unity is strength" underscores the power of teamwork. When people function as a team, it strengthens loyalty, unity and collaborative efforts toward common goals. "Esprit de Corps" enhances synergy, suggesting that the combined output of a group surpasses individual efforts (one plus one makes eleven). This fosters harmony, mutual understanding, team spirit, unified action, and a sense of belongingness to the organisation.

Merits of Administrative Management

Fayol's theory significantly contributed to modern management. The notion that "Managers are not born but can be made" holds true, indicating that management theory can be taught to cultivate effective managers.

1. Fayol played a pioneering role in differentiating management functions from other business functions.
2. He was the first to emphasise the universality of management principles.
3. His contributions form the foundation of management thought, with the functions of management offering a systematic understanding of the management process. This theory is also recognised as the management process approach.

Limitations of Administrative Management

1. It may not be suitable for organisations in the rapidly changing environments. Adhering to management principles always can be challenging. For instance, the principle of centralisation may not be effective in dynamic settings. Modern organisations often embrace participative management, challenging the universality of Fayol's principles.
2. The theory places excessive emphasis on formal structure of organisations, neglecting the informal needs of workers.
3. Developed during a period of relatively stable environments, the theory may not seamlessly apply to contemporary management, which heavily relies on interacting with dynamic environments.

Despite the limitations, Fayol's contributions remain significant, and his principles continue to be widely applied in management practices.

Scientific Management and Administrative Management

Points of Similarities: The two theories are similar with respect to the following:

1. Both theories represent pioneering work in the field of management, serving as the cornerstone of managerial understanding.
2. They share common focus on strategies to enhance output and productivity.
3. They both underscore the importance of addressing primary needs, often met through financial incentives.
4. They emphasise on formal job structures to fulfil individual and organisational requirements.
5. Both theories portray organisations as independent entities with limited or no significant interaction with the external environment.
6. They contribute to the development of essential management principles crucial for industrial progress.
7. Practical experience in their respective companies forms the basis for the development of theories.
8. Both Taylor and Fayol believe in acquisition of managerial qualities, advocating that organisations should actively cultivate these skills.

Points of Differences: The theories differ on the following grounds:

1. Taylor is recognised as the pioneer of scientific management, whereas Fayol is known as the father of Administrative Management Theory.
2. Taylor emphasises on productivity within the shop level, whereas Fayol directs his focus on the entire organisation.
3. Taylor's primary focus is on enhancing productivity, while Fayol's emphasis is on effective administration and management of the organisation.

Taylor (Father of Scientific Management)	Fayol (Father of Principles of Management)
Increase production at the shop level	Develop principles to coordinate activities throughout the organisation.
Improve output through work simplification and standardisation.	Increase overall production at the organisational level.

Management perspective is bottom-up, studying from the lower levels to the top.	Top-down view, examining management from the higher levels to the lower.
Based on scientific observation and measurement.	Based on personal experience later translated into universal truth.
Covers narrow perspective of management.	Has wider perspective and, therefore, wider applicability.

III. Weber's Bureaucracy Theory

Max Weber, a notable German sociologist belongs to the scientific school of thought. He has contributed to the study of bureaucracy through topics such as specialisation of job, scope, merit system, uniform principles, structure and hierarchy.

Max Weber
Max Weber, a notable German Sociologist belongs to the scientific school of thought.

Max Weber, a German sociologist, made significant contribution to management, economics, philosophy, and sociology, with his most notable being bureaucratic management. During times when organisations were typically managed through traditional or charismatic authority, based on birth class or personal appeal, Weber argued for a more rational approach to management.

He introduced the concept of rational-legal authority as opposed to charismatic or traditional authority, emphasising the need for organisations to be managed in a systematic way. Rational-legal authority is *rational* because it involves formal authority-responsibility structures aimed at achieving predetermined goals and *legal* because authority is derived from position rather than personal appeal, class, or reference. The authority is bound by a set of rules and regulations.

To facilitate rational operations in large organisations, *Weber* conceptualised an ideal bureaucracy characterised by features such as efficiency, objectivity, unity, and discipline.

Features of Bureaucracy Theory

1. ***Division of Labour:*** Jobs are broken into smaller, specialised tasks. Each unit understands its area of expertise and recognises boundaries.
2. ***Scalar Chain:*** Organisations adopt a hierarchy where orders flow from top to bottom, and obedience moves from bottom to top. The hierarchical structure supports effective communication, coordination, and control within the organisation. Lower units are overseen by higher units, facilitating delegation as authority moves downward.
3. ***Appointments Based on Merit:*** All appointments are based on merit of the individuals for the respective jobs.
4. ***Formal Rules and Procedures:*** Written rules and regulations ensure consistency, coordination, and uniformity in behaviour. They provide a reference for decision-making. Each person understands the expected outcomes of their actions in specific situations.
5. ***Impersonal:*** All individuals are treated equally, regardless of their position or status. Impartiality governs the management of people and events. Relationships are guided by rules and authority, and decision-making relies on rational factors rather than personal considerations.
6. ***Professional Officials:*** Managers are not owners but qualified professionals, appointed on the basis of merit. They are governed by rules and regulations, and lack personal, vested interests in the organisation.
7. ***Official Records:*** All decisions are documented in official records, preserved for reference.

Weber's ideal bureaucracy views organisations as structured entities with designated tasks and clear authority-responsibility relationships. Members, regardless of their positions, are expected to uniformly adhere to these structures.

Merits of Bureaucracy Management

1. ***Rationality and Efficiency:*** They are rational and ideal forms of organisation that contribute to operational efficiency.

2. ***Optimal Resource Utilisation:*** Management ensures optimal use of resources through formal chain of command.
3. ***Depersonalisation and Fair Treatment:*** The depersonalisation characteristic leads to uniform and fair treatment for all individuals within the organisation.
4. ***Increased Efficiency and Growth:*** Bureaucratic structures enhance efficiency through knowledge, unity of command, individual subordination, and minimised frictions and tensions, facilitating the growth of large-scale organisations.

Limitations of Bureaucracy Management

1. ***Neglect of Social Needs:*** Excessive focus on formal rules and procedures overlooks the social needs, desires, and sentiments of individuals.
2. ***Impact on Creativity:*** Bureaucratic systems hinder creativity and innovation due to impersonal approach in dealing with people. Allowing some flexibility in rules can enhance decision-making.
3. ***Disregard for Informal Organisation:*** Bureaucratic structures often ignore the role of 'informal organisation,' which both supplements and complements formal organisations.
4. ***Restricted Communication:*** The hierarchy of authority limits open communication, which may be effective in various decision-making situations.
5. ***Procedure Orientation over Goals:*** Strict adherence to rules, regulations, and procedures make the organisation overly procedure-oriented rather than goal-oriented. People may be evaluated on rules rather than results, making rules the primary focus, and objectives secondary.
6. ***Coordination:*** Job specialisation, where tasks are divided into specific categories, creates isolated compartments, and complicates control. Highly specialised roles may struggle to coordinate with other activities.
7. ***Conflict:*** This approach fosters conflict between the organisation and individuals. While people prefer open and interactive work environments that encourage innovation, bureaucratic organisations often prioritise rules and regulations. These structures, thus, oppose the fundamental nature of human beings.
8. ***Closed-system Perspective:*** Bureaucratic organisations adopt a closed-system perspective, limiting interaction with the environment. Their rigid structures

lack adaptability to environmental changes, as everything adheres strictly to established rules. In contrast, modern organisations thrive on constant interaction with the environment, necessitating a continuous flow of information in and out.

The bureaucratic structure is not suitable for today's rapidly changing and dynamic environment. Weber did not categorise it as inherently good or bad. He did not claim the existence of an 'ideal bureaucracy' in practice. He proposed that creating a bureau for each important job could lead to efficiency in large operations. However, Weber did not anticipate the potential abuses that could arise as organisations outgrew their founders.

Weber is credited with introducing a formal and systematic concept of authority. His belief in rational and efficient economic behaviour dominating human conduct remains relevant in many organisations today.

Questions

I. Long Answer Questions

1. Explain the classical theory of management. How does it contribute to management thought?
2. Explain the techniques used by Taylor in promoting scientific management at the shop level.
3. Explain Henri Fayol's administrative management theory. How have the principles of management contributed to Fayol's theory?
4. Compare and contrast the contribution of Taylor and Fayol to classical theory of management.
5. Explain Max Weber's contribution to classical management thought.
6. Define 'scientific management'. Explain its aims and features. Discuss the principles of scientific management.

II. Write short notes on:

(i) Functional foremanship
(ii) Job analysis
(iii) Differential wage system
(iv) Mental revolution in scientific management

III. Multiple Choice Questions

1. Taylor's theory covers the concepts of
   (*i*) Behavioural theory
   (*ii*) Modern theory
   (*iii*) Classical theory
2. Principles of management are introduced by
   (*i*) Frederick Taylor
   (*ii*) Henri Fayol
   (*iii*) Peter F. Ducker
3. Max Weber is associated with
   (*i*) Bureaucracy theory
   (*ii*) Scientific management theory
   (*iii*) Administrative theory
4. He is known as the father of modern management theory
   (*i*) Frederick Taylor
   (*ii*) Elton Mayo
   (*iii*) Henri Fayol

Answers

1. (iii) 2. (ii) 3. (i) 4. (iii)

IV. Case Study

Mr. Rohit is a great scholar and manager. His style of management is followed as an example in other organisations. He is respected by peers and co-workers for his sincerity, commitment and loyalty. He spends ample time with his peers and subordinates solving various managerial problems and delegates them authority for decision-making in specific areas.

As president of the company, he developed principles and philosophies of management for all the departments in consultation with each departmental head and concerned subordinates.

Though he prefers a persuasive style of leadership, he expects perfection in work. He cannot tolerate mistakes, laziness and slackness in performance. His ideas of perfection make people believe that he is intolerant and strict.

Questions

1. Which theory of management does Mr. Rohit believe in?
2. What is people's perception about his management style?
3. Do you recommend change in his style of management?

❑❑❑

11

Chapter

Fundamentals of Planning

Whatever failures I have known, whatever errors I have committed, whatever follies I have witnessed in private and public life have been the consequence of action without thought. — *Baruch, Bernard M.*

11.1 MEANING

In the world of business, things are always changing and bring great chances for success or challenges. Managers cannot just hope for the best and ignore potential problems. They must plan and be prepared to act when things get tough. Opportunities, threats, risks, and uncertainties are all part of planning. Managers need to be proactive, thinking ahead and making decisions before problems become too big.

Planning creates a roadmap for success in business. It makes choices about what to do from different options to be ready for whatever might happen in the future. It considers the why, what, when, where, who and how of the organisation.

- 'Why' represents the objective of the organisation.
- 'What' represents the actions taken to achieve the objective.
- 'How' represents policies, rules, budgets etc. to achieve the objective.
- 'When' represents the time frame.
- 'Who' represents the people involved.
- 'Where' means planning for domestic, national or international markets.

"Planning is selecting information and making assumptions regarding the future to formulate activities necessary to achieve organisational objectives."

– *Terry* and *Franklin*

"Planning involves the definition of objectives and planning of operations in terms of policies, plans and budgets which will establish the most advantageous course for the company. Planning also requires that managers keep currently informed on all matters which will contribute to improve planning and performance in the position."

–Louis A. Allen

"Planning involves selecting missions and objectives and the actions to achieve them; it requires decision-making, that is, choosing from alternative future course of action. Plans, thus, provide a rational approach to achieving pre-selected objectives."

–Koontz and *Weihrich*

11.2 FEATURES OF PLANNING

1. **Primary Function of Management:** Planning is the first function of management. If the plan is wrong, everything else goes wrong. The team structure, what people do, how motivated they are, and how leaders lead—all depends on good planning.
2. **Adaptive to Environment:** Planning helps business survive in the changing world. It makes companies ready to adjust to what competitors are doing, what people like, and what is happening in the economy.
3. **Future Oriented:** Planning is looking ahead. It anticipates changes, exploits opportunities and meets challenges through forecasting that fills the gap between where we are and where we want to go.
4. **Goal Oriented:** Planning is goal oriented. It lays down the goals and makes plans to achieve them.
5. **Pervasive:** Planning is done for all types or sizes of the organisation. Whether it is business making money or a small group working for non-profit activities, planning happens at all levels—top, middle, and low.
6. **Intellectual Process:** Planning is a complex process and a smart way of thinking. It looks at what happened before, what is happening now, and what might happen in the future. As people use their judgment, intuition, and imagination to make plans, it is an intellectual process.
7. **Efficient:** Planning aims at getting the most out of resources without spending too much. Managers make sure that the gains are more than the costs.
8. **Flexible:** Plans can go wrong if unexpected things happen. Planners need to be ready to change the plans when the situation changes.
9. **Planning and Decision-making:** Planning involves decision making. Choosing out of multiple goals, ways to achieve out of available alternatives, sources from where funds will be raised, optimum allocation of resources are some of

the choices that run the organisation. Planning continuously involves decision-making.

10. **Feedback:** Planning and control go together. Planning sets up the goals, and control makes sure the goals are achieved. Control keeps plans on the right path by giving feedback on the plans. If things are not going as planned, it helps to look back at the plans and see what needs correction.
11. **Open System Approach:** Organisations are open systems that take inputs from the environment and produce output to reach their goals. The open system approach helps organisations deal with happenings around them and move from where they are to where they want to be in the future.

11.3 IMPORTANCE/OBJECTIVES OF PLANNING

1. **Achievement of Objectives:** Planning provides the path for goals with minimum waste of time, money and energy. It bridges the gap between present and future through optimum utilisation of time and money.
2. **Fulfilment of Commitments:** Organisations have long-term and short-term commitments towards society, depending on their nature which can be fulfilled through planning. A defence organisation, for example, has long-run commitments while a retailer has short-term responsibilities.
3. **Facilitates Decision-making:** Decision-making is "the process of choosing a course of action from two or more alternatives." Planning facilitates decisions like what to produce and how to produce, allocation of resources over functional areas, and helps to decide a course of action that will optimise the situation. Planning is the basis for decision-making: present and future.
4. **Stability to Organisations:** Planning helps organisations stay steady in the changing world. It determines how the organisation will be structured, who will be a part of it, how everyone will be motivated and how things will be kept on track. It promotes team strategy to ensure everyone works together.
5. **Overall View of the Organisation/Co-ordination:** Planning coordinates everyone and everything in the company. It makes sure individuals and departments work well with each other. It also connects what is happening inside the company with the outside world.
6. **Optimum Utilisation of Resources:** Organisations operate within constraints of resources such as time, money, and manpower. Planning strategically distributes these resources across key objectives and functional areas (production,

personnel, finance, and marketing), based on their priority and ensures they are utilised effectively, leading to creation of valuable outputs. Efficiency in resource utilisation becomes a crucial factor in driving organisational success.

7. **Develops Managers:** Planning involves imagination, thought and creativity and develops conceptual and analytical skills to co-ordinate internal activities with external environment.
8. **Promotes Innovation/creativity:** Planning includes forecasting, predicts chances for success, and encourages innovative ideas, concepts, products, and relationships.
9. **Basis for Control:** Planning establishes benchmarks and control assesses performance, compares it against standards, and corrects any deviations, enhancing future planning. Without plans, there is no control. Thus, planning serves as the foundation for effective control.
10. **Reduces Risk:** Risk occurs when there is some information about the future, but it is not entirely reliable. Planning lessens risk by forecasting and promoting to seize opportunities and tackle potential problems. This helps in dealing with the challenging environment of fast technological shifts and global competition.
11. **Morale Boost:** When plans succeed, individuals become more committed to organisational tasks. This leads to successful organisations and higher standards for the next planning phase.
12. **Facilitates Delegation:** Thoughtfully designed plans focus on strategic matters while entrusting routine tasks to lower levels. This makes delegation easier and effective.

11.4 LIMITATIONS OF PLANNING

1. **Unwillingness to Set Goals:** This may arise because of the following reasons:
   i. ***Multiple options:*** Planners may hesitate to set goals due to the challenge of choosing one from several alternatives. Committing to one goal often means giving up others.

   ii. ***Fear of failure:*** Future-oriented goals have uncertainties. Risk averse people avoid setting goals they fear they may not be able to achieve.

   iii. ***Limited knowledge:*** Effective plans need to align with the demands of the environment, such as suppliers, customers, and competitors. Insufficient knowledge about the organisational structure makes planning difficult.

iv. ***Lack of confidence:*** Lack of confidence in setting ambitious goals affects establishing challenging goals, resulting in suboptimal planning.

2. **Unwillingness to Change:** Resistance to change often stems from fear of the unknown. People tend to stick to the current situation if they are content with their existing setup. According to Paul R. Lawrence, there are three main reasons why individuals resist change:

   i. ***Uncertainty about causes and effects:*** People are generally hesitant towards change when they lack clarity about why changes are being introduced and how these changes will impact their authority and responsibilities within the organisation.

   ii. ***Reluctance to give up current benefits:*** Individuals have psychological resistance to change when they are satisfied with the present situation. Their contentment with existing benefits makes them resistant to changes whose potential advantages are unclear.

   iii. ***Weaknesses in the proposed change:*** The feasibility of change may be hindered by limitations within the existing system that are not conducive to the proposed changes. Rigid rules, for instance, can lead to internal inflexibility in the formulation of plans.

3. **Environmental Factors:** The environmental factors encompass the expected conditions in which plans are designed, including assumptions about the future. The rapidly changing environment necessitates frequent adjustments to plans. Unforeseen, external, and uncontrollable environmental factors can disrupt the plans.

4. **Constraint on Resources:** Even with innovative ideas, inadequacy of resources may affect translating those ideas into action.

5. **Lack of Information:** Absence of complete and accurate information about the future affects alignment of plans in achieving reality.

6. **Group Dynamics:** Effective plans can be generated in groups, but certain barriers within groups can hinder the planning process:

   i. ***Acceptance of high-risk projects:*** Group members may collectively endorse high-risk projects that they would hesitate to support individually. This can lead to suboptimal project outcomes.

   ii. ***Conformity to superiors' ideas:*** Lower-level members often conform to ideas of their superiors, even if they have superior alternatives. This can result in overlooking potentially better ideas.

iii. ***Dominance of certain groups:*** Dominant groups within a team may prioritise their ideas, suppressing a diverse range of perspectives and compromising the quality of planning.

iv. ***Shortcutting planning processes:*** Groups may opt for shorter planning routes instead of analysing complete information. This can undermine the depth and accuracy of the planning process.

v. ***Lack of planning skills:*** Inadequate skills, judgment, and creativity contribute to sub optimal planning.

vi. ***Restriction of creativity:*** Plans outline a predetermined course of action, discouraging deviations to avoid criticism. This stifles creativity as individuals may refrain from exploring innovative approaches.

vii. ***Environmental changes:*** The fast-paced evolution of the environment, including government policies, labour laws, competitor strategies, and technology, necessitates continuous updates to plans. Unforeseen external factors can impact the effectiveness of planning.

11.5 WAYS TO OVERCOME LIMITATIONS

1. **Scientific Goal Selection:** To overcome reluctance in relinquishing alternative goals, planners conduct cost-benefit analysis for each option and accept goals whose returns outweigh the costs.
2. **Scientific Methods:** Addressing the fear of non-attainment of goals involves scientific goal selection process that facilitates accurate predictions and practical implementation of plans. Flexibility in plans is essential to adapt to changing situations.
3. **Communication System:** Knowledge gaps can be reduced through a robust communication system, ensuring that individuals at all levels are informed about organisational activities. An effective management information system can address this challenge.
4. **Forecasting:** Environmental uncertainties can be reduced by forecasting changes to understand their impact on organisational goals.
5. **Confidence:** Planners need confidence to establish rational, realistic, challenging and achievable goals. Top-level management sets comprehensive goals, while lower-priority goals are formulated at lower levels in consultation with superiors.
6. **Help Members Accept Change:** Resistance to change can be overcome through the following measures:

i. ***Explanation of change:*** Planners articulate the reasons and outcomes of change, enabling members to understand the benefits associated with it.

ii. ***Comparison of benefits:*** By comparing existing benefits with future ones, reluctance to relinquish current advantages is addressed, fostering a willingness to embrace change.

iii. ***Participative planning:*** Involving members in the planning process minimises the impact of potential weaknesses. Participative planning encourages engagement and collaboration, making it easier for individuals to accept change.

7. **Set Responsibility:** Assigning clear responsibility for plans enhances their realism. Strategic plans fall under the responsibility of top-level management, while middle and lower levels are accountable for tactical and operating plans, respectively.
8. **Encourage Group Participation:** Planning should foster participation, allowing individuals to collaboratively formulate and implement plans. Inclusive involvement strengthens the planning process.
9. **Prepare Contingency Plans:** Organisations should develop contingency plans to address unforeseen situations. It prepares the organisation to adapt to unexpected challenges.

11.6 PROCESS OF PLANNING

1. **Need for Planning:** The necessity for planning is determined through environmental analysis. Organisations evaluate their strengths and weaknesses in relation to external opportunities and threats. When opportunities (demand for a new product), or threats arise (competition with a similar product), the organisation responds based on its strengths or converts weaknesses into strengths.

   Resources are allocated to the specific area, and a structural arrangement for planning is established, incorporating a communication system and decision-making centers. This ensures a targeted and effective approach to address organisational needs.
2. **Identify Goals:** Once the need for planning is established, planners identify the objectives they aim to accomplish. For example, if sales are declining because of inadequate promotion policies, effective advertising and promotional management becomes the objective. Clearly defined goals facilitate optimal

allocation of resources and efficient implementation of plans. Objectives are established for the entire organisation, individual departments, and various levels within each department. This forms a structured framework for goal setting across the organisation.

3. **Analyse Present Situation:** Planners conduct comprehensive analysis of the organisation's internal and external environments. Internal environment represents resources (physical, financial, information, and human) and external environment represents the economic, political, legal, and technological forces.

   Internal environmental information is derived from past records, statistical data, and financial statements and external environmental data are derived from financial journals, economic surveys, RBI bulletins, research reports, and other relevant sources. Appraisal of the organisation's strengths, weaknesses, opportunities and threats helps in developing plans about the organisational surroundings.

4. **Identify Barriers to Planning:** For planning to be effective, managers identify areas where existing objectives can be continued, modified, or abandoned. They also identify new areas where objectives need to be formulated. This proactive identification of obstacles and strategic planning adjustments ensures a successful planning process.

5. **Develop Planning Premises:** The primary purpose of planning is to achieve future objectives. Anticipated future conditions, known as planning premises, include forecasts and assumptions. Market dynamics, consumer preferences, and the political and economic environment serve as the premises for plan development. They reduce the risk of failure by considering various scenarios under different sets of assumptions.

6. **Develop Alternative Courses of Action:** Since there is no single best approach, the planning process explores all possible alternatives. However, a criterion is established to limit the number of alternatives. For example, a criterion could be capital investment, where alternatives requiring more than ₹75 lakh are eliminated from consideration.

7. **Evaluate Courses of Action:** Each alternative undergoes a cost-benefit analysis to ensure thorough evaluation that aligns with the organisation's goals and environmental factors.

8. **Select a Course of Action:** The optimal course of action is chosen, and the plan is complemented by sub-plans known as derivative plans. Production plan,

for instance, may have derivative plans for purchases, production planning and control. The selected plan should be flexible, cost-effective, and acceptable to those involved in its implementation.

9. **Feedback:** Planning is successful if its implementation is effective, and goals are achieved. Feedback involves continuous review of plans. Plans should have adaptability, and deviations beyond acceptable limits should be addressed. This might necessitate adjustments in the planning steps, the implementation process, or a complete reconsideration of the planning itself.

11.7 FEATURES OF A GOOD PLAN

1. **Integration:** A good plan integrates short-term needs with long-term goals, aligning all efforts towards overall objectives.
2. **Market Research:** Prior to plan formulation, planners conduct thorough market research, recognising the potential disparity between what customers say and what they do.
3. **Economy/Financial Constraints:** Plans that excessively rely on financial budgets may falter if expected revenues fall short. Comprehensive analysis of future costs and benefits is essential in designing effective plans.
4. **Coordination:** A sound plan coordinates the efforts of all functional areas, ensuring alignment with objectives at every level. Lower-level objectives contribute to higher-level goals, maintain clear direction and connection between actions and outcomes.
5. **Consistency:** Plans are consistent and adaptable to the environment and organisational resources. Frequent alterations at higher levels can hinder effective implementation at lower levels.
6. **Flexibility:** While consistent, plans should be flexible enough to adjust to environmental changes, allowing for reviews based on unforeseen circumstances.
7. **Acceptability:** Even the best plans can fail if not effectively implemented. Plans must be acceptable to those who formulate them and those responsible for implementation.
8. **Participative:** Plans gain acceptance when subordinates participate in the planning process. Involving employees from different departments and levels fosters good ideas, commitment, loyalty, and dedication to planned activities.

9. **Based on Planning Premises:** As plans aim to achieve future goals, they rely on accurate forecasts based on planning premises.
10. **Effective Communication System:** Successful planning necessitates interaction among people at all levels within and outside the organisation. A sound plan is built on a well-designed communication system, incorporating inputs from everyone to ensure effective implementation.

11.8 TYPES OF PLANS

Goals are the ends and plans are the means to achieve the ends. Goals and plans are closely related. Plans can be classified as follows:

I. Classification based on Levels

1. Strategic Plans
2. Tactical Plans
3. Operational Plans

II. Classification based on Use

1. Single Use Plans
   (*i*) Programmes
   (*ii*) Budgets
   (*iii*) Strategies
   (*iv*) Projects
2. Standing Plans
   (*i*) Policies
   (*ii*) Procedures
   (*iii*) Methods
   (*iv*) Rules

III. Classification based on Time

1. Long-term Plans
2. Medium-term Plans
3. Short-term Plans

IV. Classification based on Functional Areas

1. Production Plans
2. Marketing Plans
3. Financial Plans
4. Human Resource Plans

11.9 PLANS BASED ON LEVELS

1. Strategic Plans

Strategic plans are made by top-level managers in collaboration with board members and middle-level managers. They are designed to attain strategic goals by distributing resources across various areas. They are comprehensive and guide functional areas of the business. They focus on growth, diversification, change etc.

The questions most answered through strategic plans are:

i. What are the ways in which overall goals can be achieved?
ii. How to allocate resources over different areas of the enterprise?
iii. How to respond to external environment?
iv. How to co-ordinate internal strengths and weaknesses with the external environment?

2. Tactical Plans

Tactical plans support and execute strategic plans, facilitating the attainment of departmental goals. They are formulated by middle-level managers in collaboration with lower-level managers and typically pertain to intermediate timeframes.

They are more specific and answer the following questions:

i. How to deal with competitors?
ii. How to deal with changing demand?
iii. How to increase product share in the market?

3. Operational Plans

Operational plans aim to realise operational goals of the enterprise. They are made by lower-level managers in collaboration with middle-level managers, are more specific, and define the tasks for different sections. While resource allocation is addressed in strategic plans, operational planning ensures their efficient utilisation. They focus on short timeframes and involve tasks such as meeting delivery schedules, adjusting production timelines, and budgeting costs.

	Strategic Plans	Tactical Plans	Operational Plans
Focus of attention	Strategic Goals	Tactical goals	Operational goals
Level of Managers	Top-level managers	Middle-level managers	Lower-level managers
Timeframe	Long period of time, normally more than 5 years	Intermediate period, between 1 to 5 years	Less than one year
Scope	Overall organisational goals.	Departmental goals	Goals of units of each department
Environment	Relate witn the external environment	Focus on external and internal environment	Focus on internal environment (effective use of resources)

The plans and goals are as represented:

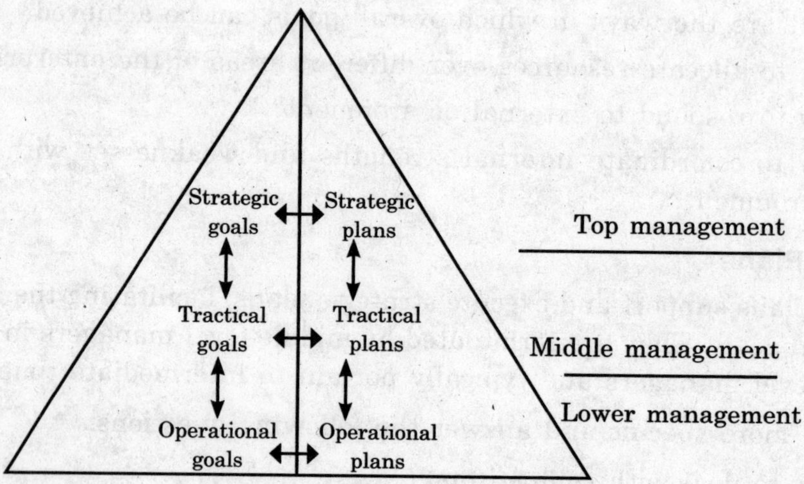

Levels of goals and plan

Source: K.M. Bartol and D.C. Martin; Management © 1991, p.161.

11.10 CLASSIFICATION BASED ON USE

I. Single Use Plans

II. Standing Plans

Single-use plans involve activities that are not repeated, created to achieve a specific objective. Examples include Programmes, Budgets, Strategies, and Projects.

Standing plans are designed for recurring activities, made to achieve overall goals. Commonly used standing plans include Policies, Procedures, Methods, and Rules.

I. SINGLE-USE PLANS

Single-use plans are made for specific objectives and conclude once the goal is met. They are short-lived and tailored for non-recurring activities. For instance, if a company aims to install a machine, the plan outlines the purchase strategy—whether to buy or lease, opt for a new or secondhand machine. Decision-making considers returns and costs, and once the machine is acquired, the plan is completed. These plans are designed for objectives unlikely to be repeated and address non-repetitive and distinct issues. Various types of single-use plans include programmes, budgets, strategies, and projects.

1. Programmes

Programme is a series of activities designed to achieve a specific objective, encompassing steps, time requirements, and allocated resources for each activity. Specific objectives, policies, procedures, methods, and budgets are incorporated into each programme to support its expenses.

It is "a comprehensive plan that includes future use of different resources in an integrated pattern and establishes a sequence of required actions and time schedules for each in order to achieve stated objectives." — *Terry and Franklin*

Steps in Making a Programme

i. The total workload is divided into parts.

ii. The parts are organised in a sequential order, establishing relationships to facilitate coordination.

iii. Each part is assigned based on skills and abilities of individuals, determining specific responsibilities.

iv. The approach is outlined, and resources are organised for accomplishing each step.

v. The time required for each part is determined, recognising that delays can increase costs.

vi. Schedules for each step are established to ensure optimal utilisation of resources.

2. Budget

Budget outlines the inflow and outflow of financial resources over a specified period. It establishes the standard of performance, assesses performance against estimated levels and reports on deviations. It is, thus, a tool to control and guide upcoming actions.

The timeframe, known as the planning horizon, is often divided into shorter sub-periods. For instance, a yearly budget might have monthly sub-periods, and a monthly budget can be broken down into weekly activities. This sub-division coordinates activities across different periods, identifying deviations before the end of the budgeted timeframe.

Types of Budgets

Budgets can be broadly classified as follows:

1. **Operating Budgets:** They pertain to operational activities of a business, and include the following:
   i. *Expense Budgets*: They plan expenditure, which can be fixed or variable.
   ii. *Revenue Budgets:* They forecast earnings derived from business activities.
   iii. *Profit Budgets*: They project profits, representing the difference between revenue and expense budgets.
2. **Financial Budgets:** They forecast the sources and application of funds, and include the following:
   i. *Capital Expenditure Budgets*: They indicate the sources from where funds will be raised for investments.
   ii. *Cash Budgets*: They predict cash position throughout the budgeted period, ensuring smooth flow of cash. They identify cash shortages and surpluses, allowing for adjustments to raise or invest cash.
   iii. *Balance Sheet Budgets*: They project assets, liabilities, and capital over the budgeted period, providing a comprehensive overview of the financial position.

3. Strategy

Strategy is "determination of the purpose and the basic long-term objectives of an enterprise and adoption of courses of action and allocation of resources necessary to achieve these aims."

Strategy involves selecting a course of action to attain long-term goals through continuous interaction with the environment. It provides direction to plans, in response to environmental threats or opportunities. When objectives and programmes are established, strategy unifies and allocates resources to achieve these objectives. It aligns resources with the current context to enhance overall effectiveness.

Features of Strategy

i. It aligns business operations with environmental concerns.

ii. Strategy impacts become apparent over a significant duration. Short-term losses do not necessarily indicate imperfect strategies; long-term outcomes determine success.

iii. Strategy ensures the best use of resources. Limited resources are assigned based on priority.

iv. It is a comprehensive plan applicable to all organisations, across functions and levels.

Merits of Strategies

i. Strategies provide a plan of action to achieve a specific objective.

ii. They distribute resources strategically across key business areas.

iii. They harmonise the internal and external business environments.

iv. They facilitate growth amidst changing conditions.

4. Projects

Project is a coordinated plan involving specific, limited activities aimed at achieving a significant, one-time objective. It is part of a larger programme with a distinct goal to be accomplished, supported by resources (physical, financial, and human resources) and budgets.

Each project plan is led by a project manager responsible for completing the project within specified time and resource constraints. Upon project completion, the workforce is disbanded, and the project plan concludes. Examples of project plans include creating ad campaigns, constructing infrastructure like bridges and dams, acquiring land and buildings, and procuring machinery.

Features of a Project

i. Project has a specific objective that contributes to an overall goal. For instance, project designing an advertisement campaign aims to boost sales.

ii. It is unique and non-repetitive. Once the objective is met, the plan concludes. For example, a project to construct a building exists until construction is ongoing. After completion, the plan no longer applies. If another building is to be constructed, a new project plan is needed.

iii. Projects must meet assigned time and cost constraints. Delays result in substantial financial losses. Construction projects, such as buildings, dams, or bridges, involve significant costs, and delays can lead to cost overruns.

vi. Projects are supported by goals, policies, procedures, rules, and budgets to support the interdependent tasks.

v. Policies guide project selection and implementation based on defined parameters. Procedures outline the steps to execute a policy and budgets provide financial support to the project by arranging funds at the right time and cost.

II. STANDING PLANS

"Standing plans are directives that serve to increase organisational effectiveness by standardising many routine decisions."

They standardise repetitive activities, enable routine decisions to be made at lower levels, allowing top managers to focus on strategic issues. They address situations that frequently occur within the organisation, saving time, money, and effort by providing a predefined approach to recurring problems. For instance, each time an employee takes leave, they follow the established leave rules.

Merits of Standing Plans

i. Standing plans offer standards, enabling delegation.

ii. They promote coordination by providing a predetermined approach to recurring issues.

iii. Standardised decisions increase efficiency.

iv. They serve as a ready reference, facilitating prompt decision-making.

v. They save time, money, and energy by offering a swift basis for action.

1. Policies

"A policy is a verbal, written or implied overall guide setting up boundaries that supply the general limits and discretion in which managerial action will take place."

Policy serves as a comprehensive guide for action, represents the intentions set by top-level managers, to be followed by all branches, departments and levels. Policies drafted by top managers address broad organisational objectives, and departmental managers establish policies for department-specific goals. Expressed in general terms, policies function as long-term plans that provide a framework for decision-making. However, they remain adaptable to suit the evolving needs and challenges faced by the organisation.

Features of Policies

1. **Consistency:** Policies at all levels and departments align cohesively towards organisational objectives. They serve as guiding principles that, to a significant extent, limit the discretion of members.

2. **Flexibility:** When necessary, discretion can be exercised. Rigid policies transform into rules. For instance, a company may choose to offer discount if competitors are doing so, even if it contradicts the established policy.
3. **Documentation:** Policies must be documented in writing to minimise confusion and misinterpretation in their application.
4. **Factual basis:** Policies are based on facts than personal biases or interpretations. They provide factual foundation for decision-making.
5. **Relevant to recurring events:** Policies are designed for recurring situations. Based on past occurrences, they offer general guidance for action each time a specific situation repeats.
6. **Feasibility:** Policies should be easily comprehensible. Complexity exaggerates issues rather than resolving them.

Merits of Policies

1. **Guidance and solutions:** Policies offer broad guidelines for action, providing predefined solutions for various problems within the organisation.
2. **Strategic focus:** Managers primarily focus on strategic matters, with day-to-day issues addressed at middle and lower levels based on policies set by top managers.
3. **Fast decision-making:** Policies facilitate fast decision-making, allowing problems to be resolved at the level where they emerge.
4. **Organisational effectiveness:** The presence of policies contributes to overall effectiveness of the organisation.
5. **Delegation:** Top managers can delegate decision-making authority to lower-level managers as policies provide general guidance to action.
6. **Unity of action:** Policies ensure a cohesive approach to decision-making, promoting unity in the execution of actions throughout the organisation.

Process of Policy Formulation

1. **Identify the area:** Senior line managers, in collaboration with staff members, pinpoint areas necessitating policies, ensuring alignment with overall organisational goals.
2. **Collect information:** Policy makers gather information relevant to the policy and potential issues arising during its implementation.
3. **Generate policy alternatives:** Policy alternatives are generated as general guidelines, offering options for the formulation of the final policy.
4. **Evaluate alternatives:** All alternatives are evaluated based on costs, benefits, and their contribution to objectives. Rough drafts are circulated for input at all levels, fostering discussions and consensus.

5. **Select the alternative:** Feasible alternatives, consistent with principles, are chosen. The most viable alternative is adopted, incorporating elements from different options to form the final policy.
6. **Test the alternative:** The chosen alternative undergoes testing before full implementation, with a sample area serving as a test check. Success in the trial phase prompts communication of the policy to operating managers.
7. **Implement the policy:** Once communicated and accepted by all relevant parties, the policy is put into action.
8. **Feedback:** Regular reviews assess the impact of implementation, and adjustments are made as needed. This ongoing evaluation forms the basis for future policy development.

2. Procedures

"A procedure is a series of related tasks that make up the chronological sequence and the established way of performing the work to be accomplished."

Procedure serves as a sequential guide for implementing policies, offering a more detailed and specific approach. It outlines the precise way guidelines will be executed. Acting as a roadmap for action, procedures specify the exact steps, individuals involved, timing, and duration for accomplishing policy-related tasks. They become repetitive tools, consistently applied to handle similar situations. By streamlining tasks and preventing duplication at various stages, procedures expedite work processes and go beyond functional boundaries.

Procedures are less flexible than policies, allowing little scope for managerial discretion in their execution. Consequently, routine matters are often delegated to lower levels, enabling top managers to focus on critical issues.

Multiple departments collaborate in executing a procedure; for instance, launching a new product involves coordination among the finance department (funding), advertising department (awareness creation), personnel department (manpower provision), accounts department (transaction recording), and sales department (sales execution).

Merits of Procedures

1. **Simplified work:** Procedures streamline tasks. Top managers focus on critical activities as people follow established procedures.
2. **Efficiency:** By establishing a standard approach to work, procedures provide a consistent method for task completion.
3. **Consistency and uniformity:** Procedures ensure a consistent and uniform approach to action, promote reliability in the execution of tasks.

4. **Defined sequence:** They outline a clear sequence of activities, eliminating duplication of work and ensuring a structured workflow.
5. **Delegation:** Procedures promote delegation and skill development of lower-level managers by providing a framework for task execution.
6. **Decision-making:** By defining the sequence of work and time required for each step, procedures support quick decision-making and control in the organisational workflow.

Policies and Procedures

Policies	Procedures
It is a general guide to thinking and action.	It is a specific guide to action that defines steps to implement the policy.
It relates to overall activities.	It is more specific than policies. It relates to overall activities through policies.
It is formulated by top managers.	It is framed by middle and lower-level managers.
It can be changed at the discretion of managers.	It cannot be easily changed. It is detailed and deterministic.
Objectives are the foundation for policies.	Policies are the foundation for procedures.
Managers use skill, imagination and creativity to frame policies.	There is little scope for creativity and skill as everything is standardised.

Policies and Strategies

Policies	Strategies
They are general statements that guide decision-making.	They are specific plans to achieve specific goals.
They do not require action plans.	They are action plans.
They are standing plans for repetitive activities.	They are single use plans for non-repetitive activities.
They ensure smooth operation of the organisation.	They are influenced by competitors' actions to achieve specific objectives.

3. Methods

Method is "a prescribed manner for performing a given task with adequate consideration to the objective, facilities available, and total expenditure of time, money and effort." It represents the specific approach to execute individual steps within a procedure. It is more detailed than a procedure, focusing on the precise way to accomplish a particular task or step.

They establish standard, scientific, and specific approach to promote efficiency. For instance, in the selection procedure, cross-checking details through previous employers can be a method to verify the applicant's professional background. Methods for conducting interviews may involve face-to-face interactions or indirect methods using questionnaires.

4. Rules

Rules represent a set of actions that everyone within an organisation must adhere to, leaving no room for personal discretion. They are explicit statements specifying actions that must or must not be taken in particular situations. Enforced rigidly, rules are obligatory directions dictating specific behaviours or actions. They are documented to prevent confusion and are readily available for reference. However, strict adherence to rules can constrain individual freedom, creativity, and innovation, contributing to the development of a 'bureaucratic organisation.'

Rules may or may not be integral to a specific procedure. For instance, the rule "No smoking in the office" is not part of any procedure, while the rule "Large purchases should be made by inviting tenders" forms a part of the purchase procedure.

Rules and Policies

Rules	Policies
They are specific statements.	They are general statements.
They are rigid.	They are flexible.
Guidelines must be universally followed by all without discretion.	They allow discretion in their formulation and implementation.

Rules and Procedures

Rules	Procedures
They do not represent sequence of actions.	They represent a sequence of actions.
They may or may not form part of procedures.	They are sequence of rules.
They are inflexible.	They are more flexible than rules.
They are specific actions to be or not to be taken.	They are broader than rules.

11.11 CLASSIFICATION BASED ON TIME

Classification of plans into long-term, medium-term, and short-term is not fixed; it depends on type of business, product nature, adaptability to the environment, and production cycle. The timeframe should justify the resources invested in the plans and fulfil commitment to decisions. These plans are interconnected; short-term plans contribute to medium-term plans, which contribute to long-term plans.

1. **Long-term Plans:** These plans typically span a minimum of 5 years, focusing on overall goals across all business functions. They anticipate environmental changes, involve long-term investments, and concentrate on strategic objectives.
2. **Medium-term Plans:** Spanning one to 5 years, these plans support the long-term goals. They are associated with tactical goals. For instance, they assess the impact of advertising on sales.
3. **Short-term Plans:** Prepared for a one-year period, these plans address immediate future of the company. They are specific to functional areas and pertain to operational goals, such as organising short-term training programmes.

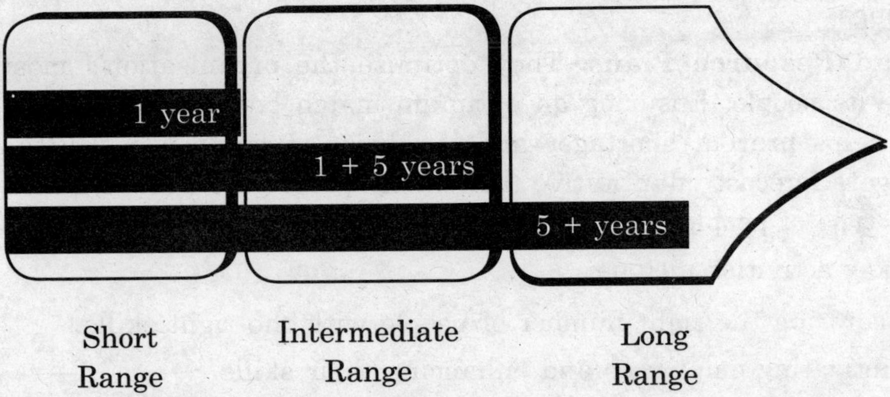

Plans

11.12 CLASSIFICATION BASED ON FUNCTIONAL AREAS

"A functional plan describes the specific actions to be taken in the immediate future by people responsible for that functional area. It usually sets forth short-term objectives, the actions to be taken to achieve those objectives, and a timeframe for the accomplishment of each action."

Functional plans are drafted to attain short-term goals in functional areas and cover a period of typically less than one year. Focused on the immediate future of functional areas, they are formulated by operating managers.

1. **Production Plans:** "Production plans consist of planning and overseeing the process of converting inputs into value-enhanced output." They include production system, efficiency of operations, location of company facilities, design of company facilities, and day-to-day process planning.
2. **Marketing Plans:** Designed by marketing managers, they "tell sales and marketing personnel who will sell what, where, when, to whom, in what quantity and how."

The company creates new products to boost market share, strategises for cash and credit sales, and establishes credit terms and policies for the sales department. Production and marketing plans rely on each other; the production department manufactures based on projected sales, and sales department sells what is produced.

3. **Financial Plans:** Finance managers create financial plans to raise and use funds efficiently, meet fixed and working capital needs of the business and enhance its financial strength. They strategise for financial adjustments in economic downturns, make provisions for cuts, and secure funds during economic upswings.

4. **Human Resource Plans:** They optimise the organisation's most valuable asset—its people. Ensuring an optimum match between employees and their roles helps prevent shortages and surpluses of manpower. Human resource managers forecast quantitative (how many people are needed) and qualitative (what type of people are needed) needs of the organisation.

Their key activities include:

i. Acquiring the right number of people with the right skills.

ii. Motivating employees and enhancing their skills.

iii. Providing training for people to adapt to the changing environment.

iv. Formulating policies for employee retention, compensation, and development.

Functional plans can also be developed for areas such as accounting, research and development, etc.

Questions

I. Long Answer Questions

1. Discuss the role of planning in business organisations. Explain the steps involved in the planning process.
2. "Planning is a bridge between the present and the future." Comment.
3. Define planning. Discuss the limitations of planning. What measures do you suggest overcoming these limitations?
4. "Managerial planning is a mere ritual in the fast-changing environment." Discuss.
5. What is planning? Describe the importance, merits, and limitations of planning.
6. Explain the barriers to planning. How can these barriers be overcome?
7. Discuss the characteristics of a sound plan.

8. Explain the meaning, importance and process of policy formulation.
   (a) What are single use plans? Explain different kinds of single use plans?
   (b) How do programmes and strategies help in achieving the objectives?
   (c) What are standing plans? Explain different kinds of standing plans.
   (d) Distinguish between policies, procedures, methods, rules and standards. How do they help to achieve the objectives?

II. Write short notes on:

(i) Procedures and rules
(ii) Methods
(iii) Types of policies
(iv) Programmes and procedures

III. Differentiate Between:

(i) Single use and Standing Plans
(ii) Policies and Procedures
(iii) Policies and Strategies
(iv) Rules and Policies
(v) Rules and Procedures

IV. Case Study

(I) "Radiant Industries" manufactures electrical stamping. It supplies 50% of its output in the domestic market and 50% in the international market.

As on date, it is doing well in the domestic market, while it is unable to capture the international market successfully. Market research has identified the following reasons for this:

1. Intense competition in the international market, as the product is not new there.
2. Quality is not upto the international standards.

However, the product is new to the domestic markets, thus, is readily acceptable here. The managing director (MD) of the company is worried about its international operations and, thus, holds a meeting with the Finance and Marketing Managers (major departmental heads) to analyse the issue.

After extensive discussion, the Marketing Manager came to the conclusion that the firm should continue working in the international markets, as he feels that the firm might face competition in the domestic market which may drive the firm out.

So, he wants to improve quality upto the international level and introduce product differentiation.

The finance manager, however, is not very pleased with this opinion; as quality enhancement upto the international levels would require huge amount of capital investment; and the firm at present is not in a position to finance it. This would require some time; thus, the marketing manager's plan cannot be implemented immediately.

The MD knows that product differentiation and quality enhancement is a long-term procedure; but going with the opinion of the marketing manager; he wants to continue its operations in the international markets.

The result was increasing losses for the company. The departmental managers then suggested the MD reduce the sales targets in foreign markets and plan accordingly. The MD didn't listen. The company came close to bankruptcy.

Questions

1. Analyse the case.
2. What reasons do you account for the company's failure?
3. What would you have done in such a situation? Suggest a strategy for the company to come out of this financial crisis

(II) The managing director of a company sent his departmental manager Mr. Arya to attend a five-day seminar on 'Developing plans for Organisational Activities.' After Mr. Arya came back from the seminar, the MD called him to his office and said, "I hope the seminar has helped you in learning to prepare plans. Please help in making plans for the following issues":

(a) You know our managers go on frequent touring in India and abroad. Most of them take their spouses along at the company's expense. We want to stop this practice.

(*b*) Many employees take advance for official expenses but do not fill the necessary vouchers in time. It is becoming difficult for the accounts department to keep track of the defaulters and keep their accounts upto date.

Questions

1. If you were the departmental manager, what plans would you make in each case?
2. Can these plans be used repeatedly ?

❑❑❑

12 Chapter

Management by Objectives

"Surround yourself with the best people you can find, delegate authority, and don't interfere as long as the policy you've decided upon is being carried out."

— *Ronald Reagan*

12.1 MEANING OF MANAGEMENT BY OBJECTIVES (MBO)

When a team works together, objectives help to contribute to the same purpose; the essence of MBO. Management objective refers to the primary goal of a management team or system that dictates the actions, decisions and regulations created by an organisation's management. Managers often share goals with employees and executives to develop a consistent purpose and strategy. It creates a collegial working relationship that helps the organisation to grow.

The term 'Management by Objectives' was first coined by *Peter Drucker* in 1954 in his book, "The Practice of Management." Management by Objectives (MBO) is an approach to enhance organisational effectiveness, performance, and motivation. It is a personnel management system, where organisations set, plan, monitor and achieve specific objectives with cooperation of employees at all levels. It is the process of setting objectives to give a sense of direction to the employees.

It is, a strategic business model with clearly defined objectives agreed upon by management and the employees. Superiors and subordinates take part in goal setting, with complete focus on transparency and ease of communication. This helps all individuals to see their achievements in connection with company's priorities and reinforce alignment between their activities and outcome, thus, increasing productivity.

Managers systemically update and delegate tasks to employees with mutual understanding and keep the goals aligned with the organisational mission. A definite set of functions is set for each employee, and their work is monitored to plan, design, and execute objectives at a definite time frame.

The memory aid for setting objectives in MBO (SMART objectives) explains how a group or organisation will achieve a goal.

- **Specific** - They target a specific area for improvement, are precise and clear to team members, partners, and other groups.
- **Measurable** - They suggest an indicator of progress, that is, how much and in what direction will change occur. The standard measure can be a number, percent, or any other unit used as a reference point to monitor change.
- **Achievable** - Objectives are within reach of partners, community, and team members, within the constraints of resources, knowledge, and time. Thoughtful discussion between managers and team members results in achievable objectives.
- **Relevant** - The objectives align with organisation's mission, vision, and values and state realistic results that can be achieved by partners, community members, and decision-makers. They help to achieve meaningful change for the focus population.
- **Time-bound** - They specify when the results can be achieved by attaching a reasonable date to their accomplishment.

MBO balances the capacity of subordinates with expectations of the organisation. Unrealistic or unachievable objectives weaken the purpose of objective setting.

The final approval of goals is based upon:

- what is attainable within the structure.
- what is consistent with the goals of other managers.
- what is consistent with the long-term objectives of the organisation.
- what is consistent with the available resources.

"The system of management by objectives can be described as a process whereby the superior and subordinate managers of an organisation jointly identify its common goals, define each individual's major areas of responsibility in terms of results expected of him, and use these measures as guides for operating the unit and assessing the contribution of each of its members." – *George S. Ordiorue*

"Management by objectives is a comprehensive managerial system *that integrates many key managerial activities in a systematic* manner and that is consciously directed toward the effective and efficient achievement of organisational and individual objectives."

– *Koontz* and *Weihrich*

"MBO is a result-centered, non-specialist, operational managerial process for the effective utilisation of material, physical, and human resources of the organisation by integrating the individual with the organisation and organisation with the environment." – *S.K. Chakravarty*

MBO is "the establishment of effectiveness areas and effectiveness standards for managerial positions and the periodic conversion of all these into measurable time bound objectives linked vertically and horizontally with future planning."–*Professor Reddin*

12.2 COMPONENTS OF MBO

1. **Specific Goals** – The goals are specific and easily understandable in terms of who will be impacted by the goals (focus population) and what kind of impact is intended on them.
2. **Realistic and Acceptable Goals** – These goals result in successful outcomes, particularly when they are challenging in nature.
3. **Joint Participation in Goal Setting** - Participation of internal stakeholders promotes setting of realistic goals with high acceptance and commitment.
4. **Feedback** - Continuous feedback helps to know whether employees sustain or redirect their efforts to reach the goal.

12.3 NATURE OF MBO

1. **Philosophy of Management:** MBO is a philosophy of management that affects management thinking. It is the way an organisation works in all divisions and levels. It cuts across all boundaries; vertical and horizontal. Human values, culture and learning are part of every organisational aspect and, thus, considered in MBO.
2. **Participation:** MBO involves managers at all levels. Goals at each level are set with the participation of managers at lower levels to ensure greater commitment to goals. The whole process of management revolves around participative objective-setting.

   Every manager frames objectives, evaluates performance, establishes relationships with superiors, peers and subordinates, with clarity about what to achieve and how.
3. **Integration:** There is integration of objectives across all levels (corporate, departmental and individual) and functional areas. It integrates objectives with resources, sub-systems and the external environment.

4. **Links Objectives to Performance:** Goals set standards to measure performance. Planning and control are, thus, the heart of MBO. This brings in place appropriate systems and procedures for delegation, resource allocation, authority-responsibility relationships, reward system etc. for every activity.
5. **Functional Approach:** It is a systematic and functional goal-setting approach. It is also known as Results management; Goals Management; Management by Results or Management by Mission.
6. **Autonomy:** MBO is a goal-setting approach. It does not interfere in the process of implementation of those goals. Every member has the freedom to accomplish the goals in his own way.
7. **Promotes Creativity:** Participation in setting goals and freedom in execution promotes creativity and innovation in the organisation. People generate ideas with diverse inputs, contributing to motivation and commitment by employees.
8. **Result-oriented Strategy:** MBO aims at results. It monitors the performance, reviews the goals and makes necessary modifications.

12.4 OBJECTIVES OF MBO

1. It promotes participation in the goal-setting process, facilitates decision-making and co-ordinates individual goals with organisational goals.
2. It improves communication amongst managers and subordinates. The superiors set targets for each team member. This leads to highly motivated and committed employees.
3. It defines responsibilities of everyone in the MBO process. This increases efficiency by specifying priorities and outcomes at each level.
4. It helps employees to understand their duties. This leads to satisfaction and avoids job mismatch.
5. Every employee contributes to objectives. They are loyal to the organisation and enjoy the work.
6. It maintains balance between objectives, translates concepts into practice and establishes accountability for results.

12.5 NEED FOR MANAGEMENT BY OBJECTIVES

1. It helps the employees to understand their duties at the workplace. They know clearly what is expected out of them.

2. It determines key responsibility areas for each employee according to their interest, specialisation, and qualification. It leads to highly motivated and committed employees.
3. It avoids job mismatch and leads to satisfied employees.
4. Employees contribute to goals in their own way and enjoy the work and the workplace.
5. It ensures effective communication, leading to a cordial atmosphere at the workplace.

12.6 PROCESS OF MBO

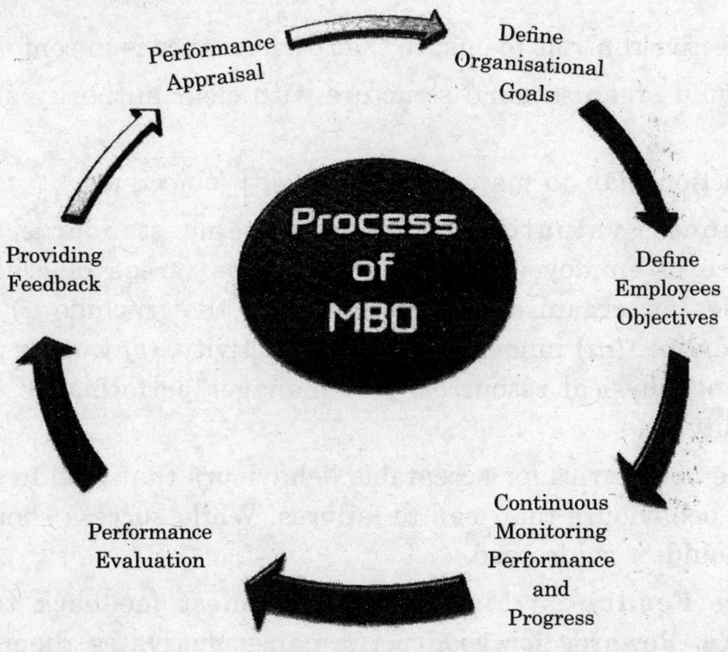

1. **Define Organisational Goals:** The company heads determine current goals of the organisation. MBO emphasises measurable, tangible, and achievable goals, keeping the organisational mission in mind.

   The goals define:
   - Why does the organisation exist.
   - What should be its activities.
   - How should the activities be pursued.

2. **Define Employee Objectives:** After setting the goals, the company determines how to reach them. Employees set their own goals which are capable of being achieved. Organisational objectives are aligned with the objectives of the employees to prevent unrealistic expectations from employees.
3. **Continuous Mointoring Performance and Progress:** The performance of employees is continuously monitored as outcomes help to determine plans. Managers keep track of progress to avoid failures at any stage.

   The following measures help to monitor performance:

   - Remove ineffective programmes where performance does not match the objectives.
   - Install effective controls to ensure that performance is in conformity with plans.
   - Design sound organisational structure with clear authority and responsibility all levels.
   - Prepare action plan to match resources with objectives.
4. **Performance Evaluation:** Companies frame standards to evaluate the performance of employees. Specific key areas (areas of critical importance) set priorities for organisational performance that include (*i*) profitability, (*ii*) market standing, (*iii*) innovation, (*iv*) productivity, (*v*) worker performance, (*vi*) financial and physical resources, (*vii*) manager performance, and (*viii*) public responsibility.

   They define boundaries for acceptable behaviours that lead to success and non-acceptable behaviours that lead to failures. While success should be rewarded, failures should be addressed.
5. **Providing Feedback:** Managers give honest feedback to employees on performance. Rewards for good performance motivates them to keep up the good work. Employees design strategies to overcome the flaws and improve performance.
6. **Performance Appraisal :** The success of plans is ensured through periodic performance reviews, where problems are identified, solutions are found, and goals are adjusted for the next MBO cycle. After defining and initiating organisational and individual goals, managers periodically assess subordinates' performance to ensure alignment with planned outcomes. The MBO approach encourages self-appraisal, where subordinates review their performance under the expert guidance of superiors. Appraisal includes praise and recognition for positive performance and identifies areas for skill and knowledge development.

However, appraisal is not used to punish non-performers or solely reward high performers. It ensures that everything goes according to plan without deviations in performance. Appraisal is used to recycle the MBO process. Successfully achieved objectives form the basis for the next MBO cycle. This cycle represents objective setting, action planning, and performance. The performance review provides the basis for the next round of objective setting and action planning.

12.7 MERITS OF MANAGEMENT BY OBJECTIVES

MBO produces positive impact on employee performance, motivation, commitment, and job satisfaction.

1. **Efficient Management:** MBO results in efficiency and people are productive at their jobs. Employees know the path to follow as there is a mutually agreed upon systematic plan adopted by every member to complete the assigned tasks. Every member works towards business-focused objectives, leading to improved communication and teamwork.
2. **Realistic Goals:** Goals provide a roadmap for action. With participative goal setting, everyone in the organisation is aware of the process and shares their perspectives and ideas. They do not just plan the goals, but plan for action. Goals serve as standards for control and people concentrate on profit influencing tasks. They understand their roles and tasks better. MBO sets straightforward business goals, and each member has a clear set of tasks to meet them.
3. **Effective Planning:** Plans provide blueprint for growth of a business. Employees are clear about the objectives and develop a systematic plan to achieve them. Result-oriented planning promotes planning by results, facilitates evaluation and corrective actions.
3. **Transparency:** All members are aware of their goals and ways to achieve them. The communication process is active between management and the employees. Measurement and appraisals are objective, specific, and equitable. There is complete transparency in knowing who is doing what, thus, increasing efficiency of the management.
4. **Communication and Commitment:** Most often, employees work for their own objectives and the environment surrounding them. Gradually, they lose their sense of commitment, followed by lack of direction, transparency, and miscommunication between the superior and subordinates. MBO bridges this gap and creates a positive work environment. It increases the quality of teamwork

and communication between the management team, as they constantly cooperate to ensure clarity in the strategies and provide regular feedback.

A better sense of understanding prevails in the organisation resulting in quality improvement and optimum use of resources. Participation improves morale, commitment, and communication. Every member is involved in planning and achieving the company goals. It reinforces a sense of responsibility and motivates them to complete the tasks in time.

6. **Accountability:** Defined goals promote accountability where everyone measures and appraises his performance. People are accountable for results. With specific, objective, and equitable goals, there is constant evaluation of results and people aim to reach their full potential. Participatory behaviour encourages team morale and productivity of the organisation.
7. **Efficient Utilisation of Human Resource:** Having the best teams is not enough. Human resources must be captured to their fullest potential with digital transformations. Sustainability in competitive markets requires delegating tasks to individuals who best suit the given role. MBO provides employees and managers to collaborate on setting goals and assigning roles through thoughtful matching of talents to jobs and utilising human resources to maximum effect.
8. **Removes Ambiguity:** It reduces role ambiguity as everyone is clear about their roles. Management structure is focused and encourages a positive work culture. Employees understand the workflow. Collaboration between manager and employees leads to effective understanding of job roles. People at all levels feel involved, empowered and indispensable with clear objectives related to the wider business strategy. Managers tailor each set of objectives to individual staff members, based on their specialisations, skills, qualifications, and career goals.

Henry L. Tosi and *Stephen J. Carroll* highlight the following advantages of an MBO programme:

1. It lets individuals know what is expected of them.
2. It aids in planning by making managers establish goals and target dates.
3. It improves communication between managers and subordinates.
4. It makes individuals more aware of the organisational goals.
5. It makes the evaluation process more equitable by focusing on specific accomplishments. It lets subordinates know how well they are doing in relation to the organisational goals.

12.8 LIMITATIONS OF MBO

1. **Illusionary Approach:** It emphasises too much on group goal setting. Individuals can have different goals. Group goal setting supersedes individual goal setting. Though goals are tailored to individual staff skills, they may not fully consider their personal and career development options.
2. **Lack of Understanding;** MBO is not easily understood by everyone in the organisation. Success can be achieved when everyone knows not just what to do but also how to do. Organisations may not be able to co-ordinate overall goals with individual goals if superiors and subordinates do not mutually agree to the goal-setting process.

   To fully appreciate the benefits of MBO, people need to understand:
   - Why is MBO being implemented.
   - What purpose will it serve.
   - How will the performance be evaluated and appraised.
3. **Lack of Focus:** MBO is not always considered a comprehensive philosophy. Some relevant parts of the company are often ignored, like company culture, work ethos, and interpersonal activities. It ignores the prevailing culture and working conditions of the organisation. Focus is more on goals which employees are expected to achieve without bothering much about the circumstances at the workplace. Employees are just expected to perform and meet the deadlines.
4. **Stressful for Employees:** MBO can cause strain to meet the goals set by management. With a measurable, business-aligned set of goals, staff can feel under pressure. Excessive focus on business goals can detract from other important business operations.
5. **Lack of Creative Environment:** Individuals compare their performance at the workplace. They may indulge in unproductive tasks to outperform their fellow workers. The workplace environment is not conducive to innovation and creativity.

- Group goal achievement is more difficult. When the goals of one department depend on the goals of another department, coordination becomes a problem.
- It takes a few years for MBO to produce effective results.
- Some companies set high goals, which can be difficult for the employees.
- Appraisals are sometimes made on personality traits rather than performance.
- Effective interaction between superiors and subordinates may not be possible due to status difference or interpersonal skills.

12.9 EFFECTIVE MBO

MBO is not merely a technique for achieving success but a broader management philosophy that requires a shift in the organisation's values and culture. To effectively implement MBO and address its limitations, certain guidelines can enhance its success:

1. **Top Management Support:** Top managers should not only set objectives but actively engage in reviewing the performance of operating managers. Continuous guidance and support are crucial to sustain the MBO programme.
2. **Training:** Knowledge gaps can be overcome through training programmes. MBO is a means to an end, not the end itself. Defining clear purpose and adoption of appropriate techniques are key to success. Training helps individuals comprehend the concept and philosophy of MBO, fostering a change in attitudes and behaviours. This leads to organisational structural changes. Altered behaviours establish new authority-responsibility relationships, allowing individuals to adapt to the new roles effectively.
3. **Purpose of MBO:** Objectives should be formulated through comprehensive understanding and consensus among managers at all levels. Clearly defined goals play a crucial role in establishing achievable performance standards. Having a clear purpose enables organisations to enhance productivity and face the challenges of a competitive environment. This promotes long-term planning, performance evaluation, and overall productivity.
4. **Feedback:** Top managers, while setting goals in consultation with lower-level managers, regularly review subordinate performance, typically on a quarterly basis, to ensure alignment with planned objectives. Feedback provides guidance for performance improvement and continuous learning. It serves as valuable input for strategic management by addressing gaps between the current state and desired outcomes.
4. **Participation:** As MBO involves participation of subordinates in the goal-setting process, it is crucial to encourage increased involvement. Participation fosters commitment and alignment of individual goals with organisational goals. It results in mutually agreeable performance levels, acceptable to both superiors and subordinates.

   However, the degree of participation should be carefully considered. Subordinates should have the necessary skills and knowledge for meaningful involvement. Their readiness for self-appraisal through feedback and acceptance of responsibility for performance, whether positive or negative, must be ensured for effective implementation of MBO.

6. **Inter-departmental Coordination:** MBO instills commitment among team members, motivating them to strive for optimum performance. However, excessive commitment can sometimes lead to unhealthy competition. People may focus on individual or departmental goals, competing for limited resources. Successful MBO implementation requires inter-departmental cooperation. Individuals must recognise that organisational success results from coordinated efforts of all departments, rather than individual achievements.

Example of Management by Objectives

A company wants to increase sales by ₹50 lakh, ROI to 15 % and shareholders' earnings to 6%. The General manager, Sales discusses with regional managers of all zones, who further discuss with their district managers. Goals are set for individuals of each sales department and progress is periodically reviewed.

Thus, heads of the department collaborate and assess the results. By evaluating successes and failures, they promote changes and define goals for the future. A series of superior-subordinate relationships involves setting objectives at every level through negotiations and collaborations.

Questions

I. Long Answer Questions

1. What do you understand by MBO? How can MBO programme be made effective?
2. MBO was introduced in a business organisation but it failed. Cite the possible reasons responsible for such a failure.
3. Explain the process and utility of MBO programme.
4. Explain the meaning and process of MBO.
5. How is MBO programme conducted in a business organisation? What are the limitations of MBO?
6. Briefly explain the meaning and advantages of 'Management by Objectives' (MBO).

II. Write short notes on:

(i) MBO

(ii) Approaches to MBO

III. Multiple Choice Questions

1. MBO means
   (*i*) Management before objectives.
   (*ii*) Management by objectives
   (*iii*) Management by ordinance
2. The concept of MBO was introduced by
   (*i*) Peter F. Drucker
   (*ii*) F.W. Taylor
   (*iii*) Henri Fayol
3. MBO approach to goal setting follows
   (*i*) Top-down approach to setting objective
   (*ii*) Bottom-up approach to setting objectives
   (*iii*) Both
4. In MBO, superiors and subordinates work on objectives
   (*i*) Jointly
   (*ii*) Independently

Answers

1. (ii) 2. (i) 3. (iii) 4. (i)

❑❑❑

13 Chapter

Organising Function

"For every minute spent in organising, an hour is earned."

13.1 MEANING OF ORGANISATION

Organisation is "the process of identifying and grouping the work to be performed, defining and delegating responsibility and authority, and establishing relationships for the purpose of enabling people to work most effectively together in accomplishing objectives."

"Organisation defines the part which each member of an enterprise is expected to perform and the relations between such members, to the end that their concerted endeavour shall be most effective for the purpose of the enterprise."

Organising is the "process of defining the essential relationships among people, tasks and activities in such a way that all the organisation's resources are integrated and coordinated to accomplish its objectives efficiently and effectively."

Organising is the arrangement of relationships within an organisation, creating a network of connections, particularly in terms of authority and responsibility. This outlines the relationships between various positions and individuals, emphasising the roles of people.

Tasks are distributed across different units or departments, and individuals are assigned specific responsibilities to optimise the organisation's well-being and individual objectives. Relationships within the organisation occur both vertically and horizontally. Vertically, it involves authority-responsibility structure at different levels within the same department, horizontally, it encompasses authority-responsibility structure across different departments at the same levels.

13.2 NATURE OF ORGANISATION

1. **Structure of Relationships:** Organisation entails a system of well-defined tasks, incorporating authority and accountability. Formal structure is

established through delegation. While formal relationships are designed within the organisational structure, spontaneous informal relationships arise through constant inter-personal interactions.

2. **Managerial Function:** Organising is a managerial function that integrates human and non-human (physical) resources. It plays a crucial role in facilitating other management functions, such as planning, directing, and staffing.
3. **Ongoing Process:** Organising is a continuous process, involving a series of steps from determination to accomplishment of objectives. It adapts and evolves in response to changes in the environment.
4. **Encourages Teamwork:** It encourages teamwork, where individuals contribute collectively towards a common goal. Tasks are divided among team members, fostering coordination and effective group activities.
5. **Foundation of Management:** The success of any institution relies on its sound organisation. Clearly defined roles, division among members, and transparent authority structure form the foundation of successful management.
6. **Goal-oriented:** Every organisation is established with a specific objective. Activities are distributed among members, departments are created, and continuous monitoring occurs to achieve these objectives. Organising is inherently a goal-oriented process.
7. **Adaptive to Change:** The organisation structure remains open to environmental changes, both internal and external, demonstrating adaptability in response to evolving circumstances.
8. **Situational:** No single structure can be deemed the best, as it varies based on the nature of activities, size of the organisation, and relationships among individuals. The organisation structure functions as an open system designed to meet the requirements of the evolving environment.

13.3 PROCESS OF ORGANISING

1. **Determination of Objectives:** Establishing an organisation serves a specific purpose. To attain its goals, the organisation outlines tasks essential for success. For instance, if the objective is exporting goods, the organisation identifies the nature and type of goods, target countries, and coordinates with foreign buyers. The initial phase in organising is determining the workload.
2. **Division of Activities:** Task division is important as one person cannot handle all activities. Work is segmented into smaller units and assigned based on

members' abilities. Division of work enhances output. For instance, *Adam Smith* demonstrated that while one person could produce 20 pins a day, specialisation in various tasks enabled 10 individuals to produce 48,000 pins daily. It boosts efficiency, as repetitive tasks lead to increased proficiency. It also helps in training, as breaking down complex tasks allows training of semi-skilled workers for specific roles.

3. **Grouping of Activities:** Departments like sales, finance, and accounting consist of individuals performing similar tasks. This grouping of activities into departments is known as departmentation. Each department operates under a set of rules, procedures, and standards.
4. **Define Authority and Responsibility:** Authority and responsibility are defined within each department, led by its in-charge, whose competence aligns with department's requirements. The department head delegates responsibilities to members, establishing a clear structure where individuals understand their superiors, subordinates, and reporting relationships.
5. **Co-ordination:** Co-ordination becomes crucial when departments start functioning, preventing conflicts. It delineates relationships among people in different positions and optimises resource allocation.
6. **Reviewing and Re-organising:** Regular reviews and re-organising are integral to the organising process. Constant appraisal allows adjustments to adapt to environmental factors and changing circumstances.

13.4 IMPORTANCE OF ORGANISING

1. **Facilitates Administration:** Top managers delegate responsibilities to middle and lower-level managers, enabling them to focus on strategic administration. Key elements of organising, such as division of work, grouping of activities, distribution of authority, and coordination, contribute to streamlined administration by top management.
2. **Growth and Diversification:** A well-organised institution is adaptable to change, responsive to growth, and capable of diversification. It can expand its operations effectively.
3. **Creates Synergies:** Division of work promotes synergy, where the collective effort of a group is more than the sum of individual achievements. Departments collaborate and coordinate their tasks, creating efficient and productive outcomes.

4. **Establishes Accountability:** Clearly defined reporting relationships ensure that every individual understands their superiors and subordinates, promoting accountability to immediate bosses and commitment to broader organisational goals.
5. **Optimum Use of Technology:** In the era of technological advancements, well-organised structures optimise the use of technology to remain competitive in dynamic market conditions.
6. **Facilitates Communication:** The efficiency of an organisation relies on effective communication among its members. A well-organised structure establishes a strong communication system, enhancing overall efficiency.
7. **Facilitates Creativity:** By providing a sense of achievement and encouraging creative thinking, a sound organisation structure promotes innovative ways of working.
8. **Improves Interpersonal Relationships:** A well-structured organisation contributes to improved interpersonal relationships by aligning tasks with individuals' abilities and skills. Assigning the right person to the right job promotes satisfaction and positive relationships among team members.
9. **Facilitates Coordination:** Effective coordination is facilitated by a thoughtfully designed structure, bringing order and system to work. It ensures harmonious collaboration across different levels and departments, aligning individual goals with organisational objectives, internal environment with external environments, and financial resources with non-financial resources.
10. **Facilitates Teamwork:** Teamwork is encouraged by the organisational setup, where individuals work collaboratively to optimise resource utilisation. The organisation fosters a collective perspective, where individuals view goals from a group standpoint, aligning organisational objectives with individual aspirations.
11. **Facilitates Control:** Organisation structure facilitates control by providing direction and ensuring adherence to plans. Clearly defined objectives, coupled with regular feedback, ensure conformity to planned course of action.
12. **Increase in Output:** Division of work into specialised departments enhances efficiency and promotes output.
13. **Optimum Allocation of Resources:** Resources are allocated based on priority, ensuring individuals work on tasks that align with their strengths. The organised structure prevents duplication of work, eliminates overlapping, and ensures that everyone contributes collectively toward organisational goals.

13.5 ORGANISATION CHART

As organisations grow in size and complexity, they add more departments, sub-units, and employees. This growth increases the distance between top executives and lower-level employees, making interactions more complicated. To help everyone understand the positions, departments, sub-units, and their relationships, visual maps called organisation charts are used. These charts provide a clear understanding of each person's position in the organisation relative to their superiors and subordinates. They clearly define the authority, responsibility, and accountability structure within the organisation. It is a "line diagram that depicts the broad outlines of an organisation's structure."

Organisation charts "show in visual form the various major positions or departments in the organisation, the way the various positions are grouped into specific units, reporting relationships from lower to higher levels, and official channels for communicating information." *– Alferd D. Chandler*

An organisation chart represents how a company is organised using boxes and lines. The boxes show the activities a company performs and the people who perform these activities. The lines indicate the relationships among them, following the official chain of command and communication channels. A typical organisation chart looks like this :

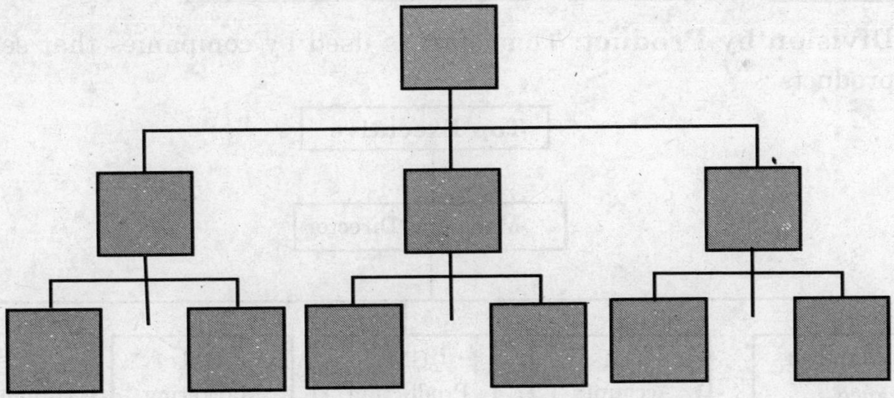

Organisation Chart

What Does Organisation Chart Show

Organisation chart shows the following aspects of a company's structure:

1. ***Division of work***: The organisation's workload is divided into smaller units, with activities at each level shown in boxes.
2. ***Chain of command***: The lines of authority flow from top to bottom, showing the relationships between superiors and subordinates.

3. ***People who perform the activities***: The boxes sometimes include the names of the people who perform the tasks.
4. ***Levels of management***: While top executives hold ultimate responsibility, authority is delegated down the hierarchy, creating management levels. The sample chart above shows three levels of management.
5. ***The basis of division***: Organisation charts are prepared based on how organisational activities are divided. The different bases for creating these charts include:
   i. **Division by Functional Areas:** The chart is based on the functions performed by the organisation.

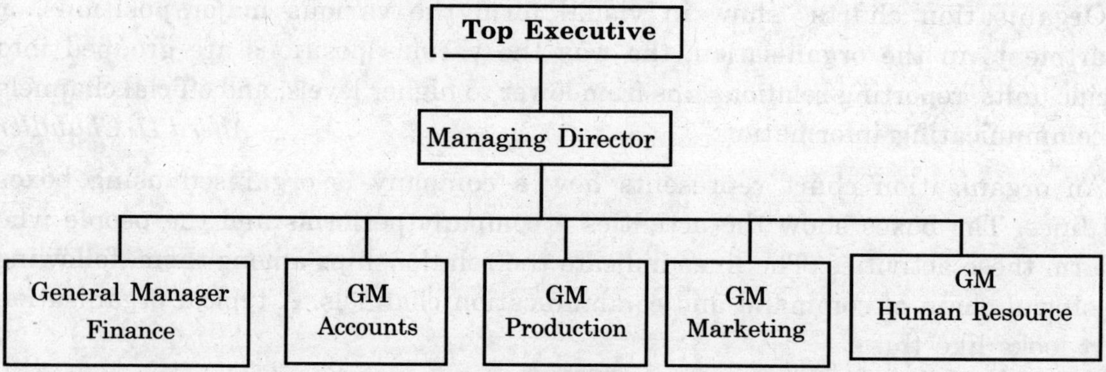

   ii. **Division by Product:** This chart is used by companies that sell multiple products.

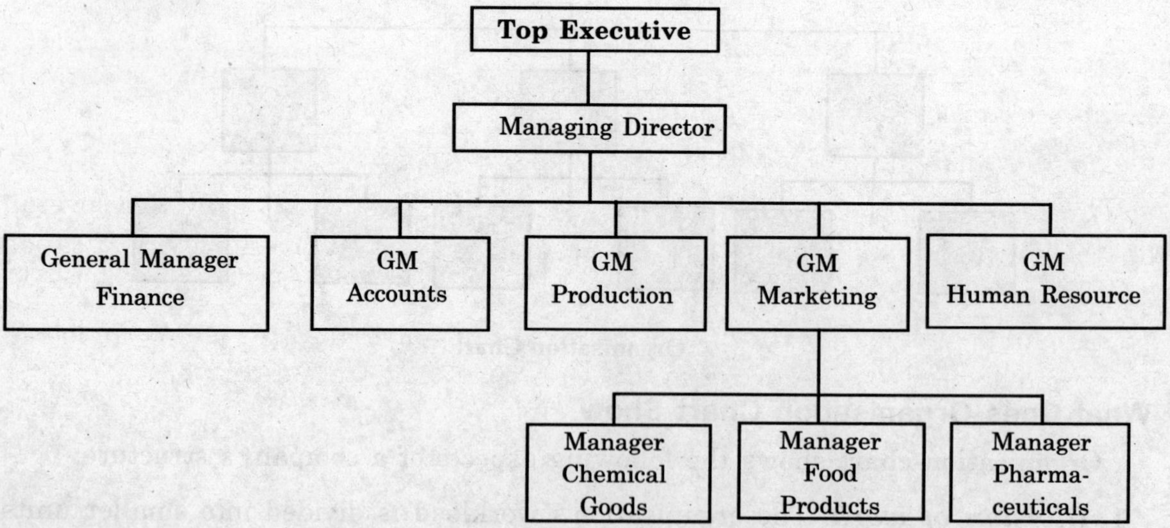

iii. Division by Customers: This chart is used by organisations that sell goods to different types of customers.

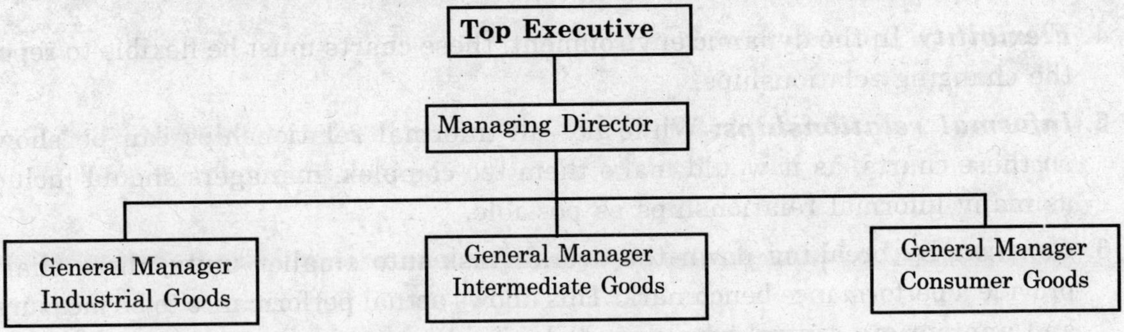

iv. Division by Geographical Area: This chart depicts the structure of organisations that sell goods in different regions.

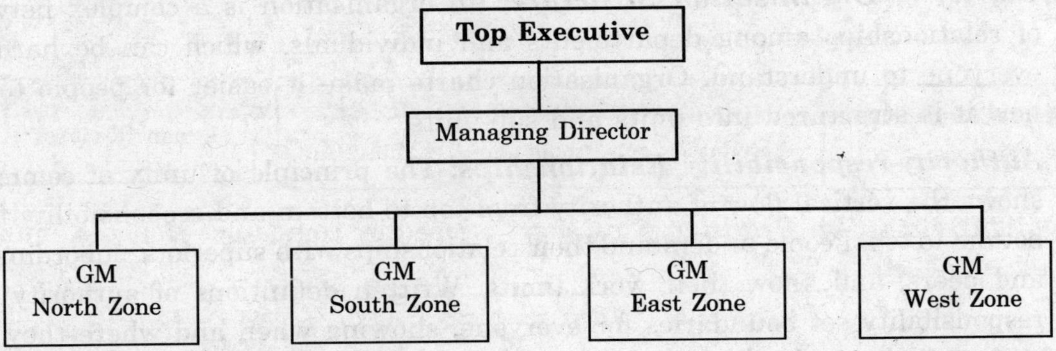

Principles of Organisation Charts

Organisation chart is based on the following principles:

1. ***Clear definition of jobs***: The charts are prepared keeping in view overall jobs of the organisation. Every job has a suitable position on the organisation chart.
2. ***Authority-responsibility***: The authority and responsibility for each job at different levels must be clearly shown on the organisation charts.

3. ***End result areas***: The charts represent the activities (jobs) performed at different managerial positions and the end-results (or the objectives) expected of each position.
4. ***Flexibility***: In the dynamic environment, these charts must be flexible to report the changing relationships.
5. ***Informal relationships***: While not all informal relationships can be shown on these charts, as it would make them too complex, managers should include as many informal relationships as possible.
6. ***Control***: By breaking down the overall task into smaller units, these charts provide a performance benchmark. This allows actual performance to be measured and appropriate control measures to be implemented.

Merits of Organisation Charts

Organisation charts have the following merits:

1. ***Clarity of Organisation Structure***: An organisation is a complex network of relationships among departments and individuals, which can be hard for everyone to understand. Organisation charts make it easier for people to see how it is structured into units and sub-units.
2. ***Authority-responsibility Relationships***: The principle of unity of command shows the vertical flow of authority from top to bottom and responsibility from bottom to top. People understand their relationships with superiors, subordinates, and peers, and know their work limits. Written definitions of authority and responsibility set boundaries for everyone, showing when and where they can use creativity and initiative in their tasks. Clear authority and responsibility help with control, as everyone is accountable for their assigned tasks.
3. ***Location of Experts:*** If a problem arises in any functional area of the organisation, these charts help identify the right person to solve it. They also assist in evaluating the performance of experts and training them to improve.
4. ***Location of Potential Areas of Conflict:*** Work is divided to match each person's skills and expertise. Care is taken to ensure no task is left unassigned and no duplication occurs. This helps prevent overlapping of activities.
5. ***Scope for Organisational Improvement:*** Conflicts among people in the existing structure can be identified, helping to improve organisational relationships.

Limitations of Organisation Charts

Organisation charts suffer from the following limitations:

1. ***Blueprint of Formal Relationships***: As organisations evolve to meet the demands of the changing environment, their structure must adapt accordingly. Organisation charts serve as a blueprint of formal authority and responsibility relationships. However, they remain effective if they can swiftly adjust to changing circumstances.
2. ***Broad View of Organisation Structure***: Organisation charts provide a general overview of how an organisation operates. They do not show the specific tasks or activities assigned to each role.
3. ***Reporting Informal Relationships:*** Organisation charts display formal relationships within an organisation, outlining who reports to whom officially. However, alongside the formal connections, informal relationships also emerge based on social interactions and norms. While formal and informal organisations work together, not all informal relationships can be represented on organisation charts. They can be partially shown on the organisation charts as follows:

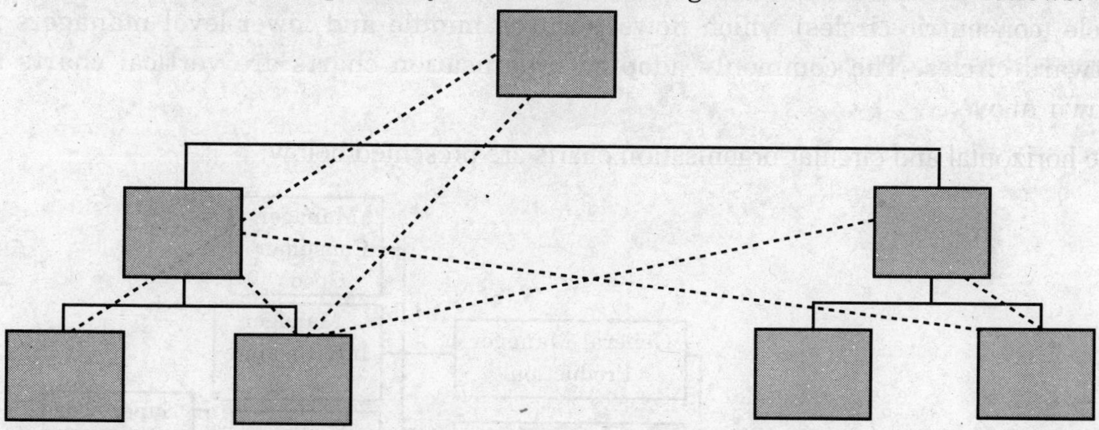

The dotted lines show informal relationships amongst organisational members.

4. ***Misinterpretation of Charts***: Sometimes, people do not understand these charts the way they are meant to be. This defeats the purpose of the charts.

"Organisation charts are demoralising because they reinforce the idea that all authority and ability rest at the top of the organisation. Proper training of organisational members can help the top executives overcome this problem."

—*Robert Townsend*

5. ***Extent of Authority***: Organisation charts illustrate how authority is distributed among managers at various levels. However, they do not indicate the full scope of authority each manager holds. It is hard to overcome this limitation because the precise extent of authority cannot be easily measured.
6. ***Dynamic Environment***: Organisation charts display formal relationships among people at the time they are made. However, they might not fully reflect changes in reporting relationships due to the fast-changing business environment. As a result, these charts may not always show the exact relationships.

Kinds of Organisation Charts

Organisation charts are broadly of the following types —

1. Vertical organisation charts
2. Horizontal organisation charts
3. Circular organisation charts

Vertical charts show the flow of authority from top to bottom; horizontal charts show this flow from left to right and circular charts show top position in the innermost circle (concentric circles) which flows towards middle and lower-level managers in outward circles. The commonly adopted organisation charts are vertical charts as shown above.

The horizontal and circular organisation charts are presented below:

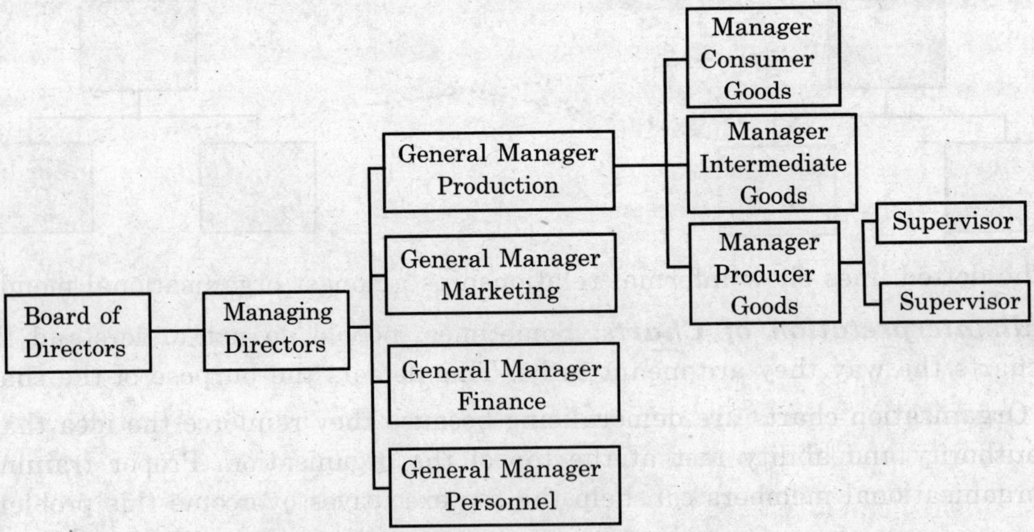

Horizontal Organisation Chart

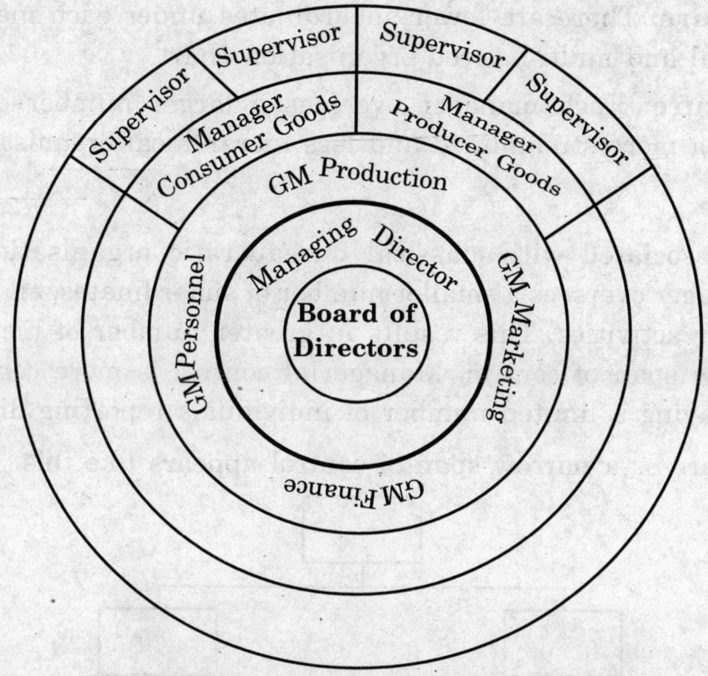

Circular Organisation Chart

(These charts can be extended for other department also, here they show extension for production department only)

13.6 SPAN OF MANAGEMENT

The effectiveness of a superior in managing subordinates is crucial for organisational output, considering the complexity of activities and relationships within the organisation. Managing all subordinates under one superior is impractical; therefore, there is need to establish an optimum limit on the number of subordinates a superior can effectively oversee.

This limit is referred to as the "span of management" or "span of control." In the 19th and mid-20th century, management experts suggested that a manager could effectively handle around 5 or 6 subordinates at the upper level. Once managers reached this point, they faced problems of being overloaded with tasks, trouble in organising and coordinating, and challenges in maintaining control. However, determining the exact number of employees that managers can effectively supervise is no longer straightforward. The span of management is situational, based on the number of employees a manager can supervise.

I. Tall Structure: There are fewer subordinates under each manager, creating a hierarchical and multi-layered organisation chart.

II. Flat Structure: Each manager oversees a larger number of subordinates, resulting in a more streamlined and less hierarchical organisation chart.

I. Tall Structure

Commonly associated with classical bureaucratic organisations, in the tall structure, a manager oversees a smaller number of subordinates, allowing for tighter control over their activities. This results in greater number of hierarchical levels, known as narrow span of control. Managerial control is more concentrated, with each manager having a limited number of individuals reporting directly to them.

A tall structure or a narrow span of control appears like this.

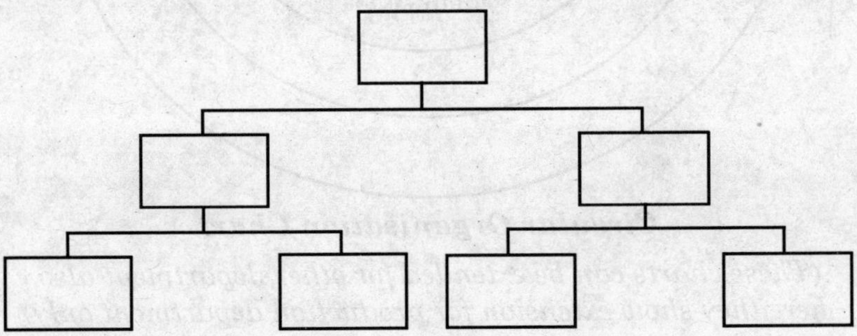

Merits of a Tall Structure

1. Managers can closely monitor and oversee the activities of their subordinates.
2. It improves communication between superiors and subordinates, facilitating efficient exchange of information.
3. Personal relationships between superiors and subordinates are promoted, creating a conducive environment for collaboration.
4. Control over subordinates becomes more feasible, enabling managers to maintain a more direct approach to supervision.

Limitations of a Tall Structure

1. Numerous levels in the organisation structure complicate coordination.
2. A higher number of managers is required to supervise subordinates, leading to increased overhead expenditures such as salaries. Consequently, this form of structure is costlier.

3. The growing gap between top managers and workers hinders the communication process, causing delays and inefficiencies.
4. Decision-making becomes challenging due to many hierarchical levels, resulting in slower and more complex process.
5. Superiors have limited time for strategic matters, impacting the organisation's overall strategic focus.
6. Employees working under strict control experience centralised decision-making, limiting their creative and innovative contributions.

"The most common and most serious symptom of mal-organisation is multiplication of the number of management levels. A basic rule of organisation is to build the least possible number of management levels and forge the shortest possible chains of command." — *Peter F. Drucker*

To address the drawbacks of a tall structure, many organisations opt to downsize, which involves reducing the number of levels in the hierarchy. Downsizing is "the process of significantly reducing the layers of middle management, expanding spans of control and shrinking the size of the work force." By downsizing, organisations aim to enhance communication, decision-making, and overall operational effectiveness. Many companies downsize their work force through restructuring. It is "the process of making a major change in organisation structure that often involves reducing management levels and also possibly changing some major components of the organisations through divestiture and/or acquisition."

II. Flat Structure

A shift from tall structures to flat structures occurred when a larger number of subordinates were placed under the supervision of a single superior. *James C. Worthy,* a consultant at L. Sears, Roebuck and Company, pioneered this transition. In a flat structure, there are fewer hierarchical levels, creating a more streamlined organisational framework. This adjustment aims at improving communication, decision-making, and operational efficiency within the organisation. A structure where span of control for each managerial position is 4 appears as follows:

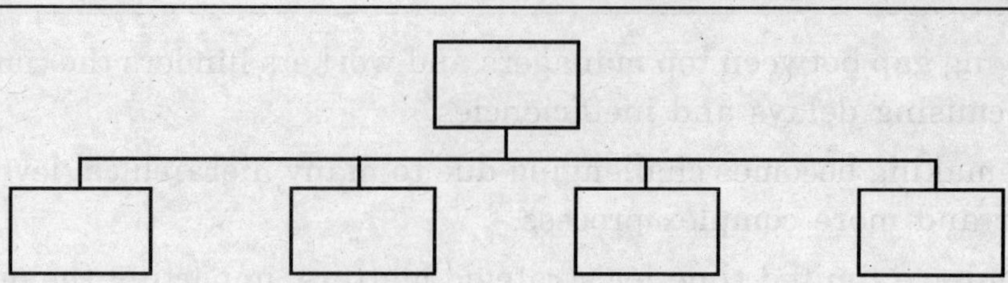

To illustrate, if organisations A and B, both have 256 workers and the span of control for each managerial position is 2 for company A and 4 for company B, there will be 9 levels in company A (requiring 128 supervisors at the lowest level, 64 at the next higher level and so on) and 5 levels in company B. A narrow span of control creates more levels in the organisational hierarchy than the wide span of control.

The levels in case of organisation B (5) where span of control is 4 appears as follows:

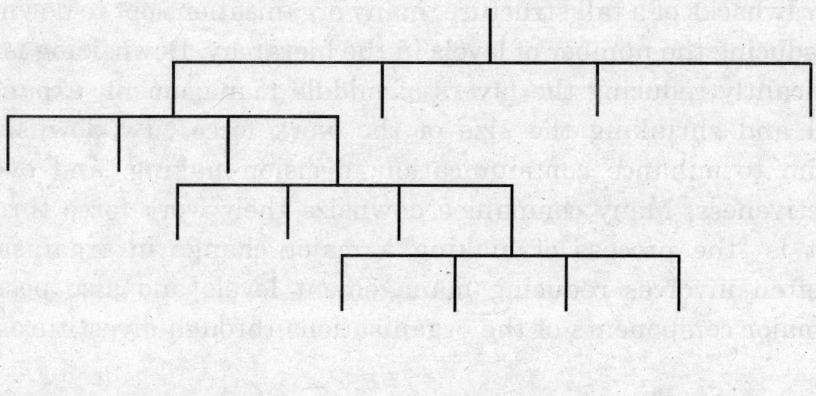

1st level (1 executive)
2nd level (4 executives)
3rd level (16 managers)
4th level (64 workers)
5th level (256 workers)

(The span of 4 prevails for each functional area at each level). The figure represents the span for only one functional area and one level).

Merits of a Flat Structure

1. The cost is lower as fewer managers are needed to supervise organisational activities.
2. Decision-making is effective as superiors delegate authority to subordinates, allowing them to focus on strategic matters. Decentralisation of decision-making streamlines the process.
3. Subordinates are entrusted with tasks they are considered capable of, leading to efficient work performance.
4. Communication is effective due to the reduced number of hierarchical levels.

5. The structure encourages innovative abilities of top management, promoting a dynamic and creative organisational environment.

Limitations of a Flat Structure

1. Coordinating the activities of subordinates might be difficult for managers in this structure.
2. To prevent the negative impact on organisational productivity due to decentralisation of control, proper training for subordinates becomes essential.

Both tall and flat structures have their positive and negative aspects and determining the exact number of subordinates a manager can effectively handle remains challenging. Management theorists like *David D. Van Fleet* and *Arthur G. Bedeian* argue that the span of control and organisational efficiency are not necessarily linked. Empirical studies support the idea that the span of control is situational and depends on various factors.

Some research suggests that flat structures yield better results because decentralised decision-making involves less top-down control, fostering initiative and job satisfaction. Larger groups are believed to be more adept at solving complex problems through group decision-making, benefitting from a diverse range of skills.

Contrarily, other studies indicate that tall structures can be more effective. With fewer members in a group, consensus-building and thorough evaluation of decisions are more achievable. High group cohesiveness in tall structures leads to greater commitment to decisions, increased satisfaction, and reduced conflicts among members.

In ultimate analysis, the effectiveness of organisation structure depends on the specific context and circumstances.

Factors Affecting Span of Management

1. ***Competence of Managers*****:** The competence of managers plays a crucial role in determining the span of management. Those who excel in decision-making related to motivational plans, leadership styles, communication channels, and control techniques can effectively supervise a larger number of subordinates.
2. ***Nature of Work*****:** If employees engage in similar and repetitive tasks, managers can oversee a larger number of subordinates, allowing for a wide span of control. Conversely, non-repetitive and challenging work requires narrower span of control.

Changes in work, driven by dynamic environment, support a narrow span, as superiors frequently need to direct subordinates. Stability in work favours a wide span of management, as superiors' guidance is not frequently required for routine work processes.

3. ***Assistance to Managers***: Availability of technical or secretarial support proves valuable in gathering and processing information for decision-making. This allows managers to save time in communication, oversee a larger number of subordinates, and dedicate attention to strategic organisational matters.
4. ***Competence of Subordinates***: Competent subordinates can manage their roles independently, require less frequent directions from superiors, enabling managers to effectively manage a larger group of subordinates.
5. ***Plans and Policies***: Well-defined plans that articulate organisational and individual goals, accompanied by clear policies, allow superiors to oversee a larger group of subordinates, resulting in a wide span of control. In cases where standing plans are well-established, subordinates understand broad guidelines for decision-making in similar and repetitive situations. This reduces the need for subordinates to consult superiors for similar problem-solving scenarios, enabling superiors to manage a larger group efficiently. However, if decisions primarily rely on single use plans like programmes, budgets, or projects, managers may need to be frequently consulted, resulting in a narrower span.
6. ***Organisational Level:*** Top executives, handling crucial and specialised activities, typically have a narrow span. At lower levels, the span can be wider since supervisors primarily deal with routine tasks.
7. ***Authority-responsibility Structure***: A well-defined structure where responsibilities are clear, individuals work within their assigned roles and seek directions, when necessary, allows superiors to supervise a larger number of subordinates. Conversely, lack of clarity in the authority-responsibility structure, roles, accountabilities, and reporting relationships hinder managers from supervising a large group of subordinates, resulting in a narrower span.
8. ***System of Control***: Effective control techniques support decentralisation, allowing decisions to be made at the relevant levels. Extensive delegation, along with clarity in job responsibilities and authority-responsibility relationships promotes freedom in decision-making. Consequently, the span of control can be wide.

9. ***Financial Factors*:** A narrow span, requiring more managers, tends to be a costly structure. Conversely, a wide span may lead to organisational inefficiencies. Striking a proper balance between the costs and benefits becomes crucial.

The span of management may be narrow or wide depending on different situations. Even within the same organisation, the span can differ across functional areas and levels. It is common for the span to be narrow in the finance department and wide in the marketing department at the same level. The span may vary across different organisations, even for the same functional areas and levels. The situational nature of the span of management emphasises its flexibility and adaptability to specific organisational contexts.

Graicunas Theory

French management consultant, *V.A. Graicunas*, introduced a theory on span of management which explains three kinds of relationships that a superior can have with subordinates. He suggested the number of subordinates under one superior based on mathematical formulae as follows:

Kind of Relationship	Formula	No. of Subordinates	No. of Relationships
1. Direct relationship (one-to-one relationship)	n	2 3	2 3
2. Cross relationship	$n(n-1)$	2 3	2 6
3. Group relationship	$n\left(\frac{2^n}{2}-1\right)$	2 3	2 9
Total number of relationships	$n\left(\frac{2^n}{2}+n-1\right)$	2 3	6 18

Graicunas identifies three types of relationships:

1. Direct single relationships
2. Direct group relationships
3. Cross relationships

1. ***Direct Single Relationship***: This represents direct relationship of the superior with his subordinates individually. If there are 3 subordinates (A, B and C) under one superior (X), there will be three direct single relationships, represented by the formula n. These are relationships between X and A, X and B, and X and C.

2. ***Direct Group Relationships***: This is the relationship of superior with subordinates jointly. All possible combinations of superior-subordinate relationships exist in group relationships. It represents interaction of the superior with one or more subordinates while others (one or more) assist the relationships.

   For one superior (X) and three subordinates (A, B, C), there will be 9 direct group relationships:

   X and A with B assisting

   X and A with C assisting

   X and B with C assisting

   X and A with BC assisting

   X and B with AC assisting

   X and C with AB assisting

   X and AB with C assisting

   X and AC with B assisting

   X and BC with A assisting

   The number of relationship (9) is represented by the formula $n\left[\frac{2^n}{2}-1\right]$.

3. ***Cross Relationships***: While the subordinates work under the same superior, they also interact amongst themselves. These are the relationships amongst subordinates mutually. Based on the formula n (n –1), with 3 subordinates, 6 such relationships will be formed. These are between:

   A and B

   B and A

   A and C

C and A

B and C

C and B

With every increase in the number of subordinates by one, increase in the number of relationships is by more than one. While, with 2 subordinates, the total number of relationships is 6, with 3 subordinates, it is 18.

The theory emphasises on the number of relationships rather than importance of relationships. Based on Gaicunas' theory, some management thinkers also suggested numerical limits on the span of management, ranging from 3 to 9 for top managerial positions and 8 to 30 for supervisory management. Managerial effectiveness is judged by the situational factors more than the number of subordinates.

13.7 PRINCIPLES OF ORGANISING

Principles serve as guiding rules for managerial thinking and action. The following principles are observed in organising:

1. **Unity of Objectives:** All organisational activities align with its objectives set for each level and functional area, developing clear understanding. Mutual support among objectives at different levels is crucial for overall goal attainment.
2. **Organisational Efficiency:** Organisational goals should be achieved efficiently, emphasising optimum use of resources. Maximum output with minimum inputs is the goal, ensuring resources are distributed effectively across various functional areas.
3. **Division of Labour:** Breaking down the main task into smaller units enables individuals to focus on their responsibilities, thereby enhancing overall output. The work division should align with individual skills, promoting specialisation and organisational productivity.
4. **Authority-Responsibility Relationships:** Authority and responsibility are inter-linked. Responsibility implies obligation to fulfil assigned tasks, requiring corresponding authority to be delegated. Tasks assigned (responsibility) must align with the given authority. Authority without responsibility leads to misuse, while responsibility without authority results in suboptimal performance.

5. **Delegation:** Work is divided, and specific tasks are assigned to subordinates with the accompanying authority to efficiently execute those tasks. Top managers delegate some of their duties to lower levels, allowing them to focus on critical organisational matters. This accelerates organisational processes and promotes growth in the dynamic, competitive business environment.
6. **Scalar Chain:** Scalar chain represents the hierarchical line of authority where authority flows downward, and responsibilities flow upward. The chain promotes communication across different levels and facilitates decision-making. Each person in the chain is aware of their superior and subordinate roles.
7. **Span of Control:** Span of control refers to the number of subordinates a supervisor can effectively manage. The specific number varies based on factors like managerial competence, nature of work, control systems, and subordinate capabilities. While the exact number a manager can oversee is not fixed, supervising fewer subordinates results in taller structures, and larger number leads to flatter structures.
8. **Unity of Command:** Each subordinate should have a single supervisor. Clear lines of authority ensure that individuals receive instructions exclusively from their immediate supervisor. This instils discipline and order, preventing confusion and indiscipline that may arise when receiving orders from multiple superiors.
9. **Balance:** Achieving balance is crucial among different organising principles. This includes maintaining equilibrium between centralisation and decentralisation, a narrow and wide span of control for a well-functioning organisation structure.
10. **Flexibility:** An organisation should be adaptable, making structural changes in response to shifts in environmental factors. Flexibility ensures that the organisation remains responsive and resilient in the face of changing conditions.
11. **Management by Exception:** Every issue need not be reported to top managers. Only significant deviations from the norm should be reported up the hierarchy. Routine matters can be effectively addressed by middle and lower-level managers, promoting the development of lower-level managers.
12. **Simplicity:** Organisation structure should be easily understandable by everyone. Clarity regarding roles, authorities, and responsibilities associated with each job enhances efficiency. A simple structure promotes cooperation, coordination, and effective communication.

13. **Departmentation:** Departmentation involves organising activities into specialised groups or departments, each tasked with specific functions. Similar activities are grouped in a department led by the departmental manager.

14. **Decentralisation:** Decentralisation empowers lower-level managers and enhances organisational efficiency by distributing decision-making responsibilities across various levels of management.

15. **Unity of Direction:** Similar activities, like production or marketing, are grouped under one unit, led by the departmental manager. He guides departmental members to work collectively toward a shared objective—the departmental goal.

16. **Cooperation:** Cooperation promotes teamwork and shared focus on a common objective. Every individual and department collaborate to help the organisation reach its goals.

Questions

I. Long Answer Questions

1. Define the term 'Organisation'. Explain the steps involved in organising.
2. What is the importance of organising? Describe the steps involved in the process of organising.
3. Define organisation chart. How are they supportive of the organisation structure?
4. What do you mean by span of management? Explain the factors which affect an effective span of management.
5. How do tall and flat structures emerge out of span of management? State their merits and limitations.
6. Define 'organisation'. State the principles of organising.

II. Write short notes on:

(i) Span of control

(ii) Organisation chart

(iii) Flat organisation structure

III. Multiple Choice Questions

1. The number of subordinates that a manager can efficiently manage is
   (*i*) Span of control
   (*ii*) Unity of command
   (*iii*) Unity of direction
2. Wide span of management represents
   (*i*) Tall structure
   (*ii*) Flat structure

Answers

1. (*i*), 2. (*ii*)

❑❑❑

14
Chapter

Formal and Informal Organisations

14.1 FORMAL ORGANISATION

Formal organisation is a deliberately planned system consisting of clearly defined roles, each carrying a specific level of authority, responsibility, and accountability. The structure includes formal rules, regulations, and communication channels to facilitate effective collaboration toward achieving organisational objectives, conflict resolution and overall control of activities.

Features of Formal Organisation

1. ***Deliberately Created Structure***: Formal organisation is intentionally designed to establish clear relationships among individuals in different positions.
2. ***Job-oriented***: It prioritises jobs over individuals, assigning tasks and defining relationships to achieve organisational objectives.
3. ***Division of Work***: Work is distributed based on skills and abilities of individuals. It enhances specialisation and overall output.
4. ***Departmentation***: The foundation of organisation structure lies in departmentation. This involves breaking down work into smaller units and regrouping them into larger units (departments) based on similarity of activities. Departmentation establishes responsibilities of departmental heads.
5. ***Formal Authority***: Authority is closely tied to the position and the person occupying that position, representing the right to give commands, make decisions, perform tasks, and allocate resources.
6. ***Delegation***: The division of work into units and its assignment down the hierarchical chain is known as delegation. This involves assigning tasks and authority to subordinates who assume responsibility for those jobs.

7. ***Coordination***: Managers harmonise the activities of individuals, units, and departments, all working collaboratively toward formal organisational goals. Coordination is the process of linking activities of various departments to ensure a cohesive approach.

Merits of Formal Organisation

1. Organisation structure outlines goals and establishes authority-responsibility relationships to achieve those goals.
2. It ensures optimum use of resources.
3. Division of work facilitates an efficient communication system.
4. Organisational hierarchy prevents task overlap, ensuring each individual or department has distinct responsibilities.
5. Career paths and promotion opportunities are clearly defined within the formal structure.
6. Low rates of absenteeism and turnover are maintained due to clear objectives, policies, and strategies.
7. The structure aligns organisational goals with those of individuals, fostering synthesis of individual, group, and organisational objectives.

Limitations of Formal Organisation

1. Excessive focus on rules can stifle creativity and innovative thinking.
2. Social needs may go unmet in a formal chain of command, as interactions are limited to official matters.

14.2 THEORIES OF FORMAL ORGANISATION

Organisation theory is the study of organisations and its people. It explains the nature of people and the basis of their decision-making.

There is no unified set of organisation theory that explains organisation principles and practices. Different theories have evolved with different assumptions and features.

Organisation theories are as follows :

I. Classical Theory

II. Human and Participative Theories

III. Contingency Theory

I. Classical Theory

Meaning: It considers organisations as closed systems with very little or no interaction with the environment. It emphasises on task more than people.

It has the following characteristics :

1. Organisation structure focuses on ***division of work.*** Work is broken into smaller units so that it becomes simple and specialised to perform. Division of labour is done for all the tasks at all the levels of the organisation.
2. It advocates ***functional departmentation.*** Major functional departments are production, personnel, finance and marketing. Every activity is allotted to specific department. Functional process also promotes line and staff relationships. The major functional departments are line departments and sue assists line managers in carrying out the line activities.
3. It strongly supports ***hierarchy of relationships or scalar chain.*** *One* subordinate should have one boss. People take orders from their seniors in command and issue directions to their subordinates. Final decision-making authority vests at the top. This promotes co-ordination amongst levels in different functional areas. It also reduces conflicts as every individual reports to a single superior. Obligation is defined and results can be measured.
4. There is ***narrow span of control*** as the relationships are hierarchical. People are directed to work. They do not assume responsibilities on their own. Formal plans, motivational factors and communication channels are designed to get the work done.

Main contribution to classical theory has come from Taylor, Fayol, Weber, Oliver Sheldon, Chester Barnard etc. Based on the nature of authority, three types of organisations are : Line organisation, Line and Staff organisation and Functional organisation. *(See Chapter 15).*

Limitations of Classical Theory

Though classical theory promotes discipline, it is not a complete theory of managing organisations as focus is more on tasks than people. The theory is found inadequate on the following grounds :

1. It assumes organisations to be closed systems with little or no interaction with the environment. Organisations are open systems that actively interact with the environment. There is constant 'give and take' between organisations and

the environment. Organisation structures change with change in environment to meet their stated goals.

2. Classical theory assumes all organisations to be designed on similar principles like division of work, specialisation, scalar chain etc., while it is not actually so. Business is based more on networking and knowledge management which cuts across vertical and horizontal boundaries. Depending upon how much an organisation interacts with its counterparts abroad, the structures keep changing everytime a new relationship is formed either in terms of adding or deleting an alliance.
3. Classical organisations are based on universality of principles of management. This does not apply to modern organisations. Unity of command, for example, does not hold true in the world of specialisation. People are highly specialised and subordinates receive orders from various specialists like human resources manager, finance manager etc. This gives rise to functional structures which follow principles contrary to those followed in the classical theory.

This theory represents a static form of organisation that does not interact with the environment. In practice, no organisation can ignore the influence of environment.

It also ignores the behavioural aspect of organisations. It considers people as resources rather than human beings. Informal groups, social interactions and group thinking are ignored. It is, thus, not an acceptable theory of organisation.

However, this theory has provided a ground work for contemporary organisations to change the principles according to needs of the environment. The theory perhaps developed in times when organisations had little interaction with the environment, employees' social needs were not strong and, therefore, the focus was more on formal relationships.

II. Human and Participative Theories

Meaning: The classical theory of organisation was opposed in 1950's when behavioural theories emerged on the management scenario. The classical theory was criticised for being highly mechanistic, formal and impersonal. *McGregor* introduced Theory *Y,* which focused on human relationships to achieve organisational goals.

Hawthorne experiments conducted by *Elton Mayo* supported social and informal interactions amongst work groups.

The human theories focused on *people* to achieve the *tasks.* There was shift from *task-oriented approach* to *people-oriented approach.* They are comparatively less mechanistic, impersonal and formal than the classical theory.

They design organisation structures to suit the needs of people and synthesise individual goals with organisational goals.

Features of Human and Participative Theories: Following are the important features of these theories:

(a) People do not wish to be directed. They self-direct and control their activities.

(b) Plans are made in consultation with subordinates. Participative styles of management are adopted.

(c) People not only accept responsibility; they also seek responsibility.

(d) People use imagination, creativity and innovativeness in performing the organisational tasks.

(e) Both organisational resources and human potential are fully utilised.

(f) It improves productivity along with employee satisfaction.

(g) They harmonise individual goals with organisational goals rather than focus only on organisational goals.

(h) They view subordinates as innovative, creative and challenging and, thus, advocate a wide span of control.

(i) Human behaviour is determined by social and psychological factors and not just physiological factors.

(j) People work as a team and not individuals. They look after each others' needs and also needs of the organisation.

(k) Informal organisations (or groups) co-exist with formal structures.

The human and participative theories, thus, focus on informal interaction amongst members that satisfy their psychological needs. This gives rise to flat, decentralised structure which smoothens the process of communication, decision-making and control.

However, it is not free from limitations. Some of its limitations are as follows :

1. People have different needs and, therefore, motivated by different factors. There can be conflicting opinions on various aspects of organisational working.
2. Human beings is one of the factors in designing the organisation structure and not the only factor. There is over emphasis on informal relationships.

III. Contingency Theory

Managers may choose a theory to adapt the organisation to its surrounding environment.

The following factors affect which theory to adopt:

1. ***Nature of People*** : People who are lazy, lack responsibility, do not work on their own, want to be guided, and have strong lower-order needs, are governed by classical theory of organisations. People who enjoy their work, seek greater responsibility, exercise self-direction and control, and want to satisfy their higher-order needs prefer participative theory to organising.
2. ***Type of Task and Technology*** : Classical form of organisation is preferred when goods are produced through mass production technology while participative theory is more suitable where job-order (small scale) or continuous technology is adopted. If organisation uses different types of technology, it may adopt different structures depending upon the processes used for different parts of the company.
3. ***The Environment*** : Organisations differ in structure depending on their environment. Firms which operate in dynamic environment are more flexible and, therefore, adopt participative theory while firms that operate in stable environment generally adopt classical organisation.
4. ***Degree of Change and Uncertainty***: Change is a continuous phenomenon. Changes in environment cause changes in the organisation structures. Change in attitudes, perception and knowledge from simple to complex shifts the organisation structure from classical to participative.

   As society develops, managers become creative and trained. Skilled labour is available, specialisation increases and, therefore, a shift is observed from classical to participative organisation structure.

Factors Affecting Contingency Theory

Features	Classical Theory	Participative Theory
Nature of People	Lazy, with little or no desire to assume additional responsibility	Active with desire to assume and seek additional responsibility
Technology	Mass-production technology	Job-order and continuous technology
Environment	Stable	Dynamic
Change	Change is not observed	Changes are observed in the environment

14.3 INFORMAL ORGANISATION

Informal organisation refers to unplanned and unofficial social interactions among individuals. It operates independently of formal principles but is an inherent component of formal organisation. As formal organisations expand, the coexistence of informal relationships becomes inevitable.

E. Wight Bakke calls the creation of informal organisation a fusion process. "When an individual and an organisation come together in such a way that the individual is a participant in, and a member of, the organisation and the two are mutually dependent on each other, both are reconstructed in the process. The organisation to some degree remakes the individual and the individual to some degree remakes the organisations."

Informal organisation is "any joint personal activity without conscious joint purpose, even though contributing to joint results."

It is "a network of personal and social relations not established or required by formal organisation but arising spontaneously as people associate with one another."

Features of Informal Organisation

1. ***Unplanned Structure***: Informal structure emerges spontaneously during casual interactions where people discuss interests, attitudes, hobbies, and beliefs, fostering unplanned relationships.
2. ***Social Needs***: It addresses social and personal needs by connecting individuals who share common thoughts, feelings, and interests, reinforcing friendship, love, and support within informal organisations.
3. ***No Formal Structure***: Relationships evolve based on changing interests, and there is no hierarchy of superiors and subordinates. Communication occurs in various directions: vertical, horizontal, and diagonal.
4. ***Informal Leaders***: Informal leaders emerge through group consensus and significantly influence group activities, contributing to formal goals.
5. ***Informal Communication System***: The communication system is informal, flowing in all directions—vertical, horizontal, and diagonal—connecting people throughout the organisation. It operates faster than formal channels, though rumours may spread alongside formal messages.
6. ***No Rules and Regulations***: Without fixed rules and regulations, informal organisation adapts its guidelines based on the current needs.

7. ***No Fixed Tenure***: Formed and dissolved at the will of the people, informal organisations do not follow a specific legal dissolution procedure.

Merits of Informal Organisation

1. ***Enhances Social and Cultural Values***: Members share thoughts and cultural beliefs, strengthening organisational bonds and commitment to goals.
2. ***Alleviates Top Managers***: Social interactions foster cooperation, eliminating the need for formal motivation from managers.
3. ***Augments Managerial Capacities***: Members provide support to managers beyond the official chain of command.
4. ***Social Satisfaction and Security***: Members fulfil social needs for interaction, friendship, love, support, recognition, and acceptance. Informal organisation also offers relief from work-related stress.
5. ***Communication Efficiency***: Informal communication is faster than formal channels, allowing people to discuss problems and solutions before seeking final approval from superiors.
6. ***Healthy Relationships***: It promotes understanding among members, contributing to formal organisational goals.
7. ***Stimulates Creativity***: Individuals explore their creativity and implement new ideas throughout the organisational hierarchy.
8. ***Self-control***: Employees set targets to regulate their activities, eliminating the need for top-down control.
9. ***Quick Feedback***: Managers receive prompt feedback on decisions through informal communication channels, helping in the assessment of policy implementation.

Limitations of Informal Organisation

1. ***Conformity***: Members establish their own norms and standards. Excessive adherence to group norms can be detrimental if they conflict with the interests of the formal organisation.
2. ***Attitude of Leaders***: If leaders prioritise personal interests over group interests, informal organisation can work against formal goals.
3. ***Role Conflict***: Individuals may face role conflicts when group goals differ from formal objectives, leading members to prioritise group goals.

4. ***Rumour***: Rumour, unverified information that spreads through the grapevine, can rapidly circulate false information throughout the organisation, creating challenges due to the absence of secure evidence.

5. ***Resistance to Change***: Informal groups tend to strongly protect their goals and values, resisting deviations from established norms. This can make implementing new policies challenging.

11.4 FORMAL AND INFORMAL ORGANISATIONS

Nature	Formal Organisation	Informal Organisation
Formation	They are deliberately created structures.	They are created to achieve personal goals.
Structure	Formally structured authority-responsibility relationships.	Lacks formal structure and emerges spontaneously in response to formal structure of an organisation.
Objective (Purpose)	Achieve formal organisa tional goals.	The objective is social satisfaction.
Emphasis	Official authority-responsibility structure. It flows from top to bottom.	People and their relationships. Authority moves from leaders to followers.
Power	Attached to position.	Attached to person.
Chain of Command	Authority comes from top management.	Authority comes from knowledge and skills of group leaders.
Social Acceptance	They arise out of formal authority-responsibility structure.	They arise out of social acceptance and recognition.
Stability	Relationships remain stable, not influenced by incoming or outgoing of members.	Change in members can result in instability.
Flexibility	Lack flexibility. Interactions are typically based on positions.	Highly flexible.
Behaviour of Members	Behaviour norms and standards are framed by managers.	Behaviour norms and standards are framed by group members.
Leadership	Managers are leaders due to their official positions.	Leaders are selected by the members.
Governance	It is regulated by rules and regulations.	No fixed rules exist; group norms govern the groups.
Control	There are strict measures of control.	Group norms and values are the controlling measures.

Nature	Formal Organisation	Informal Organisation
Communication	Official communication channel; vertical in direction.	Unofficial communication channel; flows in all directions.
Interaction	Interactions are based on authority, responsibility, and accountability.	Interactions are based on power and social status.
Winding up	Winds up according to legal procedures	Winds up at the will of members.

Questions

I. Long Answer Questions

1. What is a formal organisation? State the theories of formal organisation.
2. What is informal organisation? Explain its merits and limitations.
3. What are informal organisations? How do they emerge in a formal organisation?
4. Differentiate between formal and informal organisations. Do informal organisations necessarily emerge out of formal organisations?

II. Write short notes on:

(i) Formal and informal organisation

(ii) Classical theory of organisation

III. Multiple Choice Questions

1. Informal organisations are
   (*i*) Flexible
   (*ii*) Inflexible
2. Informal relationships can be
   (*i*) Horizontal
   (*ii*) Vertical
   (*iii*) Random
   (*iv*) All of these

Answers

1. (*i*), 2. (*iv*)

IV. Case Study

(I) Mr. Arya is the senior manager of production department of Sunglass Co. Ltd. One of his subordinates, Mr. Gupta, is an intelligent, hardworking and conscientious worker. His knowledge of various subjects makes him popular amongst employees of the organisation. People come to him for solving their official and personal problems, so much so that they surpass their hierarchical superiors. Managers of other departments get offended and report the matter to the managing director.

Questions

1. What type of organisation is this? State its features.
2. Can the managing director stop the employees from approaching Mr. Gupta for getting their problems solved? If not, how best can he manage such an organisation?

(II) Group Behaviour of Unions

Modern Textile Limited is one of the leading textile mills in the South, having a work force of more than 1500 employees, engaged in the manufacture of cotton yarn of different counts. The company has a well-established distribution network in different parts of the country. It had modernized most of its plants, with a view to improving productivity and maintain quality. To maintain good human relations in the plants and the organisation as a whole, it extended all possible facilities to the employees. Compared to other mills, the employees of Modern Textiles Limited were placed in reasonably high wage brackets. The company has a general manager, followed by a line of executives incharge of different functional areas. The Industrial Relations Department was headed by the Industrial Relations Manager with supporting staff. The company earned profits every year and distributed reasonable amounts as bonuses to the employees. The employees were represented by six trade unions - A, B, C, D, E and F (unions are alphabetically presented based on membership) - out of which the top three unions were recognised by the management for the purpose of negotiations. All the unions maintained good relations with the management individually and collectively. In a particular year when the bonus issue was placed before the management, it had a series of discussions with all recognized unions and finally announced a bonus, which was agreed upon by all recognised unions. The very next day when the management prepared the representatives, while unions A and C signed the same, the leader of union B refused to do so and walked out, stating that the amount declared as bonus was not sufficient. The next day, union B issued a strike notice to the management asking for a higher bonus. The management tried its level best to avoid an unpleasant situation, but in vain. As a result, one morning, members of union B went on strike. They were joined by members of union D. During the strike, the management could probe the reason for the deviant behaviour of union B leader: it was reported that leader of union A, soon after the first meeting had stated in the presence of a group of workers "because of me the management has agreed to declare this much amount of bonus to the employees. Some representative unions, particularly union B, had miserably failed in its talks with the management for want of initiative and involvement". This observation somehow reached the leader of union B on the very day it was made, as a result of which he felt insulted. Soon after identifying this as the reason for B's strike all the management in the presence of the Industrial Relations Manager brought about a compromise between the union leaders, A and B. Immediately after this meeting, the strikers (members of union B and D) had resumed work and the settlement was signed for the same amount of bonus, as was originally agreed upon.

Questions

1. Was the leader of union A justified in making remarks that caused offence to the leader of union B?
2. Could the strike have been avoided had A not made his remarks before a group of workers?
3. If you were the manager, what would your long-term strategy be for ensuring that inter-union differences do not recur on issues affecting the welfare of workers?

❑❑❑

15 Chapter

Organisation Structure

Organisation structure is not simply about creating an organisational design. It is also about how the organisation is aligned with other aspects, functions, processes and strategies within the business. When looking at organisation structure, the context within which the business exists must be taken into consideration.

15.1 ORGANISATION STRUCTURE

Organisation is "establishing effective behavioural relationships among persons so that they may work together efficiently and gain personal satisfaction in doing selected tasks under given environmental conditions for the purpose of achieving some goal or objective."

"An organisation's structure specifies its division of work activities and shows how different functions or activities are linked; to some extent it also shows the level of specialisation of work activities. It also indicates the organisation's hierarchy and authority structure and shows its reporting relationships."

"Organisation structure is the formal pattern of interactions and coordination designed by management to link the tasks of individuals and groups in achieving organisational goals."

15.2 ELEMENTS OF ORGANISATION STRUCTURE

1. **Objectives and Plans:** The organisation structure is designed to align with its plans and goals. It guides activities towards achieving its objectives.
2. **Specialisation:** Activities are grouped based on similarities, forming departments that lay the groundwork for the organisation structure.
3. **Standardisation:** Ensuring uniformity and consistency, standardisation brings stability to the organisation structure. Management develops policies, procedures, and programmes for coordinated departmental work.

4. **Coordination:** Units must achieve common goals. Coordination ensures that individual objectives contribute to the overall organisational goals.
5. **Centralisation and Decentralisation:** Decision-making authority determines the structure. Centralised structures have top managers making decisions, while decentralised structures involve middle and lower-level managers.
6. **Environment:** The organisation structure is adaptable, changing with shifts in economic, social, technological, and political factors.
7. **Staffing:** Jobs and departments are filled with personnel, establishing authority-responsibility relationships to maintain the structure.

15.3 MECHANISTIC AND ORGANIC STRUCTURES

1. **Mechanistic or Classical Organisation Structure:** This is a formal setup with clear roles, policies, schedules, chain of command, and vertical communication. The emphasis is on organisational goals, with limited interaction with the external environment.
2. **Organic or Behavioural Organisation Structure:** These structures adapt to the environment, employing a participative decision-making style. Communication flows both vertically and horizontally, and internal control is emphasised.

Mechanistic Structure	Organic Structure
It is pyramid shaped with authority centralised at the top.	It is flat shaped with authority decentralised at lower levels.
It follows hierarchy of command.	It does not follow hierarchy of command.
There is narrow span of control.	There is a wide span of control.
There is intense division of labour into specialised tasks.	Work is divided into general tasks with little or no specialisation.
Individual goals are different from organisational goals.	There is synchronisation of individual goals with organisational goals.
Tasks are performed according to position. People at lower levels perform comparatively simpler tasks.	Tasks are assigned according to capabilities/ skills and not positions.
Communication is hierarchical; orders, instructions, and commands flow from top to bottom.	Communication is a network. It flows as suggestions, advises and information than orders.
Subordinates are loyal to superiors and the organisation. They obey orders.	There is commitment to goals and not just obedience.
Appropriate for organisations operating in stable environment.	Suitable for organisations operating in dynamic environment.

15.4 FACTORS AFFECTING ORGANISATION STRUCTURE

1. **Strategy:** Strategy determines a course of action. Organisation structure is tailored to meet the demands of the chosen strategy, making strategy a prerequisite to organisational structure.

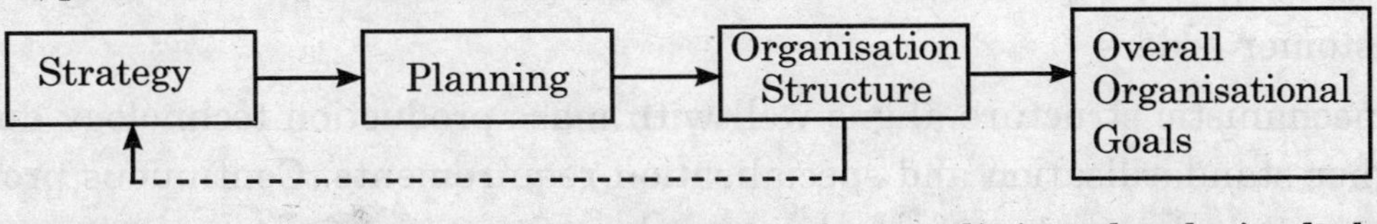

- ***Create a strategy***: Develop a strategic plan outlining the desired objectives and actions.
- ***Administrative problems in executing the strategy with the existing structure:*** Challenges may arise when attempting to implement the strategy using the current organisational structure.
- ***Decline in performance***: Ineffective strategy execution may lead to decline in organisational performance.
- ***Change in organisational structure***: Recognising the need for alignment, the organisation may undergo structural changes to better support the chosen strategy.
- ***Effective strategy execution to improve performance***: Adjusting the structure according to strategic requirements enables more effective execution, enhancing organisational performance.

2. **Technology:** Technology plays a significant role in shaping organisation structures, as demonstrated by *Joan Woodward's* research on 100 London-based firms. She identifies three types of technology:

i. Mass Production Technology

- Used for creating identical products on a large scale, such as automobiles.
- Products are standardised but assembled differently to meet diverse customer needs.
- Homogeneous yet heterogeneous due to variations in assembly (e.g., different car models).

ii. Continuous Production Technology

- Applied in processes where inputs are continuously transformed into outputs (e.g., pharmaceuticals or paper).
- Highly automated, requiring minimal human intervention.

iii. Unit or Small-Scale Production Technology

- Utilised for goods meeting constantly changing consumer preferences, like garments.
- Producing small quantities with individual production runs, catering to specific customer orders.

A mechanistic structure aligns well with mass production technology due to its higher standardisation and specialisation requirements. Continuous production or small-scale production technology benefits more from organic structure, accommodating the dynamic and varied nature of these processes.

3. **People:** People are a crucial asset, significantly influencing organisation design. Both superiors and subordinates, along with their behaviour patterns, thoughts, needs, and motivators, play an important role in shaping the organisation structure. It is a reciprocal relationship where the organisation fulfils individual needs, and individuals contribute towards organisational requirements. The organisation structure should be supportive and fulfil the needs of people, fostering positive behaviour patterns in the workplace.
4. **Tasks:** Tasks are the actions that bring plans to life. Organisation structure should be designed to enable individuals to engage in jobs with significant task features. These include skill variety, task identity, task significance, autonomy, and feedback. Creating a work environment with high task characteristics enhances job satisfaction and reduces turnover and absenteeism.

   Organisations where individuals are involved in activities with high task characteristics have organic structures and organisations with tasks of lower complexity are designed as mechanistic structures.
5. **Decisions:** The authority for decision-making and flow of information significantly shape organisation structure. Centralised decision-making aligns with mechanistic structures, while decentralised decision-making supports organic or behavioural structures.

   The decision-making environment reflects the variables, known and unknown, influencing the decision-making process. In environments of certainty, mechanistic structures are preferred as they offer clear hierarchies. In uncertain conditions, organic structures are more suitable as it requires free-flowing communication across various levels.

6. **Informal Organisation:** Informal organisations naturally coexist alongside formal structures of organisation. Informal groups arise from social values, cultural norms, religious beliefs, and personal preferences, forming an integral part of the organisational setup.

   In environments where informal relationships hold significant influence, organic structure is well-suited. Conversely, when formal relationships dominate, mechanistic structure is preferred. Striking a balance between formal and informal elements is important for a harmonious and effective organisational environment.

7. **Size:** Relationship between size and organisation structure is as follows:

	Small	Large
Job specialisation	*Less* - People do many tasks.	*More* - Seek efficiency through specialising.
Standardisation	*Less* - Primary need just to get by.	*More* - Significant need to keep things simple.
Decentralisation	*Less* - The boss can see all and decide all.	*More* - Many varied, complex decisions regularly required.

Source: *Adapted from John A. Pearce II and Richard B. Robinson, Jr., Management, McGraw Hill Book Company 1989, P. 365*

   With the increase in size of the organisation, it moves from organic to formal or mechanistic structure.

8. **Environment:** The organisation structure is significantly influenced by the nature of its environment. The level of interaction determines how open or closed an organisation is. Closed or mechanistic structure is suitable in stable environment, requiring a rigid and controlled approach to operations. Organic structure is more appropriate in dynamic and changing environment. This entails a flexible and adaptable approach to meet the uncertainties of the dynamic environment.

9. **Managerial Perceptions:** Choice of structure aligns with the perceived qualities and characteristics of the workforce. Managers opt for organic structure when they see subordinates as active, dynamic, and talented individuals. Mechanistic structure is preferred when managers perceive subordinates as less enterprising.

Factors	Mechanistic Structure	Organic Structure
Strategy	Organisations are stable.	Organisations are dynamic.
Technology	Mass-production technology.	Continuous or unit production technology.
People	Unskilled and inexperienced.	Skilled and experienced.
Tasks	Low task characteristics.	High task characteristics.
Decisions	Centralised decision-making.	Decentralised decision-making.
Informal Groups	Informal relationships are ignored.	Informal relationships are recognised.
Size	Large	Small
Environment	Stable	Dynamic
Managerial Perception	Managers have low opinion about subordinates.	Managers have high opinion about subordinates.

15.5 ORGANISATION FORMATS/THEORIES

I. **Classical Organisational Formats:** They view organisation "as a process of construction in which a great number of small work units are built into jobs, departments, divisions and finally a whole institution." — *Keith Davis*

Organisations arrange their activities into units and establish departments. These structures help streamline tasks and responsibilities within the overall framework of the organisation.

II. **Modern or Contemporary Organisational Formats:** Classical formats facilitate division of work, specialisation, and departmentalisation. However, they tend to overlook horizontal relationships (social values) among individuals, essential to consider when structuring an organisation.

While classical formats provide the foundation for organisation structure, modern formats prioritise flexibility and environmental adaptability. They address the need for a more dynamic and socially responsive organisational framework.

I. Classical Theory of Organisation

Line Organisation

Line and Staff Organisation

Functional Organisation

II. Modern Theory of Organisation

Project Organisation

Matrix Organisation

Committee Organisation

Networking Organisation

(This chapter discusses only the classical theory of organisation).

15.6 CLASSICAL ORGANISATION FORMATS

I. Line Organisation

In a line organisation, decisions are made by superiors and conveyed to subordinates, establishing a top-to-bottom flow of information known as line authority or direct operative authority that grants the right to have control over subordinates. Managers with line authority are termed line managers, and they adhere to the scalar chain, ensuring a unidirectional flow of authority, orders, commands, and instructions from top to bottom, with responsibility flowing from bottom to top.

"The clearer the line of authority, from the ultimate management position in an enterprise to every subordinate position, the clearer will be the responsibility for decision-making and more effective will be the organisation communication."

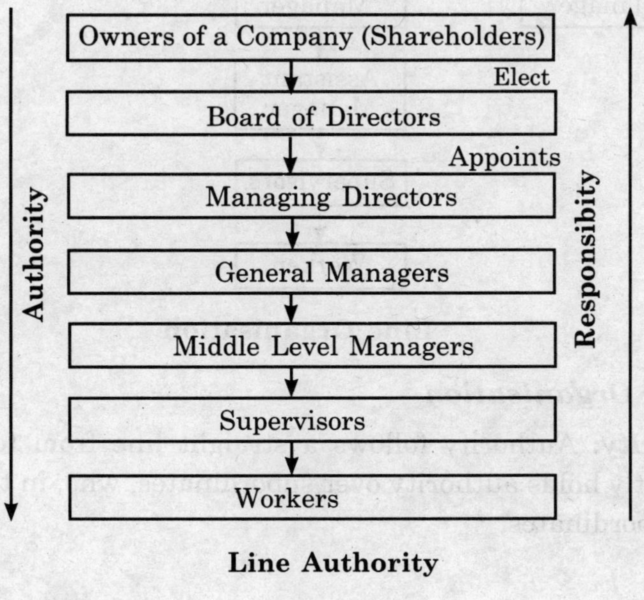

Line Authority

The role of line management depends on the nature of organisations. In a manufacturing company, line departments include production, finance, and sales, while staff departments cover purchase, personnel, research and development (R&D), and legal functions. In contrast, in a legal consultancy firm or a Research and Development Organisation, legal functions and R&D departments constitute the line departments.

While the production department serves as line department in manufacturing organisations, the purchase and accounts departments form line departments for the production department. This arrangement reflects the diverse structures tailored to specific needs of different types of organisations.

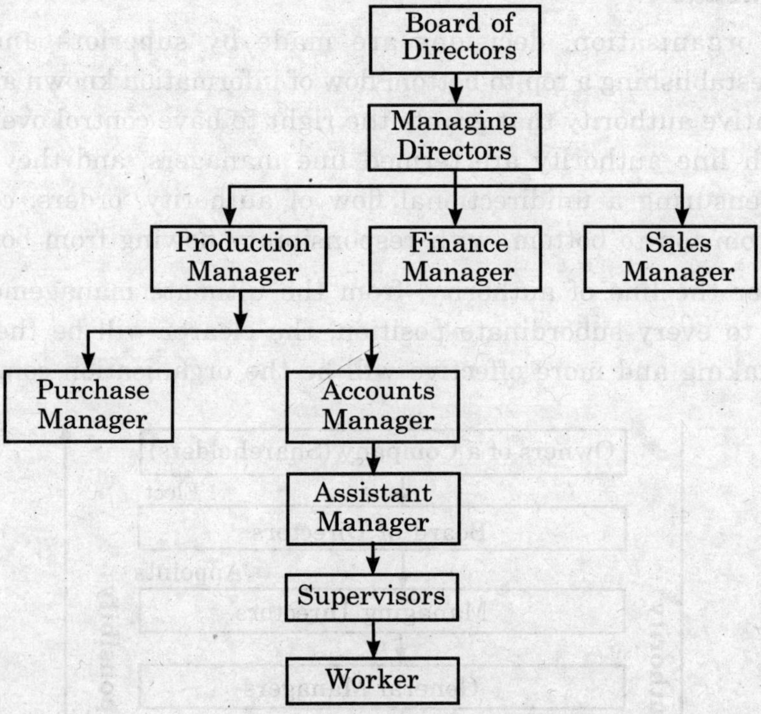

Line Organisation

Features of Line Organisation

1. **Line Authority:** Authority follows a straight line from top to bottom. Each superior directly holds authority over subordinates, who, in turn, have authority over their subordinates.

2. **Scalar Chain:** Superiors pass on responsibility and authority to subordinates, creating a hierarchical scalar chain where delegation extends down the organisation structure.
3. **Communication:** Directives and commands move from top down, while responsibilities, suggestions, and concerns flow from bottom up. The formal chain of command connects superiors and subordinates, facilitating structured communication within the organisation.
4. **Responsibility and Accountability:** Everyone within the hierarchy has clearly defined and singular responsibility and accountability. Tasks are unitary, that is, one task is assigned to one person, and multiple individuals cannot be held accountable for the same task. This structured approach confines the scope of action for each position and its holder.
5. **Independent Relationships:** Individuals in functional areas at the same level operate independently. They report to superiors within the hierarchy, and all department heads are accountable for their respective departmental outcomes. As the organisation expands, operations become more intricate, and staff specialists assist line managers in their responsibilities.

Merits of Line organisation

1. **Simple:** This structure is straightforward. Each person understands their responsibilities and the superior to whom they are answerable.
2. **Goal-oriented:** The focus is on tasks. Jobs and relationships revolve around objectives with minimum emphasis on social interactions. Orders, instructions, work groups, responsibilities, and accountability—all are geared towards goals.
3. **Economical:** Especially suitable for small organisations, this structure is cost-effective as individuals concentrate on contributing effectively to objectives.
4. **Order:** Clearly defined authority and responsibility bring order to tasks. Unity of command and direction promotes discipline, with every superior having control over subordinates.
5. **Control:** Direct contact between superior and subordinates ensures control by a single superior.
6. **Speed:** One-to-one relationships exist between superiors and subordinates, and most decisions are made by superiors. Staff and expert advice are typically not necessary, making decision-making less time-consuming.

7. **Clarity:** There is a clear division of authority, responsibility, and accountability, promoting discipline within the organisation.
8. **Develops Managers:** Decisions are made independently, without staff assistance, fostering the ability to make practical and optimum decisions. This cultivates managerial development.
9. **Effective Communication:** Communication flows upwards and downwards. Links are not bypassed in the scalar chain, reducing filtration, preventing rumours, and maintaining the authenticity of information.

Limitations of Line Organisation

1. **Inflexible:** This structure prioritises hierarchical relationships without considering the external environment, making it inflexible.
2. **Ignores Social Values:** While line organisation emphasises hierarchical relationships, social values play an important role as a complement to formal relationships.
3. **Lack of Expert Advice:** Specialised expertise is not readily available. Top managers make all decisions, strategic or operational.
4. **Overburden:** Top executives bear a heavy workload, impacting their efficiency. The line structure is more suitable for small organisations.
5. **Lack of Commitment:** Subordinates adhere strictly to instructions, and the environment of cordiality and mutuality is often missing.
6. **Coordination:** Absence of horizontal relationships, open communication, and participative decision-making makes coordination challenging in line organisation.

This structure is suitable for small organisations with simple tasks, fewer levels, and a limited number of subordinates. Communication flows vertically, control is centralised at the top, and operations are manageable. However, as organisation expands and operations become more intricate, staff specialists assist line managers in their roles.

II. Line and Staff Organisation

The line manager is accountable for achieving organisational goals. In smaller groups, one person may achieve this, but in larger organisations, it is not feasible for one individual to handle this responsibility alone. An organisation that incorporates both line and staff positions is known as line and staff organisation. Line authority involves direct control, while staff authority provides support to line positions. Line authority directly relates to the work at hand, staff authority is indirectly linked to it. Line position aligns with the organisational hierarchy, while staff positions offer specialised knowledge to address specific issues. The person in staff position is called 'staff executive.'

Line managers exercise direct authority, and staff authority serves as auxiliary, advisory, or supportive. However, staff specialists have direct authority over people in their departments. While staff can recommend actions to line managers, they cannot enforce these recommendations. Staff services may be provided to a specific position, department, or the entire organisation.

	Line Position/Authority	Staff Position/Authority
Purpose	Responsible for major goals of the organisation.	Assist line managers in accomplishing the goals.
Authority	Direct authority over subordinates.	No direct authority over line departments.
Direction of Authority	Flows from top to bottom, vertical in direction.	Flows amongst managers of functional areas; horizontal in direction.
Nature of Function	Primary	Supportive
Source of Power	Derived from organisational hierarchy— can use positive and negative motivation.	No formal authority. Power derived by virtue of professional knowledge and skill.

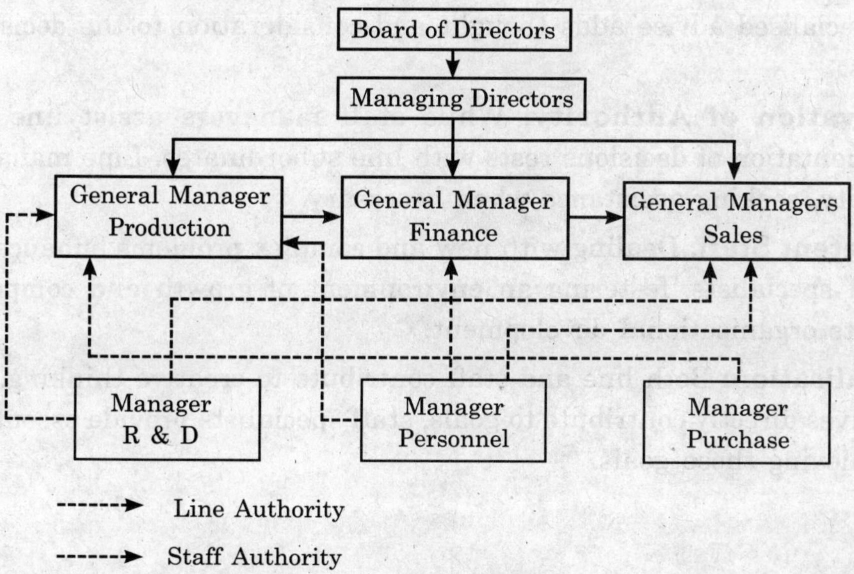

Line and Staff Organisation

Features of Line and Staff Organisation

1. The line is responsible for attaining primary goals, staff offers specialised advice to support the achievement of these goals.
2. Specialised staff members provide recommendations to line managers based on their expertise.
3. Line managers have the discretion to accept or reject staff advice. The nature of staff advice is suggestive and not obligatory.
4. Line and staff positions lack formal authority-responsibility connections. Line managers seek advice from staff, which they may or may not adhere to. Staff members do not have the authority to insist on implementation of their advice.

Merits of Line and Staff Organisation

1. **Reduces Workload:** Line executives benefit from staff support, enabling them to focus on strategic issues.
2. **Overall View of the Problem:** Staff specialists assist line managers, offering the best solutions to problems. Line executives develop analytical skills by observing staff specialists taking a holistic view of the organisation.
3. **Quick and Better Decisions:** Staff specialists contribute to quick and informed decisions since line managers cannot handle all decisions alone. Their skilled and specialised advice adds thought and consideration to the decision-making process.
4. **Reservation of Authority:** While staff managers assist line managers, implementation of decisions rests with line subordinates. Line managers retain authority, seeking assistance when necessary.
5. **Competent Staff:** Dealing with new and complex problems enhances the skills of staff specialists, fostering an environment of growth and competence that supports organisational development.
6. **Specialisation:** Both line and staff contribute to creative thinking. While line executives directly contribute to goals, staff specialists provide essential support for achieving those goals.

Limitations of Line and Staff Organisation

1. **Complexity:** Line and staff relationships are intricate, lacking clarity in authority description. The undefined areas lead to confusion within the organisation.
2. **Line and Staff Conflict:** Despite staff serving as an advisory body to line managers, conflicts emerge due to differing approaches to problems. Personal conflicts may escalate into organisational conflicts.
3. **Coordination:** Ambiguous roles create coordination challenges between line and staff activities.
4. **Frustration:** Staff specialists operate as a recommendatory body, and their advice may or may not be accepted by line executives. This can be frustrating for staff specialists.
5. **Centralisation:** As ultimate decision-making authority resides with line managers; the organisation tends to be centralised. This hampers creativity at lower levels, limiting innovation and initiative.

This structure is expensive and best suited for large organisations with intricate activities that demand expert advice. It offers professional guidance to line managers without undermining their authority. The effectiveness of this structure relies on maintaining harmony between line and staff specialists. Collaboration and cooperation between these experts are crucial for the successful functioning of the organisation.

III. Functional Organisation

As organisations expand, the addition of new departments and specialisation of activities lead to creation of sub-departments. Top managers find it challenging to oversee all activities, resulting in the development of functional organisation. This structure allows delegation of authority to control specified activities in other departments. For instance, Human Resource manager makes human resource policies not only for the human resource department but for production, finance, and marketing departments as well.

Functional authority refers to the right to give orders in a department other than one's own, focusing on specific processes, practices, policies, or other matters related to activities in different departments. This leads to individuals receiving orders from multiple functional heads, violating the principle of unity of command.

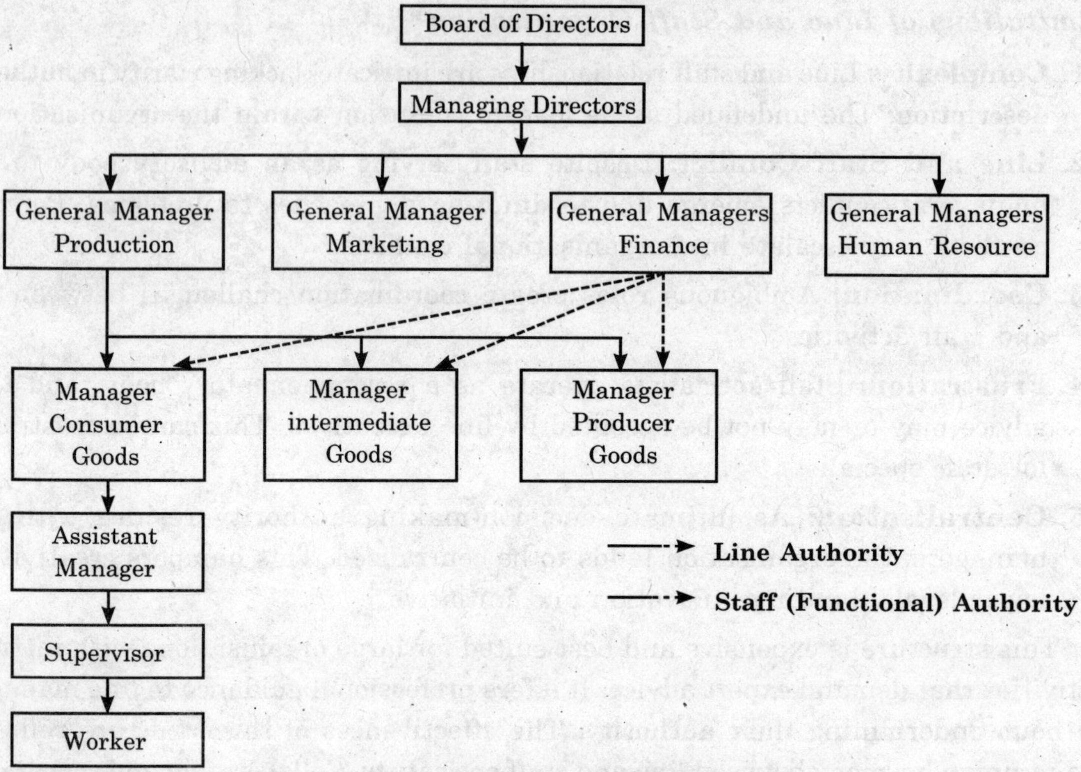

(Functional Authority in Line Organisation)

The manager of consumer, intermediate and producer goods receives orders not only from General Manager, Production (line manager) but also from General Managers of marketing, finance and personnel (functional managers) departments.

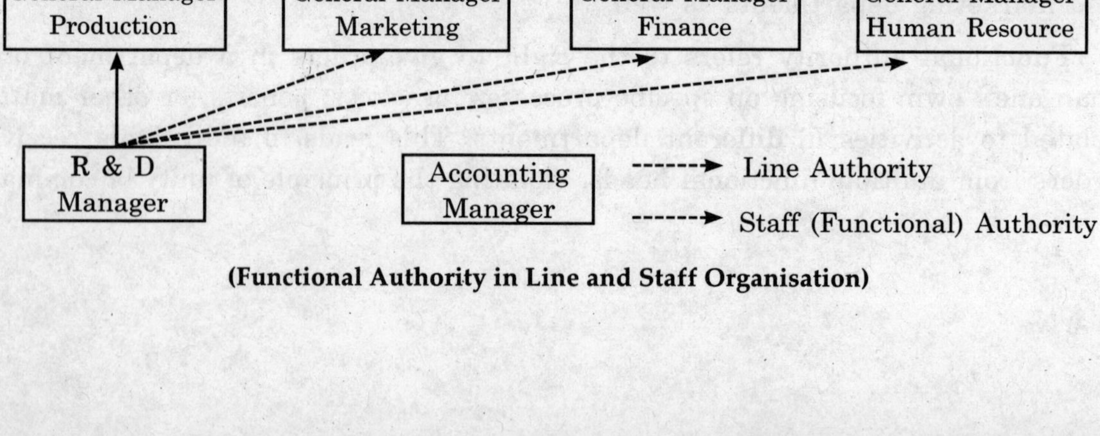

(Functional Authority in Line and Staff Organisation)

The figure shows functional authority of R&D manager (staff specialist) over different functional areas. Similar authority can be exercised by the accounting manager.

Features of Functional Organisation

1. The organisation is segmented into functional departments.
2. Specialised knowledge of functional managers is distributed and utilised across all departments.
3. Unity of command is compromised when an individual receives directives from two or more supervisors.

Merits of Functional Organisation

1. **Specialisation:** Each functional head has authority over all departments in their specific functional domain. For instance, finance manager oversees financial activities across all functional areas, focusing on their specialised area of work.
2. **Economical:** Centralising resources at the decision-making point, such as the personnel department addressing staffing needs for all departments, proves cost-effective. This prevents resource duplication compared to individual handling of functional needs by each department.
3. **Reduces Burden of Functional Heads:** Functional heads concentrate solely on activities within their department, avoiding involvement in other functional areas.
4. **Coordination:** Each set of activities falls under the control of one head, promoting coordination. Decision-making and instructions stem from a central reference point rather than solely from line managers, emphasising a holistic organisational view.
5. **Uniformity of Operations:** Functional authority ensures consistency in work processes. The line of command and communication processes are distinctly clear.
6. **Control:** Enhanced coordination and uniformity enable control over all functional areas. Functional heads exercise control within their areas of expertise.

Limitations of Functional Organisation

i. **Violation of Unity of Command:** Unity of command is compromised when subordinates are accountable to more than one boss. Following instructions from multiple heads becomes challenging for subordinates.

ii. **Coordination:** Coordination becomes problematic when functional heads concentrate on departmental goals, potentially leading to goal displacement. Efficiently managing financial needs and reallocating funds to all departments may be unfeasible in a large organisation.

iii. **Complex Relationships:** A significant gap exists between decision-makers and implementers, violating unity of command and causing slow communication. Functional heads may find it challenging to exert sole control, complicating relationships between superiors and subordinates.

iv. **Centralisation:** As organisations grow larger and the gap between superiors and subordinates widens, functional organisation tends to become centralised. Lower-level personnel often escalate problems to top positions.

v. **Inflexibility:** The constraints of functional organisation make it inflexible. Changes cannot be easily implemented at the levels where decisions are carried out, preventing the creativity of operational-level individuals.

The functional structure is well-suited for small organisations with few hierarchical levels. It is also suitable for organisations with a limited range of products. It is not ideal for organisations with diverse operations, introducing new products that demand different decision-making skills. In extreme cases, this situation may lead to conflicts between departments.

Questions

I. Long Answer Questions

1. What is line organisation? Differentiate between line organisation and line and staff organisation.
2. Distinguish between line and functional organisation.

II. Write short notes on:

(i) Functional organisation

(ii) Line organisation

(iii) Line and Staff positions

III. Multiple Choice Questions

1. Organisations where line managers seek expert assistance are
   (*i*) Line Organisations
   (*ii*) Line and staff organisations
   (*iii*) Functional organisations
2. Organic structures are suitable in
   (*i*) Stable environment
   (*ii*) Dynamic environment
3. Mechanistic structures focus on
   (*i*) Formal relationships
   (*ii*) Informal relationships
4. Unity of command is violated in
   (*i*) Line organisation
   (*ii*) Line and staff organisation
   (*iii*) Functional organisation
5. Staff specialists provide
   (*i*) Advisory function
   (*ii*) Directive function
6. Line structure is suitable for
   (*i*) Small Organisations
   (*ii*) Large organisations

Answers

1. (ii) 2. (ii) 3. (i) 4. (iii) 5. (i) 6. (i)

IV. Case Study

Radiant Industries Ltd.

Radiant Industries Ltd. wants to operate in the national and international markets. It appoints Mr. Gupta and Mr. Anand to guide on how best it can design its organisation structure. It puts forth the following propositions to Mr. Gupta and Mr. Anand:

(a) Competition is getting intense both in national and international markets and we want to maintain our competitiveness in the concerned markets.

(b) We want to increase efficiency at tactical and operating levels.

(c) We want to diversify into as many geographical locations as possible.

(d) We want to maintain quality control on our products.

(e) We want our workers to specialise in their respective areas of operations.

Questions

1. What kind of organisation structure do you think Mr. Gupta and Mr. Anand will design for the company. State its relative merits and limitations.
2. Do you suggest any change in the organisation structure if the company wants to operate only at the national level where competition is not intense?

❑❑❑

16 Chapter

Line and Staff Relationships

16.1 INTRODUCTION

In a basic organisation, authority flows from top to bottom. As an organisation grows, it needs better performance and efficiency at each level, which is hard to achieve with just a vertical command structure. To improve this, special staff are added to support the line command, creating a line and staff structure.

16.2 LINE AND STAFF AUTHORITY

Line authority is held by superiors over their direct subordinates, creating a chain of command from top to bottom. Those with line authority are called line managers. In a small and simple organisation, line managers perform their duties without needing help. However, as organisations grow larger and more complex, line managers need assistance from staff to make organisational decisions. Staff provides various services to line managers, helping them with planning, controlling, policy making, and advising on legal, financial, and administrative matters. Departments like production, marketing, finance, and personnel are considered line departments, while accounting, R&D, and public relations are considered staff departments. Line and staff managers form a specific relationship called the line and staff relationship that greatly affects the organisation's efficiency. Line and staff roles support each other and guide the way an organisation functions.

16.3 FEATURES OF LINE AND STAFF

The Nature of Line

1. ***Direct Authority***: Line managers exercise direct and close control over the organisation's principal activities, like production, sales, and operations. They make critical decisions which impact the core functions directly.

2. ***Primary Objectives***: They are primarily about getting the critical things done in the organisation. It involves meeting production targets, making more sales, and taking care of customer satisfaction.
3. ***Decision-making***: Line managers make most of the critical operational decisions that apply to the business.
4. ***Operational Focus***: It ensures the organisation attains short-term results and operational effectiveness to achieve its immediate objectives.

Staff Dynamics

1. ***Advisory Role***: They have specialised knowledge to advise, support, and guide the line managers. They deal with specialisations like finance, human resources, IT, and legal affairs.
2. ***Support Functions***: Support functions support the primary or core operations in making well-informed decisions and handling resources effectively.
3. ***Strategic Focus***: More involvement in long-term planning and strategy development is the focus of staff managers to help the organisation meet future challenges and opportunities.
4. ***No Direct Authority***: Staff managers do not directly control operations, unlike the line managers. They exert influence through recommendations and expertise.

16.4 DISTINCTION BETWEEN LINE AND STAFF

The following table highlights the differences between line and staff:

Line Managers	Staff Specialists
Part of the organisational hierarchy.	Not part of the organisational hierarchy.
Responsible for achieving overall organisational objectives.	Help line managers achieve organisational objectives.
In charge of operating departments.	In charge of service departments.
Have direct authority over people in their departments.	Do not have direct authority over people in line departments; provide advisory services.
Provide operative and executive services.	Provide advisory services.
Enjoy legitimate power.	Enjoy referent and expert power.
Authority flows vertically downwards.	Authority flows in all directions: vertical, horizontal, and diagonal, based on where advice is needed.
Make organisational decisions.	Help implement these decisions effectively.
Accountable for final decision-making results.	Not accountable for final results.

16.5 IMPORTANCE OF STAFF

Staff specialists provide the following services to line managers:

1. They improve the quality of decisions made by line managers by filling gaps where line managers lack expertise. They complement the skills of line managers.
2. By sharing the workload of line managers, staff managers allow them to focus on strategic organisational issues.
3. Being experts in their areas, they provide creative and innovative ideas to line managers.
4. By offering advisory services, they ensure uniformity in the activities of line departments.

16.6 TYPES OF STAFF

The following types of staff can assist the line managers:

1. **Personal Staff:** Staff assigned to a department or individual is called personal staff. They help managers with routine tasks like managing mail and documents, handling technical issues, scheduling meetings, and setting appointments. Personal staff is especially helpful when a manager is overwhelmed with internal matters.
2. **General Staff:** General staff refers to a team of individuals who handle tasks such as planning, organising, document preparation, and forming committees under the direction of the chief executive. These staff members are usually rotated across different areas and levels within the organisation to help them understand its structure. They assist line managers of different departments with activities common to all departments, like creating reports, scheduling, and managing budgets.
3. **Specialised Staff:** Personal staff assists line managers within their area of expertise and skill, while specialised staff offer services in areas where line managers lack specialised skills. The authority is delegated to specialised staff to carry out these services, and they are accountable for the tasks assigned to them.

Specialised Staff	Specialised Staff
It assists an individual or a department in carrying out a variety of activities.	It provides services in its area of expertise to the entire organisation.
The line manager continues to be responsible for such activities.	The responsibility for such activities vests with the staff.
Line managers have the knowledge to carry out such activities.	Line managers do not have the specialised skill.
The staff does not have authority to carry out such activities.	The authority for discharging such activities is delegated to the staff.

Specialised staff can be of the following types:

(i) ***Advisory Staff***: In an advisory role, staff personnel use their expertise to solve organisational problems. These staff members act like internal consultants, and their relationship with line personnel is similar to that of a professional and a client. The advisory staff plans, advises, and gives suggestions that line managers can modify. Therefore, advisory staff do not limit the authority of line managers.

The staff prepares plans after consulting with line managers on assigned matters. Plans are, therefore, more likely to be approved. For example, creating bonus plans that help line managers announce bonus is an advisory task. Though line managers need not accept these plans, staff managers build the confidence of line managers to gain their approval to the proposals.

Line managers normally would agree to it as:

- Staff possess specialised knowledge on subjects that line managers do not have.
- Staff are seen as qualified to give valuable suggestions.
- The advice is often beneficial for the organisation.

(ii) ***Service Staff***: The service staff helps line managers by providing services that support the organisation's administration. These services are carried out by line managers, which means their authority is somewhat limited by the service staff's role. For example, the service staff handles tasks like purchasing stationery and maintaining assets and property. They perform auxiliary services that help other departments work more efficiently. The service staff ensures that line managers follow through on their decisions.

Service staff provide services that are more effectively managed by a single centralised group rather than individuals spread throughout the organisation.

(iii) ***Control Staff***: Staff personnel help set up a system to evaluate the effectiveness of organisational plans. The control staff checks whether actual performance matches the planned performance. They ensure the organisation performs as expected, smoothly and efficiently. They also limit line authority by managing the control function.

For example, in the production department, a separate staff unit can handle quality control by inspecting goods. This improves quality and reduces inspection costs. Similarly, audit staff ensures that accounts follow legal rules and regulations.

(iv) ***Functional Staff***: A line manager can delegate authority to a line or staff manager in another department to help carry out their functional tasks. This is similar to functional organisation. When authority is delegated to other departments, the original line manager's authority is limited.

For example, the sales department of a company might delegate authority to the finance department (a line department) and the accounting department (a staff department) to handle financial and accounting matters related to sales. As these activities are managed by the finance and accounting departments, the authority of the sales department is restricted.

Though the activities of line and staff managers are different, the distinction between their roles often leads to overlapping responsibilities. Line managers have formal authority over subordinates and can compel them to work. While staff managers do not have this power, they often influence employees similarly. Some experts do not even distinguish between line and staff positions.

16.7 LINE AND STAFF CONFLICT

Though the staff is an advisory body that helps line managers work efficiently, and their relationship is meant to be supportive, conflicts can arise because line and staff managers often have different approaches to organisational problems.

The conflict arises on account of the following reasons:

I. Reasons given by line managers

II. Reasons given by staff managers

III. Nature of relationship between line and staff managers

I. Reasons Given by Line Managers

Line managers are responsible for ultimate results and, thus, give the following reasons for line/staff conflict:

1. ***Practical Approach to the Problem*:** Line managers often feel that staff suggestions do not fit the organisation's actual operations. If these suggestions are implemented and fail, line managers are blamed. However, if they succeed, staff managers take the credit. This creates a situation where staff managers have authority without responsibility, leading to a mismatch between authority and responsibility.
2. ***Encroachment upon Line Authority*:** Line managers often complain that staff managers overstep by not just offering suggestions but also telling them what to do. Staff managers impose their ideas and give advice on matters even when not asked. Line managers feel that discussing these issues with staff managers takes up too much time, reducing the time they can spend on running their departments.
3. ***Lack of Overall Vision*:** Staff managers are often criticised for lacking insight into the organisation's real problems. They have specialised knowledge, but it may not help line managers achieve organisational goals. Staff managers are often unaware of the practical issues in implementing their suggestions. Even if their recommendations are good, they might not be feasible or practical.
4. ***Authority and Responsibility*:** Line Managers may feel that staff managers need not involve themselves in operational problems because they are out of touch with the practical day-to-day realities.
5. ***Perceived Value*:** Line Managers probably feel that staff managers are not very concerned with the organisation's success because they neither produce a product nor deliver a service.

II. Reasons of Conflict Given by Staff Managers

Staff managers offer the following arguments that result into line-staff conflict:

1. ***Absence of Motivation***: Staff managers feel that their suggestions are often ignored by line managers, leading to a lack of motivation to offer ideas. While line managers do ask for suggestions, they have the authority to accept, reject, or change them. This power imbalance means that staff managers' suggestions are not always given proper consideration.
2. ***Resistance to Change***: Staff managers believe their ideas are innovative and require line managers to learn new concepts and processes. However, line managers are often resistant to change their thinking and operating methods, so they do not readily accept the staff managers' ideas.
3. ***Lack of Authority***: Staff managers believe they should have the authority to implement their ideas. If their expert advice is sought, it should also be accepted. Line managers often take credit if the staff's advice leads to successful outcomes. Without authority over the acceptance or implementation of their suggestions, staff managers lack motivation to offer them.
4. ***Call for Help***: Staff managers sometimes complain that line managers seek their help when a situation becomes hard to manage. Suggestions given at this stage may not be effective. Staff should be consulted regularly, especially during the planning phase of a task, not when problems arise.
5. ***Perceived Value***: Staff managers think that although their contribution is indirect, such contributions are essential to organisational health and effectiveness in the long run and, therefore, worthy of recognition. They tend to focus on long-range planning and the exercise of best practices in their respective expert areas. However, their expert advice and strategic insights are undervalued.

III. Nature of Relationship between Line and Staff Managers

Line and staff managers have different perspectives towards the same problem. This often results in line-staff conflict.

1. ***Attitude of Line and Staff***: Line managers are action-oriented and focused on results. They often take a short-sighted approach and look for easy solutions

to problems. In contrast, staff managers analyse problems thoroughly before making decisions, consider all possible solutions, and are not constrained by time or money. They often have a critical attitude towards the organisation. Different approaches to problem-solving can lead to conflicts between line and staff managers.

2. ***Ultimate Responsibility***: Staff managers provide advice, but line managers are responsible for implementing this advice and for the results. If plans fail, line managers often blame staff managers for poor planning, while staff managers blame line managers for poor implementation. This difference in roles and perspectives leads to conflicts between line and staff managers.
3. ***Communication Barriers***: Due to differences in jargon, priorities, and styles between line and staff management, messages from one manager tend to be misunderstood or misinterpreted by the other.
4. ***Resource Allocation***: This can lead to conflicts over budget and resource allocations. Line managers typically argue for resources to meet operational needs, while staff managers advocate for investments in strategic initiatives.

Line-staff Conflict Reflecting the Attitudes of Line Managers and Staff Specialists

Line Managers	Staff Specialists
They deal with the organisation as a whole and are highly protective of it.	They are specialists in their areas of experience and do not view the entire organisation, often being critical of it.
They hold ultimate responsibility for organisational decisions and generally want simple, easy solutions to problems.	They study all possible solutions and their pros and cons, often suggesting solutions that line managers find complicated to implement.
They often have a short-sighted approach to organisational problems.	Their approach to problems is far-sighted and long-term.
They are accused of asking wrong questions at the wrong time.	They are accused of giving wrong answers that do not relate to the overall organisation structure.

16.8 RESOLUTION OF LINE AND STAFF CONFLICT

The following measures can improve the line and staff relationships:

1. **Clear Understanding of the Authority-Responsibility Structure:** Clearly defining the roles and responsibilities of both line and staff managers reduces confusion and ensures everyone knows their contribution. Line managers are responsible for achieving organisational objectives, while staff managers provide advisory support to them. Staff managers should understand they can persuade line managers to accept their decisions but cannot mandate their implementation.
2. **Timely Assistance:** Line managers should ask for help from staff managers promptly, rather than waiting until problems become difficult to solve. Staff should be included in the planning stage of activities to prevent issues from arising in the first place.
3. **Emphasis on Interdependence:** Both line and staff managers should recognise their complementary roles and acknowledge their ongoing need for each other's assistance. If staff advice is not accepted by line managers, they should explain the reasons rather than its outright rejection. Similarly, staff specialists should understand the limitations that line managers may face in accepting their advice.
4. **Patient Hearing:** Line managers should dedicate time to spend with staff, actively listen to their input, and collaborate to find the best solutions to problems. Plans devised by line managers in consultation with staff specialists are more likely to be accepted by top managers compared to those where staff involvement is limited. Establishing shared goals that require coordination between both types of managers can align short-term operational goals with long-term strategic objectives.
5. **Communication:** Regular communication between line and staff managers is essential to encourage staff to offer suggestions whenever they sense a problem. Staff should understand that line managers can reject or modify their suggestions and should prioritise the organisation's interests over personal ego. Cultivating open-mindedness is crucial for consistent communication through formal channels like regular meetings, joint task forces, and integrated project

teams, fostering active listening and mutual respect. The top management should take an active interest and communicate that there is teamwork between the line and staff managers.

6. **Completed Staff Work:** This technique involves staff specialists independently tackling a problem from start to finish. They identify the problem, analyse it, consider alternative solutions, and use their scientific judgment to arrive at the best solution without consulting line managers. This approach saves time for line managers by avoiding prolonged discussions and meetings while staff specialists provide them with a draft solution to the problem. While line managers may or may not accept the solution, in most cases, they do.
7. **Committees:** Creating committees consisting of both line managers and staff specialists can enhance relationships between them. Together, they address problem situations, understand their implications, and reach mutually agreeable solutions. Training in collaboration and conflict resolution helps each role understand the value of the other. Cross-training fosters healthier respect for different perspectives and awareness of the issues involved.
8. **Conflict Resolution Arrangements:** Formal mechanisms should be in place for arbitrating disputes with respect and reaching an agreement. Managers should be encouraged to use dispute resolution mechanisms at the early stages of disputes before they become some of the major conflicts.
9. **Nature of Relationship:** Line managers and staff specialists should recognise the nature of their relationship. Staff should understand that line managers are ultimately responsible for the end results, which may make them hesitant to implement staff suggestions every time they are offered. They should be tolerant and understand the concerns of line managers.
10. **Educate Line Managers:** Line managers should be willing to embrace change and be open to learning new concepts, theories, and processes, especially if staff suggestions are beneficial for the organisation.
11. **Feedback System:** Management should set up feedback systems to encourage constructive criticism between line and staff members and use these mechanisms repeatedly to improve processes and relations over time.

In large and complex organisations operating in dynamic environments, not having strong line and staff relationships is not feasible. Line managers rely heavily on staff assistance for optimal performance. Modern organisations function on functional relationships, emphasising the importance of staff support. Every manager, with specialised knowledge, holds authority over others in their respective areas. Rather than strictly defining who is line and who is staff, everyone depends on specialised knowledge for effective operations. The relationships among various functions like production, marketing, legal, accounting, research and development, finance, and personnel are highly interdependent and complex. The line between line and staff becomes blurred as they cannot exist without one another.

Questions

I. Long Answer Questions

1. Explain the line and staff authority. What are the types of staff that assist line managers?
2. What is line and staff authority? What are the causes of line and staff conflict?
3. State the causes of conflict between line and staff managers. How can this conflict be resolved?

II. Write short notes on:

(i) Line and staff authority

(ii) Types of staff

(iii) Resolution of line and staff conflict

III. Multiple Choice Questions.

1. The staff that offers administrative services to line managers is
   (*i*) Advisory staff
   (*ii*) Service staff
   (*iii*) Functional staff
2. The staff that ensures conformity of actual performance to standard performance is
   (*i*) Control staff
   (*ii*) Functional staff
   (*iii*) Personal staff

3. Contribution to ultimate goals is the responsibility of
   (*i*) Line managers
   (*ii*) Staff specialist
   (*iii*) Both line and staff managers
4. Line-staff conflict can be resolved by
   (*i*) Making line managers always agree to staff advise
   (*ii*) Creating healthy environment at work

Answers

1. (ii) 2. (i) 3. (i) 4. (ii)

❑❑❑

17 *Chapter*

Authority Responsibility Relationships

True creation requires authority and authenticity *Bryant Mcgill*	You must accept responsibility for your actions, but not the credit for your achievements *Denis Waitley*

17.1 MEANING OF AUTHORITY

Authority is the legitimate power to fulfill responsibilities. It involves issuing directives, allocating resources, decision-making, and commanding individuals. Authority resides in the position and empowers decision-making, granting the right to direct and influence others' actions. It serves to unite members and inspire them to collaborate towards shared objectives.

Authority, is "the right in a position (and, through it, the right of the person occupying the position) to exercise discretion in making decisions affecting others."

— *Koontz* and *Weihrich*

It is "the organisation's legitimised power that is linked to each position within the organisation. It typically involves the right to command, to perform, to make decisions and to expend resources."

— *Pearce* and *Robinson*

"Authority conditions the actions and behaviour of every management member in an enterprise and is the common cord tying together the various organisation units, thus, making possible the very existence of the organisation and the effective working together of all personnel."

17.2 FEATURES OF AUTHORITY

1. Authority involves providing directions and guiding the conduct of subordinates.
2. It encompasses the right to make decisions within established resources, rules, and regulations.

3. It is tied to one's position, constituting the legitimate right to issue commands.
4. Goal-oriented, it focuses on accomplishing tasks correctly and promptly.
5. It coordinates the actions of individuals and various departments.
6. Authority can flow from top to bottom or bottom to top, depending on its source within the organisation structure.

17.3 SOURCES OF AUTHORITY

Authority can be derived from the following sources, also known as theories of authority.

1. **Formal or Classical Theory of Authority:** This type of authority is termed "top-down authority," aligning with the organisational hierarchy or scalar chain. Authority is "the willing and unconditional compliance of people, resting upon their belief that it is legitimate for superior to impose his will on them and illegitimate for them to refuse to obey." — *Max Weber*

   Authority moves from the Board of Directors to the Managing Director, General Managers, middle-level managers, lower-level managers, supervisors, and workers. Every subordinate acknowledges the instructions of their superiors. The authority is tied to one's position and is forfeited when a person leaves the organisation. The delegation process governs the flow of authority, with each level in the scalar chain exercising authority delegated by their superiors. This form of authority is also known as formal or legitimate authority.

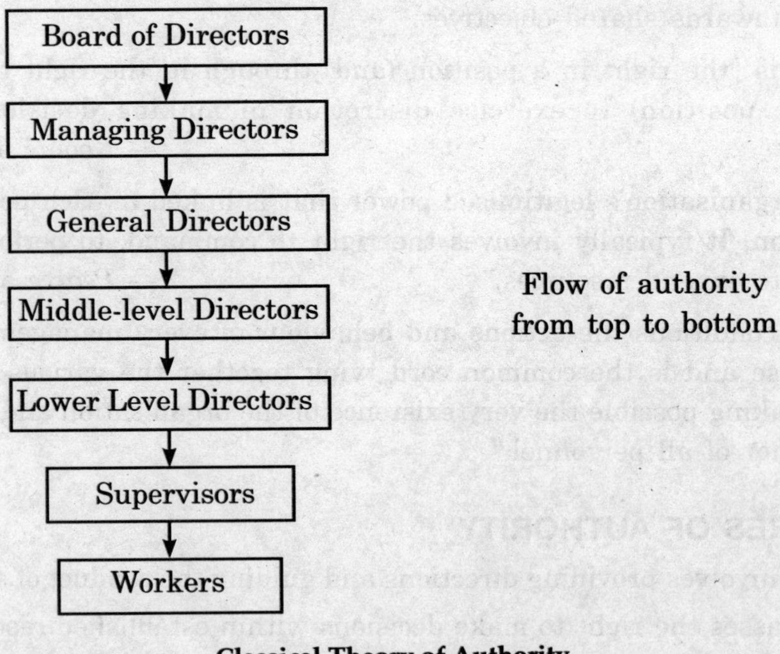

Classical Theory of Authority

2. **Acceptance Theory of Authority:** "Authority is the character of communication (order) in a formal organisation by virtue of which it is accepted by a contributor or a member of the organisation as governing ... or determining what he does or is not to do so far as the organisation is concerned." — *Chester Barnard*

This is the "bottom-up authority," where superiors exercise authority only when it is acknowledged by subordinates. *Barnard's* perspective emphasises that authority exists only when subordinates accept it. If employees reject authority, manager loses the right to direct. This theory supports informal relationships, where managers exercise authority based on the willingness of subordinates to accept it. Although employees implicitly accept authority when taking a job in exchange for rewards, this authority does not encompass all directives from the top. They agree to follow directives (authority) within a certain acceptable range.

Chester Barnard calls it "zone of indifference". *Herbert A. Simon* calls it "area of acceptance". Authority is accepted if it is in the range of acceptance. It is the area set by individuals within which they accept the authority. Outside this 'area of acceptance', superiors command authority.

"An individual will accept an exercise of authority if the advantages accruing to him from accepting plus the disadvantages accruing to him from not accepting exceed the advantages accruing to him from not accepting plus the disadvantages accruing to him from accepting; and conversely, he will not accept an exercise of authority if the latter factors exceed the former."

People establish boundaries for accepting authority, that include:

1. Actions deemed unacceptable, and consequently, individuals refuse to carry them out.
2. Actions that fall on the borderline, being both acceptable and unacceptable, creating a neutral area of decision-making.
3. Actions considered acceptable, and thus, individuals willingly execute them. These actions exist in the zone of indifference, allowing managers to issue orders pertaining to them.

According to *Chester Barnard,* a person accepts authority if following conditions are satisfied:

1. He fully understands the communication.

2. At the time of decision, he believes it is consistent with objectives of the organisation.
3. At the time of decision, he also believes it is consistent with personal objectives, and
4. He is physically and mentally adjusted to the communication and agrees to accept the communication.

Barnard maintains that command will be accepted over long-term if:

1. Managers employ recognised formal communication channels familiar to all.
2. Each member is designated a specific formal communication channel through which they receive orders.
3. The communication line between managers and subordinates is as direct as possible.
4. A complete chain of command is utilised for issuing orders.
5. Managers possess sufficient communication skills.
6. Formal communication lines are exclusively utilised for organisational matters.
7. Commands are authenticated as originating from the manager.

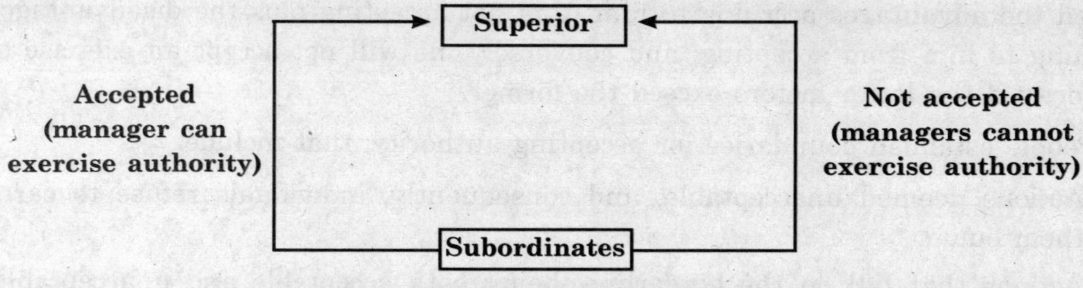

Acceptance Theory of Authority

Each individual has a unique zone of indifference, determining whether the same directives are acceptable to subordinates. The size of this zone is influenced by the benefits gained from acceptance and the losses incurred by rejecting authority. Typically, individuals at lower levels have a smaller zone of indifference, accepting most directions. This zone widens at higher levels where individuals are more involved in policymaking than implementation. Consequently, the zone of indifference expands as one progresses from lower to higher organisational levels.

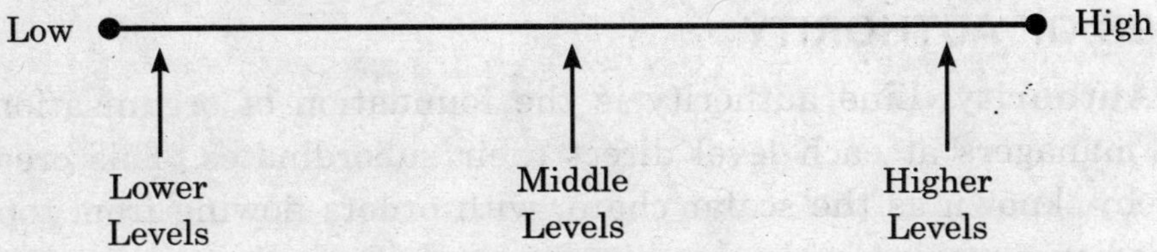

Zone of Indifference

Acceptance of authority is shaped by personal traits of leaders and their ability to persuade. However, this theory lacks popularity among management experts. It is challenging for them to conceive a scenario where a subordinate would refuse authority, considering the known consequences. Management experts generally believe there is an implicit understanding that subordinates obey their superiors.

Classical Theory of Authority	Acceptance Theory of Authority
It is normative, outlining the norms that managers adhere to when giving instructions.	It is descriptive, illustrating how managers exercise authority.
It pertains to role prescription, specifically the formal roles carried out by managers.	It concerns role behaviour, focusing on actual actions of subordinates in response to the roles prescribed for managers.
The role behaviour of employees generally aligns with the role prescription set by the superiors.	Whether role behaviour matches role prescription depends on the employees' zone of indifference.

3. **Authority of Situation:** This theory is relevant in crisis or emergency situations that require immediate action. The person present at the emergent situation takes charge, even if authority is not formally delegated through the chain of command. For instance, in the event of a fire or accident in a factory, workers can promptly use an alarm bell for emergencies or call fire/ambulance services. Therefore, even without formal authority to use the alarm bell, workers can exercise authority in the context of the situation.
4. **Competence Authority:** This authority is based on competence, skill, and knowledge rather than formal position. It acknowledges informal relationships within the organisation. Individuals from various departments and levels approach a person with competence, disregarding the official chain of command. For instance, a middle-level manager in the production department may possess expertise in tax-related matters. People facing tax issues from different departments and levels approach this manager, irrespective of their official positions.

17.4 TYPES OF AUTHORITY

1. **Line Authority:** Line authority is the foundation of organisation structure, where managers at each level direct their subordinates. This creates a clear hierarchy, known as the scalar chain, with orders flowing from top to bottom, and obedience moving in the opposite direction. Formal communication channels are established, and responsibilities are clearly defined. Line managers exercise authority based on their positions. While ultimate accountability rests with top managers, they delegate authority to middle and lower-level managers, creating a structured chain of command.

   Line authority is essential for making decisions related to functional activities within the organisation. It establishes a clear framework for superior-subordinate relationships, ensuring a well-defined structure for effective communication and decision-making.

2. **Staff Authority:** Staff authority is the right granted to specialists who support line managers and staff personnel. These specialists, not part of the official hierarchy, offer advisory services to line managers, such as legal or judiciary advice. As organisations grow larger, line managers often require assistance in dealing with complex and evolving situations. Staff specialists play a crucial role by providing support and advice to line managers on various matters. Their authority, known as staff authority, is rooted in knowledge, skill, and competence.

   Line and staff personnel work together, understanding the organisation's mission, and collaborate as a team to achieve shared objectives. Both line managers and staff specialists contribute their expertise towards overall success of the organisation.

3. **Functional Authority:** Functional authority is the privilege to issue orders within specific section of an organisation where such authority is typically absent. It pertains to task areas and is operational only for designated periods. Individuals are granted functional authority when they need to exercise some control over members in areas outside their own to fulfil their responsibilities.

Department heads receive support from staff specialists who manage activities within their departments. These specialists lack line authority over line departments but possess authority based on their expertise and competence, known as functional authority. For instance, departments like Accounting and R & D assist the production department and exercise authority over other departments.

Functional authority is not limited to specific roles; both line and staff managers can have it. For instance, a finance manager may have line authority over the finance department but exercises functional authority when overseeing financial activities in other departments. Similarly, accounting manager, closely associated with the finance department, has formal authority over line managers in other departments, enabling them to check accounts and exercise functional authority. This holds true for other staff specialists as well.

Max Weber defines three types of legitimate authority corresponding to three types of dominance or leadership.

1. **Traditional Authority:** The appeal to tradition represents the most prevalent form of authority, where people comply with traditional practices simply because "It has always been that way." This form of authority is rarely questioned, as individuals tend to follow established traditions out of habit and fear that deviation could create more problems than solutions.

   The unquestioned right of a leader to rule is the key aspect of traditional authority. People adhere to this authority because past adherence to it has provided order and continuity to the organisation. Beyond mere tradition, maintaining the stability of the social order is crucial for acceptance of this authority.

   In systems based on traditional authority, power derives legitimacy from ancient customs, and authority of the boss is often treated as an unwritten law. Throughout history, tribal leaders and monarchs have heavily relied on traditional authority, making it the most common source of legitimate power.

   Organisations emphasising continuity with the past and preservation of widely shared values and beliefs, such as established churches, higher levels of government, and courts, often exhibit prevalence of traditional authority.

2. **Rational-legal Authority:** In this type of authority, power gains legitimacy through explicit rules and procedures outlined in official rule books. Rational-legal authority relies on written laws than individual competence. Individuals possess power within legally defined limits, formally conferred upon them.

   Respect for this authority stems from followers being bound by the legitimacy of law. Legitimacy is derived from commitment to legality of power. Max Weber describes this authority in the context of the bureaucratic structure of organisations, where legal authority finds its best representation.

The core concept is that laws are established through formal procedures. The governing body operates for the entire organisation rather than catering to specific sections. Organisations characterised by rational-legal authority are often referred to as rational organisations.

3. **Charismatic Authority:** "In a system based on charismatic authority, power is legitimised by the unusual, exceptional or even supernatural qualities that people attribute to particular political, religious, or military leaders." Weber calls this extraordinary quality 'Charisma'. "The charismatic leader is seen as a person of destiny who is inspired by unsocial lofty principles or even by God. The charisma of these leaders is itself sufficient to make their authority seem legitimate to their followers".

   Many notable leaders, such as Jesus Christ, M.K. Gandhi, Hitler, and Napoleon, have been characterised by the quality of 'charisma.' Charismatic authority is an exceptional form where individuals follow a leader possessing extraordinary qualities like competence, captivating personality, perceived magical ability, revelations of heroism, and influential power of speech and mind.

   The leader is not inherently magical, but followers believe in their extraordinary qualities. The leader establishes a group of true believers who provide unwavering support. Despite its effectiveness, charismatic authority is often unstable as it relies on the unique qualities of a specific individual and lacks the guiding rules of tradition. The system becomes uncertain if the leader fails to possess charismatic qualities. Consequently, systems based on charismatic authority tend to be short-lived.

17.5 LIMITATIONS OF AUTHORITY

1. **Biological and Physical Limitations:** Managers cannot assign tasks that go beyond physical or mental capabilities of the employees. Additionally, external factors like climate or geography can also restrict managerial authority.
2. **Overall Organisational Goals:** Subordinates are unlikely to follow directions that go against overall goals of the organisation. Tasks assigned by managers should align with broader objectives of the company to ensure effective implementation.
3. **Legal Restrictions:** Organisational directives must adhere to legal regulations. For instance, companies cannot issue shares exceeding their authorised capital, as mandated by the Companies Act. Managerial authority is further limited by the company's Articles and Memorandum of Association. Legal constraints,

including those related to collective bargaining and trade unions, serve as boundaries on managerial decision-making and authority.

4. **Social Factors:** People form groups based on shared values and cultures. Directives that contradict these values are likely to face limited acceptance. Managers must be mindful of the social context to ensure effective communication and cooperation.
5. **Personal Limitations:** Acknowledging personal limitations is crucial for realistic delegation. If a manager is unable to perform a certain activity, they do not expect subordinates to do so either.
6. **Technical Limitations:** If a task is not feasible due to technical reasons, it becomes an inherent restriction on the authority to carry out that performance.
7. **Economic Limitations:** Managers must adapt to economic conditions, such as competition and pricing dynamics, that may impact feasibility and success of assigned tasks.
8. **Authority Delegation Limitations:** Authority delegation is often subject to hierarchical structures within organisations. Lower levels of the hierarchy tend to have more restrictions on authority. As one moves up the organisational ladder, these limitations decrease, allowing for broader scope of authority.

17.6 POWER

Authority is the right to give directions and power is the ability to implement those directions. Power is not solely dependent on one's position; it stems from control over resources. When an individual can change the behaviour of others, they are considered to have power. Having the right to influence behaviour implies authority. Power extends to influencing individuals, groups, teams, and departments. Those who exert influence are termed as agents and those being influenced as targets.

Power is a dynamic and social concept, shaped by interactions among people. It fluctuates with changes in situations. Power dynamics can vary, with a person having strong influence in one situation while being easily influenced in another.

Formal authority, which comes with a designated position, is often complemented by an informal system of power. Power is a broader notion that goes beyond organisational roles and arises when a person possesses superior skills or capacity to impact the actions of others. Effective managers leverage power strategically to maintain their positions within the organisation. Understanding and skilfully utilising various sources of power contribute to successful management practices.

Authority	Power
It is the formal right to issue orders, signifying a recognised position within organisational structure.	It is the capability to issue orders; the practical ability to influence and direct others.
It is linked to position in the hierarchy.	It is personal in nature, stemming from unique characteristics and capabilities of an individual rather than their position in the hierarchy.
It follows an upward trend, increasing as one ascends the hierarchy and decreasing as one descends.	It is not strictly tied to hierarchical levels, as individuals at lower levels may possess more power than those at higher levels, and the reverse can also be true.
It can be delegated to lower levels within the organisation structure.	Power cannot be delegated. It is a personal attribute to exert influence, regardless of position in the organisational hierarchy. Top of Form
Authority is usually in balance with responsibility, ensuring an equitable relationship.	It is possible for an individual with minimum responsibilities to have significant power.
Authority, being linked to position, is inherently formal.	Power, associated with individuals, can manifest in both formal and informal capacities. Legitimate power is a formal expression of authority.

17.7 NATURE OF POWER

1. **Potential to Influence:** The agent possesses the potential to influence the behaviour of the target. How this potential is utilised depends on the situation. For instance, a manager has the power to prevent employees from arriving late to the office but may not need to exercise this power if employees are aware of the expectation and arrive on time voluntarily.
2. **Dependence of Target on Agent:** The agent is considered to have power over the target when the target relies on the agent to achieve a particular goal. Power is contingent on the existence of a desired goal that necessitates the target's dependence on the agent.
3. **Control Over One's Own Behaviour:** Despite having power over the target, the agent cannot force the target to perform actions against their will. The target retains discretion over their own behaviour.

4. **Specific to People and Situations:** Power is not a general concept; it is specific to individuals and situations. Only certain people have power in particular circumstances. The exercise of power is closely tied to its source and context.
5. **Two-way Relationship:** The dynamics of power involves a two-way relationship. Those who influence are also influenced by someone higher in the hierarchy. Individuals can simultaneously be targets and agents within different relationships and contexts.

17.8 SOURCES OF POWER

I. Formal or Positional Power

Power is often tied to positions within the structure rather than individual qualities. It is established during the design of the organisation structure, although its utilisation varies among individuals.

1. ***Legitimate Power:*** Legitimate power forms the foundation of classical authority theory. Subordinates acknowledge and follow authority based on their position within the hierarchy. This type of authority, also known as formal or legitimate authority, is derived from one's designated role.
2. ***Reward Power:*** Reward power involves the ability to provide incentives. Individuals comply with directions because adherence to certain behaviours leads to rewards, which serve as positive reinforcements.
3. ***Coercive Power:*** Coercive power is the authority to penalise undesirable behaviour. People adhere to directives due to the potential negative consequences associated with coercive power. While it often maintains established standards, it may not necessarily foster their improvement. Careful use of coercive power is essential to prevent strains in employer-employee relations, as its indiscriminate application can lead to conflicts and reduced productivity.
4. ***Information Power:*** Information power involves access and control over decision-making information. Individuals possessing vital information can influence those who require it. Administrative staff, computer departments, accountants, and departmental managers control information crucial for professional updates and decision-making. This power is distributed among those who manage and disseminate key information within the organisation.

II. Personal Power

1. ***Expert Power:*** Expert power arises from an individual's knowledge, skill, competence, and expertise. The competence theory of authority is built upon expert power. Individuals possessing expertise are sought after by people from various departments and levels, irrespective of the formal chain of command. Even without formal authority, these individuals can issue directives based on their competence.
2. ***Referent Power:*** "Referent power is based on identification with a person who has desirable resources or personal traits." Also known as charismatic power, it operates through personal charisma, personality, and dynamism. This power relies on the ability to create identification, where individuals emulate those, they view as ideal, adopting their personality traits and behaviour.
3. ***Connection Power:*** Connection power is associated with an individual's ties to people, particularly those with high social and economic status. People tend to follow individuals with significant social and economic standing, granting them influence based on their connections.

The various sources of power are interconnected and often coexist within an individual. A person typically possesses a combination of powers derived from different sources. Someone with legitimate power, derived from their position, may also have coercive and reward power. Based on their position, they can offer rewards for compliance and threats for non-compliance to orders.

Individuals with expert power, owing to their knowledge and competence, are often well-suited for promotions. As they ascend the hierarchy, they gain legitimate, coercive, and reward power. However, excessive reliance on coercive power may diminish referent power, as people tend to distance themselves from leaders who employ negative forms of influence.

17.9 USE OF POWER

While power often contributes to an individual's popularity, its misuse can lead to detrimental outcomes. Improper use of power can harm the individual and the organisation. It can result in reluctance to accept challenging projects and hinder innovation. Therefore, use of power should align with interests of the organisation and the individuals involved, avoiding actions that prioritise personal gain over organisational welfare.

Effective use of power involves the following considerations:

1. ***Source of Power:*** Utilising more than one source of power is often necessary, depending on the situation. For instance, managers might employ reward power when faced with challenging workers and coercive power when dealing with employees who are unmotivated or avoid work. Professionals like doctors and lawyers consistently rely on expert power, irrespective of the behaviour of their patients and clients.
2. ***Reciprocity:*** A successful power dynamic involves mutual responses between the agent and the target, with both parties acknowledging and accepting their roles and behaviours in a manner that is mutually agreeable.
3. ***Understanding Behaviour:*** Before employing any form of power, managers should thoroughly comprehend the behaviour of their targets. Using coercive power to enforce good behaviour or reward power to address bad behaviour can be counterproductive. Aligning the use of power with specific behaviours contributes to organisational effectiveness.

17.10 RESPONSIBILITY

Responsibility refers to the tasks entrusted to individuals, representing moral commitment to work. It involves obligations, duties, or assigned tasks that contribute to the development of skills, competence, initiative, and work capabilities. Responsibility is essentially the obligation of an individual to carry out assigned activities to the best of their ability and concludes upon successful completion of the task.

It includes the following:

1. **Obligation to Perform:** Responsibility necessitates obligation of an individual to execute assigned tasks.
2. **Non-delegable:** Unlike authority, responsibility cannot be delegated. Even if a superior delegates authority for specific tasks, they remain responsible for those tasks.
3. **Parity with Authority:** Responsibility must align with the corresponding authority. Achieving effective results requires balance between authority and responsibility.

4. **Bottom-to-Top:** Responsibility flows from bottom to top within an organisational hierarchy. Every subordinate carries responsibility for assigned tasks.
5. **Defined Standards:** Responsibility should be clearly defined with established standards against which individual and collective achievements are assessed.

17.11 AUTHORITY AND RESPONSIBILITY

Authority	Responsibility
Right to issue directions.	Obligation to perform the task.
Delegated from superior to subordinates.	Superior remains answerable for the tasks assigned.
Top to bottom	Bottom to top

17.12 PARITY BETWEEN AUTHORITY AND RESPONSIBILITY

Authority and responsibility are interconnected. When an individual is assigned a task, they should also have corresponding authority to execute it. The relationship between authority and responsibility is guided by the principle of parity, ensuring that the level of authority matches the scope of responsibility. The principle of parity emphasises that when assigning a task, authority must be delegated in alignment with the responsibilities. Conversely, when assigning authority, the tasks should fall within the designated scope of authority.

While perfect parity between authority and responsibility is challenging and may not be precisely measured, the two concepts coexist and are integral to the same assignment. Maintaining balance between authority and responsibility contributes to effective task execution within an organisation.

17.13 ACCOUNTABILITY

Even when authority is delegated, those who delegate authority remain accountable for the outcomes. They are held responsible for the success or failure of the assigned tasks, and this answerability extends upwards in the organisational hierarchy. Accountability is the ultimate responsibility of managers, and it comes into play when there are predetermined standards against which results are assessed.

Accountability is the obligation to ensure that work is performed within specified performance standards, maintaining responsibility of the superior or delegator. It entails providing satisfactory reasons for significant deviations from duties or expected results.

Louis A. Allen describes it as "the obligation to carry out responsibility and exercise authority in terms of performance standards established." Importantly, accountability cannot be delegated; it rests with top authorities. While authority flows downwards, accountability moves upwards, with each level answerable to their superior. The person initiating the delegation process ultimately holds the highest level of accountability.

Questions

I. Long Answer Questions

1. Explain the terms 'authority' and 'responsibility'. Why can authority be delegated but not accountability?
2. Power and authority are not one and the same thing. Comment.
3. What do you mean by authority? State the theories of authority.
4. State the types of authority exercised by managers.
5. What is power? State the different sources of power.
6. "Authority is the legitimised power linked to each position within the organisation." Discuss.
7. Distinguish between authority and power. Also discuss the types and sources of authority.

II. Write short notes on:

(i) Authority and responsibility
(ii) Expert and referent power
(iii) Line and staff authority
(iv) Functional authority
(v) Acceptance theory of authority
(vi) Authority of the situation

III. Multiple Choice Questions

1. Final obligation of the manager is
   (*i*) Operating responsibility
   (*ii*) Accountability
   (*iii*) Authority
2. Power derived from formal position is
   (*i*) Legitimate power

(*ii*) Expert power

(*iii*) Reward power

3. Expert power is enjoyed because of

   (*i*) Ability to offer rewards

   (*ii*) Personality

   (*iii*) Knowledge

4. Authority of the situation

   (*i*) Flows in hierarchy

   (*ii*) Does not flow in hierarchy

5. 'Zone of indifference' substantiates

   (*i*) Classical theory of authority

   (*ii*) Acceptance theory of authority

   (*iii*) Competence theory of authority

Answers

1. (ii) 2. (i) 3. (iii) 4. (ii) 5. (ii)

IV. Case Study

(I) Pioneer Electronics Co. Ltd.

Mr. Anand is the general manager of sales department of Pioneer Electronics Co. Ltd. He issues orders and instructions to subordinates of his department by virtue of his position in the organisation. However, whenever he issues orders to people of his department, they do not comply with the instructions as (*i*) they do not fully understand the orders, and (*ii*) they feel that compliance to these orders will vitiate their individual goals. However, the subordinate obey the orders given by Mr. Rajlok, manager, production department.

Questions

1. Mr. Anand derives his authority from which source?
2. Under which theory (source of authority) can the subordinates refuse to accept instructions issued by Mr. Anand?
3. Mr. Rajlok has authority or power over subordinates of the sales department? Explain the difference between the two.

(II) Kenyon-Werner Company

Helen Snelling is executive secretary to Andrew Evans, a cautious, retiring, quiet man. She was transferred to his office about four months ago when the Louisville regional sales office of the company was closed. Top managers hoped to provide Evans with expert help by assi`gning Snelling, whose personnel record showed her to be capable, highly efficient, ambitious, somewhat impatient, and the possessor of a quick temper. She is 28 years old. Reporting to Evans are James Root, head of accounting; Hortense Higgins, head of order writing; Francis Green, head of production scheduling; Beth Cooper, chief of switchboard operators and receptionists; and Henry Schwartz, chief of the mailroom. James Root, age 46, knows accounting very well, but he is not a good administrator. He is inclined to let chores other than accounting work be unduly delayed and seems to have little perception of human relations problems within his unit. Well liked and accommodating, he is accepted by his employees, but the top managers do not view him as a heavy weight to assume higher management responsibilities in the company. In view of the delay displayed by Andrew Evans, Helen Snelling is inclined to take action on those matters that, in her opinion, need attention. Usually, her decisions have proven quite effective; but other members of the department object to her grabbing authority that doesn't belong to her. To illustrate, about two weeks ago, Higgins, age 50, and Snelling got into a verbal scuffle about priority in completion of the order writing for certain customers. The Issue was settled by Evans, who decided in favour of Higgins. Then he had a talk with Snelling about taking it easy and the folly of being too aggressive in business relationships. Only two days ago during the lunch hour, Snelling answered Root's telephone, took request for some records to be sent to the purchasing director, secured the wanted records from the file, and sent them to the purchasing director. Root found out about the request yesterday and spoke with Snelling about it. He stated that she was overstepping her prescribed duties and the least she could have done was to tell him about it or leave a note on his desk. Snelling said she did write him a note and was only trying to help. Root emphasised that he would not tolerate any interference by her and that he intends to report the incident to Evans. Later, in searching through papers on his desk, he found the note referred to by Snelling. It is the opinion of Snelling that the people reporting directly to Evans are taking advantage of him and have been doing so for a long time. He is so buried in detail that he delays many financial decisions. She is certain that the management personnel of the finance group are going in all different directions and that Evans doesn't realise this. In her own mind, Snelling is positive that her dealings with various heads within the finance group are for the best interests of the company. She also feels certain that the subordinates of Evans go ahead and decide issues, sometimes poorly, when the final decision should come from Evans, or at least with sanction by him and knowledge of what decision has been made.

Questions

1. What is the problem as you see it?
2. What important factors do you believe contributed to the present situation?
3. What plan of action would you recommend remedying the problem?

❑❑❑

18
Chapter

Delegation and Decentralisation

The best executive is the one who has sense enough to pick good men to do what he wants done, and self-restraint enough to keep from meddling with them while they do it."

—Theodore Roosevelt

18.1 MEANING OF DELEGATION

"An individual is only one manpower. Single-handed, he can accomplish only so much in a day. The only way he can achieve more is through delegation through dividing his load and sharing his responsibilities with others."

Delegation is "the assignment of part of a manager's work to others along with both the responsibility and the authority necessary to achieve expected results."

Delegation is the process of assigning tasks and authority to subordinates, who take on the responsibility for completing those jobs. It is a crucial process in distributing work efficiently. The effectiveness of a manager is often measured by how well they delegate.

18.2 FEATURES OF DELEGATION

1. **Continuous Process:** Delegation is an ongoing activity where managers assign tasks and may also receive delegated tasks from their superiors.
2. **Art, Not Science:** Delegating tasks does not guarantee that subordinates will perform well. There is no strict cause-and-effect relationship between assigned tasks and performance. Delegation is an art – it is about how skilfully a manager assigns tasks to subordinates.
3. **Delegation of Authority, Not Accountability:** Managers delegate both tasks and the authority to perform them, but accountability remains with the

delegators. Managers are responsible for tasks assigned to subordinates, even though they delegate responsibility and authority.

4. **Necessary Activity:** Delegation is essential for managers since they cannot handle all tasks themselves. Learning to delegate effectively is crucial for overall performance. It is not a choice but a necessity.

5. **Different forms:** Delegation can take various forms – it can move downward (to subordinates), upward (from subordinates), or lateral (between peers).

18.3 PROCESS OF DELEGATION

1. **Establish Goals:** Managers set clear goals for positions to guide individuals in their roles. All activities should be aimed at achieving these goals. Effective delegation relies on everyone understanding their responsibilities and how to accomplish them.

2. **Define Responsibility:** Once tasks are defined, responsibility is determined based on measurable results. Specific goals, like 'Selling 10,000 units per month,' provide clear direction than vague instructions like "Increase the Sales". Understanding goals and performance criteria enhance employee performance and clarify the relationship between superiors and subordinates.

3. **Grant Authority:** Authority is the right to give instructions and sets boundaries for subordinates' actions. It allows them to use resources, make organisational commitments, and issue orders. Authority should match responsibility; more responsibility corresponds to more authority and vice versa.

4. **Motivation:** Delegating tasks is not enough; managers also motivate subordinates through incentives. Recognition is a central motivator, driving people to perform better.

5. **Provide Training:** Even with authority aligned with responsibility, subordinates may need training to perform tasks effectively. Managers organise training programmes to enhance their performance.

6. **Ensure Control:** Managers establish specific standards to evaluate performance and coordinate subordinates' activities with the organisation's goals.

7. **Ensure Accountability:** Accountability is a crucial aspect of effective delegation. Managers continually monitor subordinates' work as they are ultimately accountable for results.

18.4 FORMS OF DELEGATION

1. **Top to Bottom Delegation:** Top-to-bottom delegation occurs when superiors assign tasks to subordinates. Those in higher positions pass on responsibilities to those in lower positions within the organisational hierarchy.
2. **Bottom to Top Delegation:** This type of delegation is observed in informal groups where the norms of the group align with those of the organisation. Managers motivate subordinates as members of the group rather than as individuals. The group norms essentially become the norms of the organisation in the informal delegation setting.

   "To the extent that the manager convinces the members of the group that their needs, his own, and those of the company coincide, he can motivate them to produce according to the standards he sets." – *Allen*
3. **Lateral Delegation:** Delegation can also occur horizontally, where individuals at the same level in different units collaborate. The responsibility of the functional manager is shared with colleagues from other departments at the same level. This collaborative effort involves peer groups coming together and functioning as a team.

18.5 IMPORTANCE OF DELEGATION

1. **Relief to Managers:** Managers can focus on crucial policy matters by delegating routine tasks to lower levels. This enhances organisational efficiency.
2. **Develops Managers:** Delegation allows managers to take on more responsibilities and challenging projects from their superiors, leading to skill enhancement and professional development.
3. **Develops Subordinates:** Delegation develops subordinates, making them potential managers in the future.
4. **Better Decisions:** Delegation ensures decisions are made where they matter the most. Decisions made closest to the situation result in higher-quality outcomes.
5. **Faster Decisions:** Delegated authority empowers subordinates to swiftly resolve problems, leading to quick decision-making.
6. **Specialisation:** Breaking down responsibilities and delegating based on specialised capabilities promotes specialisation and increased output.

7. **Job Satisfaction:** Meeting standards provides satisfaction and motivation for subordinates to perform better.
8. **Promotes Inter-personal Relationships:** Delegation fosters interaction and positive relationships between superiors and subordinates.

Delegation rightly enables a manager to multiply himself.

18.6 PRINCIPLES OF DELEGATION

1. **Authority, Responsibility and Accountability:** Effective delegation involves three key elements: authority, responsibility, and accountability.
2. **Parity of Authority and Responsibility:** Subordinates must be granted the authority necessary to fulfil their responsibilities. The ability to provide instructions to unit members is essential. Authority without responsibility or responsibility without authority is meaningless.
3. **Scalar Chain:** Knowing one's position in the hierarchy is crucial for assigning responsibilities. The scalar chain establishes direct authority relationship between superiors and subordinates, facilitating effective decision-making.
4. **Completeness of Delegation:** Delegation should be comprehensive, covering every aspect of the work except for tasks reserved for managers. Failure to delegate fully can result in gaps and incomplete work.
5. **Unity of Command:** The principle of unity of command dictates that each person should have a single boss. Having multiple bosses can hinder task execution. Unity of command ensures clarity regarding who must carry out whose orders, preventing conflicts and fostering responsibility for results.
6. **Absoluteness of Responsibility:** Even when responsibility and authority are delegated, the person assigning the tasks (delegator) remains accountable for the delegated tasks. For instance, if district manager falls short of achieving the sales target, the branch manager (delegator) is still answerable to the General Manager of the sales department. Delegation does not absolve superiors from ultimate responsibility, which is synonymous with accountability. While responsibility can be delegated, accountability cannot.
7. **Delegation by Results:** Managers need to clearly define the objectives of delegation, specifying what they expect subordinates to accomplish. Ambiguous directives like 'increase sales' are ineffective. It is essential to communicate the

desired outcomes of delegation, including who is responsible, when actions are expected, and so forth. Subordinates should be aware of the results expected from their actions.

8. **Delegate within Defined Limits:** Delegation must adhere to specified limits. Decisions within a manager's competent authority can be delegated, while those exceeding the authority are reported up the hierarchy. In cases where decisions involve collaboration of two or more managers, termed as splintered authority, authority is exercised through inter-departmental interaction. For example, decisions regarding innovation in product designs may require joint input from production and research and development (R&D) departments.

18.7 ELEMENTS OF DELEGATION

1. **Responsibility:** Responsibility refers to tasks assigned to subordinates. Nevertheless, ultimate responsibility, also known as accountability, lies with the person delegating the task.
2. **Authority:** Authority is essential for allocating resources, leading people, giving instructions, and making decisions to fulfil the assigned responsibility.
3. **Accountability:** Accountability persists even after delegation. Managers are accountable for the task, even though responsibility and authority may be delegated. While responsibility and authority can be passed on, accountability cannot be delegated.

18.8 BARRIERS TO DELEGATION

Barriers to delegation can be grouped under following headings:

I. Barriers Related to Superiors

Superiors often refrain from delegating for the following reasons:

1. ***Preference for Personal Involvement*:** Managers may avoid delegation because they believe they can perform tasks more effectively. They choose to handle the work themselves than entrusting it to others.
2. ***Insecurity*:** Some managers hesitate to delegate due to fear that subordinates might outperform them. This reluctance often arises when work procedures and methods lack clear definition.

3. ***Desire for Power Retention***: Certain managers seek to maintain power and control over subordinates, leading to reluctance to delegate. This behaviour is common among autocratic managers who prefer direct involvement over delegation.
4. ***Lack of Confidence in Subordinates***: Effective delegation relies on trust, and managers who lack confidence in their subordinates may refrain from delegating.
5. ***Unwillingness to Establish Standards***: Effective delegation involves ensuring that actual performance aligns with planned performance. Managers who fail to set realistic standards struggle to delegate effectively.
6. ***Personal Preferences***: Autocratic managers tend to maintain tight control over subordinates and may avoid delegation. In contrast, democratic leaders are more inclined to delegate tasks as they believe in participative decision-making.

Managers often adopt delegation practices based on their own experiences. If their superiors delegated tasks to them, they are likely to trust their subordinates and delegate as well. Conversely, if their superiors did not trust them with delegation, they may be hesitant to delegate further.

II. Barriers Related to Subordinates

1. ***Lack of Confidence***: When subordinates lack confidence, they avoid taking on additional responsibilities and prefer relying on superiors for decision-making.
2. ***Fear of Mistakes***: Subordinates may refrain from accepting responsibility due to fear that making mistakes could lead to unfavourable outcomes.
3. ***Lack of Incentives***: Effective delegation relies on motivation. Subordinates may be hesitant to accept delegated tasks if no incentives are provided.
4. ***Limited Access to Resources***: Subordinates may decline responsibilities if they lack access to necessary resources. This situation arises when the assigned responsibility is not aligned with the corresponding authority.
5. ***Convenience***: Some subordinates simply prefer superiors to make decisions for them, avoiding complexities and responsibilities associated with decision-making.

III. Barriers Related to Organisation

1. ***Size of the Organisation***: In smaller organisations with fewer roles, there may be limited opportunities for delegation as there are not many tasks to assign. This can make the organisation less responsive to delegation.
2. ***Lack of Delegation Precedent***: Some organisations refrain from delegation simply because they have never practiced it before. There is lack of history of delegation.
3. ***Centralisation or Decentralisation***: Delegation is influenced by how much decision-making authority is distributed across different units. In a centralised organisation where decision-making is concentrated at the top, delegation may not be as prevalent or effective.

18.9 OVERCOME BARRIERS TO DELEGATION

1. **Acknowledge the Necessity of Delegation:** Recognising that delegation enhances managerial capacity, tasks that can be delegated should be delegated. This allows managers to focus on responsibilities that subordinates cannot handle. This builds core competencies and benefits the organisation.
2. **Build Confidence in Subordinates:** Even in the face of mistakes, managers need to guide subordinates, maintain a continuous delegation process and express confidence in subordinates to boost morale and performance, rather than withholding delegation. Trust fosters commitment, loyalty, dedication, and positive contribution to growth. Delegation works best when supported by rewards rather than penalties.
3. **Effective Communication:** Establishing an effective communication system facilitates delegation. Well-informed subordinates are valuable assets to the organisation, contributing to effective decision-making. Open communication fosters trust between delegator and delegatees, ensuring that delegated tasks are performed to the best of the subordinates' abilities.
4. **Motivation:** Incentives serve as powerful motivators in the workplace. Assigning tasks can itself be a source of motivation, showing confidence in abilities of the individuals involved. Successful task completion brings a sense of pride and satisfaction. Transforming non-commitment into commitment requires motivation—fostering zeal, enthusiasm, and willingness to work.

5. **Effective Control System:** As the ultimate responsibility lies with the delegator, establishing achievable standards for performance measurement is crucial. Instead of refraining from delegation, the delegator should monitor delegatees' activities. A moderately lenient control system, focusing on exceptions, helps achieve standards. Managers identify major deviations, while subordinates address minor ones. Effective control prevents misuse of delegated authority.
6. **Selecting the Right Person for the Right Job:** Assigning tasks to individuals best suited for the job, matches the task with the abilities of subordinates. Adequate training enhances understanding and performance. Incorrect selection of delegatees can disrupt operations. "Round pegs in round holes" makes delegation effective, ensuring that right job is given to the right person.
7. **Empower Subordinates:** Rather than refraining from delegation due to the fear of mistakes, managers should grant subordinates the freedom to make decisions, provide them with the authority to find solutions, preventing future errors.
8. **Clarity of Tasks:** Clearly defined responsibilities in terms of expected results and understanding the job enhances performance. Delegation should be purposeful and planned, aiming to achieve specific results.
9. **Monitor Critical Deviations:** Mistakes may occur, but superiors should focus on major deviations while overlooking minor ones. This encourages commitment to work, allowing subordinates to improve without excessive scrutiny.

18.10 CENTRALISATION AND DECENTRALISATION

Delegation, centralisation, and decentralisation deal with the distribution of authority and responsibility within an organisation. Delegation involves passing responsibility from one level to another. Centralisation and decentralisation refer to how authority and responsibility are distributed across different organisational levels.

Centralisation is "the extent to which power and authority are retained at the top organisational levels," while decentralisation is "the extent to which power and authority are delegated to lower levels." "Decentralisation refers to the systematic effort to delegate to the lowest levels all authority except that which can only be exercised at central points." In a centralised structure, top management retains significant control. The extent of decentralisation depends on the organisation's size, with larger organisations tending to delegate authority to lower levels.

The balance between centralisation and decentralisation varies, determining the flow of authority down the organisational hierarchy. As an organisation grows, authority narrows at the top and extends to lower levels.

No organisation is entirely centralised or decentralised. In a fully centralised structure, all decisions come from the top and in a fully decentralised structure, complete authority is delegated to lower-level managers. These extreme structures do not exist in practice; organisations fall along a continuum with varying degrees of authority delegation.

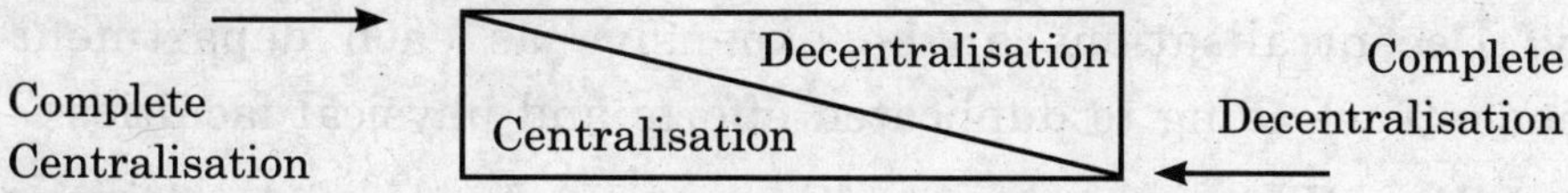

Moving from left to right on the spectrum, the degree of centralisation decreases, and decentralisation increases.

18.11 IMPORTANCE OF DECENTRALISATION

1. **Reduces top Managers' Burden:** Decentralisation lessens the workload of top managers by delegating routine decisions, allowing them to concentrate on strategic management.
2. **Develops Subordinates:** Lower-level individuals become competent at decision-making, fostering the growth of potential managers within the organisation.
3. **Fast Decision-making:** Being closer to problems eliminates the need to consult higher authorities, enabling better decision-making.
4. **Promotes Diversification:** Decentralisation facilitates diversification into multiple products and locations, reducing hierarchy levels. A broad span encourages committed employees, teamwork, and adaptability.
5. **Promotes Motivation:** A potent motivational force, decentralisation enhances efficiency, motivation, and control.
6. **Flexibility:** Decentralised organisations exhibit greater flexibility, allowing for policy adjustments at various levels in response to environmental changes.
7. **Communication:** With fewer levels in the scalar chain, communication is swifter, and information distortions are minimised.

8. **Control:** Managers establish standards for their units, fostering a result-oriented approach as autonomous units set sub-goals contributing to the larger objectives.

18.12 LIMITATIONS OF DECENTRALISATION

1. **Co-ordination:** High decentralisation challenges coordinating activities across departments, making it complex to ensure collaboration.
2. **Control:** Difficulty in coordination hampers effective control mechanisms, making it hard to manage organisational processes.
3. **Costly:** Decentralisation can be expensive as each department operates independently, leading to duplicated efforts and physical facilities.
4. **Adaptability:** When strategic decisions are decentralised, various units may respond differently to fast-paced environmental changes, making it challenging to perform organisational operations.
5. **Lack of Uniformity:** A highly decentralised organisation may lack uniform policies across units, as each unit formulates its own policies independently.
6. **Ability of Lower-level Managers:** Efficiency in a decentralised organisation depends on the decision-making skills of lower-level managers, failing which, the decentralised structure is compromised.

These issues are theoretical and not inherent in decentralisation. Well-planned efforts to decentralise bring positive results and address these challenges effectively.

18.13 FACTORS AFFECTING DECENTRALISATION

I. External Factors

1. ***Environment***: Decentralisation is preferred when customers and suppliers are widespread, competition is moderate, and markets offer ample opportunities for expansion, such as introducing new products.
2. ***Government Regulation***: Stringent government policies limit delegation of decision-making power to lower levels. In highly regulated environments, adherence to rules is crucial, resulting in lower inclination towards decentralisation.

3. ***Market Features***: Decentralisation is more feasible in homogeneous markets where companies produce similar products, allowing decision-making power to be dispersed.
4. ***Trade Union Bargaining***: The willingness of trade unions to negotiate with lower-level management results in decentralisation of decision-making power. However, if negotiations are exclusive to top management, the organisation tends to be more centralised.

II. Internal Factors

1. ***Size of the Organisation***: As organisations grow larger with dispersed units and numerous levels, making decisions independently becomes challenging and time-consuming, making coordination complex. While routine decisions can be delegated at lower levels, ensuring efficiency, top executives can focus on strategic matters.
2. ***Cost Control***: Major decisions involving significant financial outlays are typically made by top executives. Less costly decisions can be delegated to lower levels. Focus on strict cost control tends to have lower degree of decentralisation.
3. ***Philosophy of Management***: The management philosophy influences the choice between centralisation and decentralisation. Managers who seek to retain authority often prefer centralisation, while those aiming to enhance creative skills of lower levels prefer decentralisation.
4. ***History of the Enterprise***: Self-made business empires tend to lean towards centralisation, while organisations expanding through external measures like mergers and acquisitions prefer decentralisation. In cases of external growth, different managements may retain decision-making authority as per their historical practices. Autonomy in decision-making tends to favour decentralisation.
5. ***Functional Areas***: Finance and personnel tend to be more centralised, while production and marketing often lean towards decentralisation.
6. ***Ability of Subordinates***: Decentralisation is viable when lower-level individuals are innovative and inspired to work. This fosters commitment and loyalty to the organisation.
7. ***Growth of Enterprise***: Dynamic environments demand adaptability, making decentralisation essential for growing organisations. In stable organisations

where most decisions are routine, centralisation tends to be more prevalent.

8. ***Communication System*:** An effective communication system is crucial for coordinating diverse activities. Management information systems support decentralisation, facilitating smooth communication.
9. **Control System:** A well-designed control system supports decentralisation by providing regular performance appraisals and successful implementation of decisions.

18.14 PROCESS OF DECENTRALISATION

The following steps make the decentralisation process:

1. **Centralisation:** Initially, the organisation starts as a centralised structure. The power and authority to make decisions vests with the top management. As it grows, the need for delegating operating authority arises while strategic decisions are exercised by the top management. This ensures uniformity in the working of the organisation.

   Following are the strategic areas where decision-making should remain centralised:

   i. ***Planning:*** To ensure consistency and uniformity in the operations, the framework of planning consisting of policies, procedures, programmes, schedules, etc is developed by top managers. It is within the overall planning that different units make sub-plans to synthesise with the broader plans.

   ii. ***Organising:*** The organisation structure — creating departments, authority-responsibility relationships, the levels (span of control) are decided by top management and the task of working within that structure is delegated to lower levels by dividing the work into sub-units and assigning each task to different individuals.

   iii. ***Coordination:*** More the degree of decentralisation, more the problem of coordinating the business activities. Chief executive retains power to coordinate the activities of different divisions and departments. This avoids duplication of efforts at different divisions.

   iv. ***Motivation:*** People are motivated by different factors. While financial rewards are important for some, non-financial rewards of acceptance and recognition are important for others. Various motivational factors are analysed and a policy for motivating employees is made.

v. ***Control:*** Authority to make overall plans is reserved with top management. Managers also ensure that plans are achieved optimally. Setting measures of control to ensure that actual performance conforms to planned performance is centralised with the top management.

2. **Development of Managers:** Once the basic structure of organisation is designed, plans and standards for measuring performance are made and techniques of coordination and motivation are laid, managers decentralise the enterprise by delegating operating authority to lower-level managers who frame policies for their units. Though these policies do not relate to strategic matters, they are important for their units.
3. **Communication and Coordination:** Though overall coordination is done by top management; departmental managers ensure coordination of their work units through an open system of communication where information flows freely, both vertically and horizontally.
4. **Control:** While the measures of control are framed by top management (budgets, PERT, CPM etc.) to evaluate the performance of the organisation, lower-level managers also participate in controlling activities for the efficient functioning of their units.
5. **Dispersion:** Dispersion refers to geographic separation of central head office from the operating units. This minimises interference of top executives in the working of operating units. Dispersion helps to locate the units near the sources of raw materials or markets (to reduce the costs) and enhance the leadership and supervision qualities of managers in charge of their units. Increase in their skills and creativity motivates employees of their units, resulting in higher productivity.

18.15 DEGREE OF DECENTRALISATION

The important question that arises is not whether to centralise or decentralise but how much to centralise or decentralise. Some degree of decentralisation is essential. It is important to determine what kind of authority to delegate and how far down the scalar chain it is to be delegated. *John Child* describes four factors that characterise movement of organisation from one end of the continuum to the other i.e., from centralisation to decentralisation. These are:

1. **Size:** With the increase in size of the organisation, managers cannot make all major decisions themselves and, therefore, move towards decentralisation.
2. **Geographic Dispersion:** If activities are spread over wide geographical areas, top executives cannot make decisions with respect to all the functional areas and, therefore, there is a tendency to decentralise.
3. **Technological Complexity:** As a result of technological developments, top managers cannot make the decisions alone and, therefore, the movement towards decentralisation.
4. **Environment Uncertainty:** The fast-changing environment requires (*i*) careful analysis of environmental factors that affect the organisation, and (*ii*) most speedy and timely decisions by organisations to adapt to the changing environment. There is thus, need for decentralisation.

18.16 DELEGATION AND DECENTRALISATION

Decentralisation is an extension of delegation, and the two concepts differ in the following ways:

1. **Scope:** Delegation occurs between two individuals, typically from a superior to a subordinate. Decentralisation extends across all levels and functional areas. While delegation is more specific, decentralisation is a broader concept.
2. **Control:** In delegation, delegator maintains control over the activities of the delegatee. In decentralisation, control is exerted by individuals at the levels where decisions are made. It shifts to those responsible for specific areas.
3. **Interdependence:** Delegation can occur without decentralisation, as every manager must delegate to effectively manage their responsibilities. Decentralisation is not possible without delegation; it is the result of the delegation process.
4. **Autonomy:** Delegation involves performance of tasks assigned by superiors, emphasising a more directive approach. In decentralisation, managers have the autonomy to create their own plans and make decisions independently.

5. **Completeness:** Delegation is complete when authority is transferred from one person to another at any level. Decentralisation is complete when authority is transferred to the maximum extent possible, across various levels and functions.

Delegation	Decentralisation
Delegation has narrow scope as there is limited transfer of authority.	Decentralisation is wider in scope as there is wide distribution of authority.
It is complete with transfer of authority from one person to another.	It is complete when authority is delegated to the maximum extent.
Delegator controls the activities of subordinates.	Top management controls only strategic issues. Routine matters are controlled at lower levels.
Delegation is possible without decentralisation.	Decentralisation is the end-result of delegation. Delegation is prerequisite to decentralisation.
Managers of every unit implement plans devised by their superiors.	Managers of each unit have the autonomy to create and execute their own plans.
Ultimate responsibility remains with the delegator.	Responsibility rests with the decision-making units.
Delegation serves as a routine that alleviates the workload of top executives.	Decentralisation becomes essential for effective adaptation and responsiveness to change.

Questions

I. Long Answer Questions

1. What guidelines will you suggest for ensuring effective delegation of authority?
2. How would you support the view that "Delegation enables a manager to multiply himself." Why is delegation of authority not always effective?
3. Distinguish between delegation and decentralisation. What are the limitations of decentralisation?
4. What is delegation of authority? What obstacles stand in the way of effective delegation?
5. Define decentralisation of authority. What are the advantages and limitations of decentralisation?
6. Why is delegation important for the organisation? What are the barriers to effective delegation? How can these barriers be overcome?
7. "Decentralisation is nothing but extension of delegation." Discuss.
8. (*a*) Delegation is an art. Comment.

   (*b*) What are the barriers to effective delegation.

II. Write short notes on:

(i) Delegation v. Decentralisation

(ii) Centralisation v. Decentralisation

III. Case Study

Ambika Co.

Ambika Co. is a service organisation Ms. Rita is the chief executive officer of the organisation. She shows keen interest in business. However, she wants to associate herself with each and every activity of the business. Her team members feel they are not given enough freedom to decide and work on any of the activities. Most of them could not face the customers due to lack of authority to decide on issues, particularly simple issues. Now, the organisation is going in wrong direction, this is customer's comment.

Questions

1. Discuss the seriousness of the situation.
2. Suggest ways to improve the condition in the organisation.
3. Explain the importance of delegation.

❑❑❑

19
Chapter

Co-Ordination

"We all do better when we work together. Our differences do matter, but our common humanity matters more." *–Bill Clinton*

19.1 CO-ORDINATION

Co-ordination is "the process of linking the activities of various departments of the organisation."

It is "the process of integrating the objectives and activities of the separate units (departments or functional areas) of an organisation in order to achieve organisational goals efficiently."

It is "the orderly arrangement of group effort to provide unity of action in the pursuit of a common purpose." *—J.D. Mooney*

Co-ordination is "integration of the activities of individuals and units into a concerted effort that works towards a common aim." - *Pearce* and *Robinson*

Co-ordination ensures unity of action among individuals and departments. It balances differing opinions, encourages group effort, and directs activities in a unified way. Effective co-ordination relies on the interdependence of activities, using a systems approach to management where departments depend on each other. The need for co-ordination increases with the degree of interdependence. For instance, if the production department does not co-ordinate with the sales department, production may not align with sales needs. Overproduction leads to excess stock and tied-up funds, while underproduction results in lost sales revenue. Co-ordination ensures the smooth running of a business.

19.2 FEATURES/NATURE OF CO-ORDINATION

Co-ordination has the following features:

1. **Group Effort**: Co-ordination integrates the efforts of individuals and departments. It maximises group goals as well as organisational goals.
2. **Unity of Action**: It promotes unity among individual and departmental activities, ensuring everyone works toward a common goal. All activities must align with the set policies and procedures.
3. **Common Goal:** Co-ordination balances individual, departmental, and organisational goals. The work of one department supports others. For example, the sales department may want more funds for advertising, but the finance department may limit spending to control costs. Co-ordination resolves these conflicts to achieve a common goal.
4. **Continuous Process**: Co-ordination is not a one-time effort to align individual goals. It is an ongoing process that continues for as long as the organisation exists.
5. **Managerial Responsibility**: Co-ordination is the responsibility of every manager at all levels for every function (production, finance, personnel, and sales). All managers continuously co-ordinate the work within their departments.
6. **Essence of Management:** Co-ordination is not a separate management function. It is needed in every managerial task. Managers co-ordinate human and non-human resources, the internal and external environment, and all management functions. Co-ordination is the essence of management.
7. **Synthesis of Efforts**: Co-ordination integrates the efforts of people and departments at all levels. It also combines resources (physical, human, and financial) to achieve the goals.
8. **Necessary Obligation**: Co-ordination is not optional. Everyone must work toward a common goal. It is a necessary obligation.
9. **Deliberate Effort**: Co-ordination does not happen on its own. Managers must make deliberate efforts to co-ordinate departmental activities.

19.3 IMPORTANCE/NEED FOR CO-ORDINATION

Co-ordination results in the following benefits:

1. **Non-routine Jobs**: Non-routine jobs need constant flow of information, both vertical and horizontal. Co-ordination helps to perform these jobs efficiently.

2. **Dynamic Activities**: In a constantly changing world, organisations need coordination to bring together different activities, adjusting them as the environment shifts.

3. **Standards of Performance**: Managers coordinate business activities to make sure they meet high standards of performance.

4. **Interdependence of Activities**: When different parts of a company rely on each other for resources or information, coordination is necessary. According to *Thompson*, there are three types of this interdependence: pooled, sequential, and reciprocal.

   Pooled interdependence occurs when the overall performance depends on the combined efforts of departments. This happens when divisions make different products not linked to each other. For example, in a company like Reliance Industries producing textiles and electronics, the performance of one division does not rely on the other. However, the overall performance of both divisions affects the company. Resources can move between units to maintain performance. Profit from one division can offset losses in another. Coordination needs are low here.

   In *sequential interdependence*, performance of one unit depends upon the other (marketing department depends upon production department). This requires co-ordination between production and sales departments.

   In *reciprocal interdependence*, units have a give-and-take relationship. For instance, if trucks are loaded at the assembly station and unloaded at the warehouse, this requires pooled interdependence. The trucks need to be unloaded at the warehouse and returned to the assembly station for reloading. Lack of coordination in truck movement speed can waste a lot of time and resources.

   With increase in degree of interdependence from pooled to reciprocal, the need for co-ordination also increases.

5. **Specialisation**: Specialisation concentrates on very narrow areas of job. People tend to overlook overall perspective of the job. Co-ordination directs all the activities towards a common goal.

6. **Growing Organisation**: In reciprocal interdependence, units have a give-and-take relationship. For instance, if trucks are loaded at the assembly station and unloaded at the warehouse, this requires pooled interdependence. The trucks need to be unloaded at the warehouse and returned to the assembly station for reloading. Lack of coordination in truck movement speed can waste a lot of time and resources.

7. **Unity of Action**: Organisations have various types of employees, ideas, resources, goals, tasks, and skills. Coordination brings all these different elements together toward one common goal, maximising their effectiveness.
8. **Synergy**: Coordination helps the total output of a group to be greater than the sum of individual outputs. By bringing together the work of different units, coordination creates synergy, increasing the overall output.

19.4 LIMITATIONS IN ACHIEVING CO-ORDINATION

Limitations in achieving effective co-ordination are as follows:

1. **Increased Specialisation**: Specialisation can create problem of co-ordination. "People in specialised units tend to develop their own sense of the organisation's goals and how to pursue them." Higher the degree of specialisation, more difficult it is to coordinate the activities.
2. **High Interdependence Amongst Units**: As one unit depends more on another, it becomes harder to coordinate them. It is more challenging to coordinate units with reciprocal interdependence than those with pooled interdependence.
3. **Perspective:** When different departments view the same problem differently, coordination becomes difficult. For example, if a company wants to increase profits, the production department might focus on improving product quality, the sales department might push for better advertising, and the finance department might aim to cut costs. These differing opinions make it hard to coordinate efforts.
4. **Uncertainty About Future**: Changes in environmental factors can make coordination hard. Unexpected changes can disrupt plans, making coordination difficult. Internal issues like strikes and lockouts also complicate coordination.
5. **Lack of Skill:** Coordination is difficult if managers lack the necessary skills. Managers with an autocratic style may struggle with coordination.
6. **Informal Groups**: Informal groups are strongly bonded by cultural, social, and ethical values. This can impact the coordination of their activities.

19.5 TYPES OF CO-ORDINATION

Coordination can be of the following types:

1. **Internal and External Coordination**: Coordination between activities within a company is called internal coordination. Coordination with external groups (government, customers, suppliers, competitors, etc.) is called external coordination. Organisations are open systems that constantly interact with their environment. They take inputs from the environment and return outputs.

This requires full coordination between what the environment expects from the organisation and what the organisation expects from the environment.

2. **Vertical and Horizontal Coordination**: These are the forms of internal coordination. Vertical coordination is achieved amongst people at different levels. It coordinates the activities of top managers with middle and lower-level managers. It is "the linking of activities at the top of the organisation with those at the middle and lower levels in order to achieve organisational goals." Vertical coordination can be achieved through span of management, centralisation, decentralisation and delegation.

   Horizontal coordination is achieved amongst activities of different departments at the same level. It is "the linking of activities across departments at similar levels. It links the activities of four primary departments production, finance, personnel and sales".

   Horizontal coordination is needed because departments rely on each other for information or products. When departments share information, managers come up with innovative solutions.

   "The more organisations need to process information in the course of producing their product or service, the more methods of horizontal coordination they will need to use".

Methods of Achieving Horizontal Coordination

1. **Slack resources** provide extra time, money, materials, inventory, and people in each department. This flexibility helps departments adapt to internal and external pressures without waiting for more resources. For example, if a company expects to sell 10,000 units a month, it can produce 11,000 units to handle unexpected 10 percent increase in demand. Without this buffer, the company may struggle to meet increased demand, allowing competitors to attract its customers. Slack resources improve coordination between departments and units.
2. **Information systems** share data between units. Computers send information to different departments, helping with coordination.
3. **Lateral relations** allow information to be shared across different levels, not just through higher-ups in the organisation. These relations are "coordination of efforts through communicating and problem solving with peers in other departments or units, rather than referring most issues up the hierarchy for resolution."

Lateral relations can be maintained in the following ways:

i. ***Direct contact***: At middle and lower levels, employees from different departments often talk directly to solve problems. This achieves coordination without going through the chain of command.

ii. ***Liaison roles***: A liaison officer solves problems by contacting different departments directly. They act as a common link between units or departments. Even though they do not have formal authority, they coordinate diverse groups by dealing directly with departments facing issues.

iii. ***Task forces***: When a liaison officer cannot coordinate due to complex inter-departmental dependence, task forces step in to facilitate coordination. These are teams made up of members from different departments who share information about their departmental problems. Once a solution is found, the task force disbands and members return to their usual roles.

iv. ***Committees***: "Committees are usually formal organised groups with a designated membership and chairperson and regularly scheduled meetings." Committees are created to address specific, often recurring organisational issues. They help in achieving horizontal coordination among departments. For example, leave committee handles leave cases from all departments. Committee members discuss issues of their departments and find solutions that work for everyone involved.

v. ***Managerial integrators***: They are managers appointed to coordinate products, projects, or brands that involve interaction between departments. Usually, they are product, project, or brand managers. Their role is to efficiently use resources across different products or projects to adapt to changes in the environment. These coordinators typically work as staff managers, overseeing the activities of line managers. They offer guidance to departmental managers and facilitate coordination between departments. Sometimes, project or discipline coordinators are assigned to ensure projects are completed within resource constraints, especially in large organisations.

19.6 TECHNIQUES OF CO-ORDINATION

The following techniques help to achieve coordination:

(Reference to some of the techniques has been made in para 19.5).

1. **Scalar Chain**: The scalar chain shows a person's position in the organisational hierarchy, indicating their authority and responsibility. People give orders based on rules and policies. The chain of command coordinates work across levels and encourages discipline in departments.
2. **Rules and Procedures**: Rules and procedures set performance standards. Members follow these rules, avoiding the need to escalate every issue up the hierarchy. This ensures effective coordination.
3. **Plans and Goals**: Clear plans and goals help achieve coordination by ensuring that everyone in the organisation focuses their efforts towards common objectives.
4. **Information System:** People from various departments at all levels require information to make decisions. Efficient information systems, such as computers and networking, help coordinate activities across the organisation.
5. **Cooperation**: Cooperation fosters coordination. It involves members working together voluntarily as a group. When all members cooperate, it leads to the coordination of activities.
6. **Meetings**: Meetings are a useful tool for achieving coordination. They provide a platform for people to gather regularly and discuss their departmental activities. During these meetings, members talk about problems and come up with solutions that everyone agrees on. This encourages interaction, cooperation, and coordination among members.
7. **Self-coordination**: Everyone, regardless of their level or department, works toward a common goal. People and organisations are aligned in their pursuit of mutual interests, fostering coordination.

19.7 PRINCIPLES OF CO-ORDINATION

Principles are the fundamental truths on which an action is based. The following principles help to achieve coordination:

1. **Unity of Command**: Having one boss for each subordinate simplifies coordination. It is challenging when an individual has to report to multiple bosses. Unity of command ensures coordination by streamlining the activities of individuals and departments.
2. **Early Beginning**: Managers should start coordinating from the planning stage to make coordination easier later. Participative decision-making is key

to achieving coordination. It minimises conflicts, encourages commitment, and fosters harmony toward organisational goals.

3. **Scalar Chain**: This is the link between top managers and lower managers, forming a hierarchy where information and instructions move from top to bottom, and suggestions and complaints move from bottom to top. This chain promotes coordination as top managers issue orders downward, while subordinates convey suggestions and complaints upward.
4. **Continuity**: Coordination is ongoing and essential. It needs to happen constantly at every level and in every department from the beginning of an organisation's existence to its end. Coordination is not a choice; it unites members and resources, serving as the foundation for organisational success.
5. **Span of Management**: Span of control refers to the number of subordinates a manager can effectively oversee. Managers need to manage their team members effectively. Handling a large number of subordinates can make coordination challenging.
6. **Direct Contact**: Direct communication between managers and subordinates improves coordination compared to indirect or impersonal contact. Face-to-face interaction among people from various levels or departments enhances understanding of information and ideas. This promotes effective communication, understanding, and coordination.
7. **Reciprocity**: It refers to the reliance of activities on each other. For example, the production and sales departments depend on each other: more sales require more production, and *vice versa*. The degree of interdependence among organisational activities determines the need for coordination. The greater the interdependence, the greater the need for coordination.
8. **Dynamism** Coordination does not have fixed rules. As the environment changes, coordination techniques must also change. It is a dynamic concept that adapts to evolving circumstances.

19.8 CO-ORDINATION AND CO-OPERATION

Though 'coordination' and 'cooperation' are used interchangeably, they are conceptually different. Cooperation is a voluntary action to work as a group, coordination is a deliberate attempt to unify the actions of members. Coordination can be achieved if all the members cooperate with each other. Even when members cooperate, there is need to coordinate their efforts.

For example, the departmental manager wants to organise a seminar. All members of the department cooperate in organising it. Despite their cooperation, departmental manager coordinates by dividing work and giving authority to do that work.

'Coordination' and 'cooperation' are supplementary to each other. Achieving one without the other is almost impossible. The term 'coordination' is however, wider in scope and includes 'cooperation'.

Aspect	Cooperation	Coordination
Attempt	Voluntary attempt of members.	Deliberate attempt of managers.
Scope	Narrow in scope. Can exist without coordination.	Wider in scope. Includes cooperation.
Relationship	Informal relationship among members.	Formal relationship among members.
Nature	Collective action, may not need formal managerial effort.	Not a technique to achieve cooperation but to unify actions.
Concept	Collective effort to achieve a common goal.	Effort to unify the actions of members.

19.9 CO-ORDINATION-THE ESSENCE OF MANAGEMENT

When an organisation is structured and departments are designed, managers coordinate department activities to achieve organisational goals. Top managers communicate goals to departmental managers, aligning the organisation's objectives with the departmental objectives. Coordination integrates all management functions within each department. Therefore, coordination is rightly called the essence of management. It ensures that each managerial function and departmental activity contributes to the organisational goals.

1. **Coordination while Planning**: Managers ensure that different types of plans (long-term and short-term, strategic and routine), along with policies, rules, and procedures, work together harmoniously. They make sure all departments effectively follow these plans.
2. **Coordination while Organising**: Dividing work into departments, appointing people, defining their authority and responsibility, and creating the organisation structure aim to coordinate departmental activities with organisational goals.
3. **Coordination while Staffing**: Managers assign people to jobs based on their skills and abilities. Placing the right person in the right job ensures coordination among their activities.
4. **Coordination while Directing**: Directing through motivation, leadership, and communication aligns individual goals with organisational goals and ensures unity among various activities.
5. **Coordination while Controlling**: Controlling ensures that actual performance matches planned performance. Budgets and information systems coordinate organisational activities.

"Coordination is achieved by structuring the organisation in such a way as to ensure vertical coordination between hierarchical levels of management and horizontal coordination across individuals and work units at similar levels."

Coordination is essential to management. Aligning the internal environment with the external environment, and human resources with non-human resources, is everyone's task at every level, in every department. Coordination gives meaning and purpose to every task and promotes group effort to achieve goals.

Coordination is not limited to any specific department or function. All managerial functions (planning, organising, staffing, directing, and controlling) in all departments need coordination. The focus on these functions can vary over time for different departments—sometimes planning is emphasised, other times controlling. However, coordination is always essential in all departments, at all levels, at all times.

Contemporary organisations are open systems that actively and continuously interact with their environment, requiring strong coordination. Coordination is essential for organisational success. "Coordination is not an option. It is the need/necessity."

Questions

I. Long Answer Questions:

1. (a) What is coordination? Why does the need for coordination arise?
   (b) "Coordination is the essence of management." Comment.
2. Explain the term 'co-ordination'. What are the various techniques of coordination?
3. What is meant by co-ordination? Explain its importance to management.
4. Explain the meaning and principles of co-ordination.
5. What is coordination? Why does the need for coordination arise?
6. "The need for co-ordination arises because of the interdependence of activities". State different kinds of interdependence between the organisational activities.
7. How is coordination different from cooperation?

II. Write short notes on:

(i) Types of coordination
(ii) Coordination: the essence of management
(iii) Coordination and cooperation

❑❑❑

20 Chapter

Control Function

You cannot control the actions of others, but you can control the choices you make.
— *Erwin Raphael McManus*

20.1 MEANING OF CONTROL

When companies increase in size and complexity, the chances of things not going as planned go up. It becomes difficult for different parts of the company to work well together. Control ensures that what the company does matches what it was supposed to do by stopping things from going wrong.

"Controlling is determining what is being accomplished—that is, evaluating the performance and, if necessary, applying corrective measures so that the performance takes place according to plans."
—*Terry and Franklin*

"Controlling is the measurement and correction of performance in order to make sure that enterprise objectives and the plans devised to attain them are being accomplished."
— *Heinz Weihrich and Harold Koontz*

Controlling, thus, measures performance, compares it with planned performance, corrects deviations, and ensures that goals are accomplished with minimum deviations.

20.2 NATURE OF CONTROL

1. **Pervasive Function:** Managers at all levels control activities of their departments but top managers are more actively involved in it than middle and lower managers.
2. **Process:** Organisational performance is regularly monitored and deviations are corrected. It is not an after-the-event exercise, that is, acting when something goes wrong.

3. **Inevitable Function:** It is a necessary function because internal and external environmental disturbances cannot be predicted. Change is the basis of control.
4. **Associated with All Managerial Functions:** Controlling is not just about planning; it is connected to all parts of management. It helps with planning and points out problems in how the organisation is set up, how people are motivated and led. Control also checks if communication methods are appropriate.
5. **Preventive and Corrective Device:** Control stops deviations from happening and corrects them if they do. It looks at how well things are going compared to what was planned. This helps learn from the past and gives direction for the future. This makes control a way to both correct past problems and prevent future ones.
6. **Positive Function:** Control helps make a brighter future by setting realistic goals. It is not just about correcting things when they go wrong. There are two ways to control: a negative way where managers act when things fail, and a positive way where they spot problems and stop them from happening again. The positive approach believes in preventing issues than correcting them. Control focuses on results without restricting people's freedom. It is about getting things done through people, not controlling people themselves.
7. **Means, Not an End:** Control directs actions toward goals. It is a way to reach objectives and set targets for the future and not the final goal itself.
8. **Related to Management Information System:** Control relies on accurate and trustworthy information that helps to act at the right time. The Management Information System (MIS) gives this information at every level in all departments.

20.3 IMPORTANCE OF CONTROL

1. **Helps in Detecting Mistakes:** Control helps in detecting mistakes early which saves time, effort, and money because managers can correct things before, they go completely wrong.
2. **Manage Complex Situations:** As organisations grow and get more complicated, with different products and markets, a well-designed control system helps keep everything running smoothly.
3. **Monitor the Actions:** Even though employees try their best, mistakes still happen. Things can go off track, problems can be misunderstood, and wrong

decisions can be made. Control manages the plans and makes sure things are going as they should.

4. **Identify Potential of the Organisation:** Control helps organisations tackle challenges and find new opportunities. It exploits people's potential to do more than is usual.
5. **Facilitates Delegation:** When tasks are delegated, control systems make sure those tasks are done well.
6. **Facilitates Decentralisation:** When a company's activities are spread over a wide area for production, sales, and research, it is difficult to control everything from the central office. A good control system makes it easier to manage things in different locations.
7. **Coordination:** Control ensures that what people do matches the plans. It keeps everything coordinated; the way people work, the money used, and the goals of the company.
8. **Psychological Impact:** Control makes people feel the need to do their best. It creates psychological push to perform better.

20.4 RELATIONSHIP BETWEEN PLANNING AND CONTROL

Control is closely related to planning. It makes sure that performance matches with what was planned. Once the plans are put into action, people start working. They might face problems; some get corrected while others go unnoticed. The ones that go unnoticed can turn into big problems and fail the plans. To prevent these problems, managers make sure the planned activities are happening. They follow up things to make sure they go according to the plan.

"It means we must invest in developing a system for monitoring deviations from plans when they are occurring so that adjustments and corrective actions can be taken."

Planning is the first step in management, followed by organising, directing, and controlling, which makes sure things actually happened. Managers check the results to meet the targets. They also notice unusual cases so that future can be changed. Control cannot happen without plans, and planning cannot happen without a control system. They are connected. Planning sets the foundation for controlling, and controlling sets the foundation for planning. Other management functions are done according to the plans. Control looks at present and shapes the future. So, control is both looking back and looking ahead.

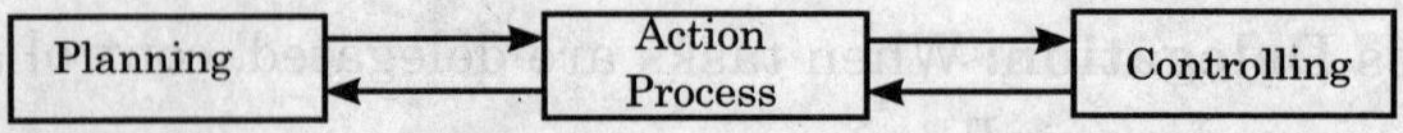

1. Planning tells what to do, and control makes sure people do it.
2. A weak control system can fail the plans, while a strong system helps plans succeed. Control helps to make changes to plans when needed.
3. Planning works best when there is a good control system, and control needs well-thought-out plans to be effective.

This can be represented as follows:

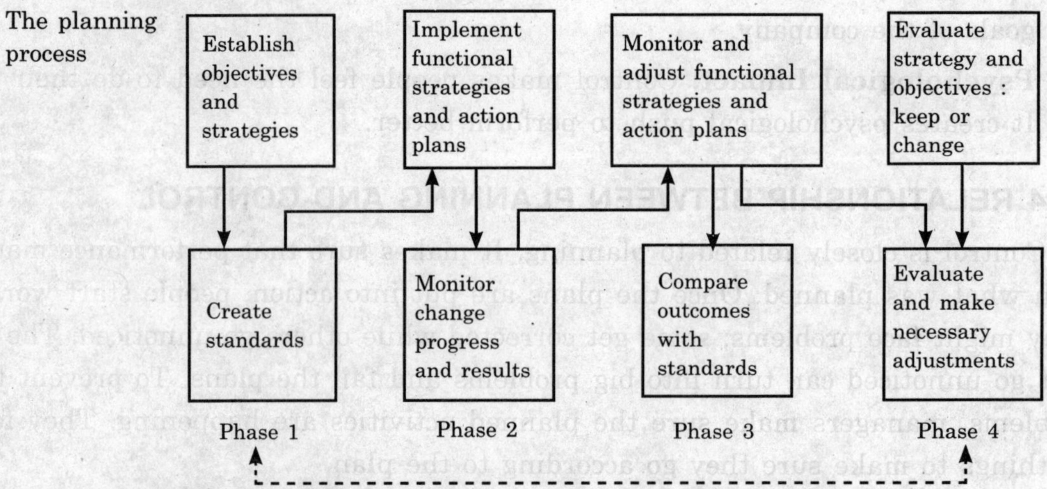

Relationship between Planning and Control

(Source: J.A. Pearce and R.B. Robinson, Jr. Management. © 1989, P. 581]

20.5 TYPES OF CONTROL

The controls associated with three components of production cycle (inputs, transformation and outputs) are:

- Feedforward Control (steering control, preliminary control or pre-control)
- Concurrent Control (screening control or yes/no control)
- Feedback Control (post-action control or output control)

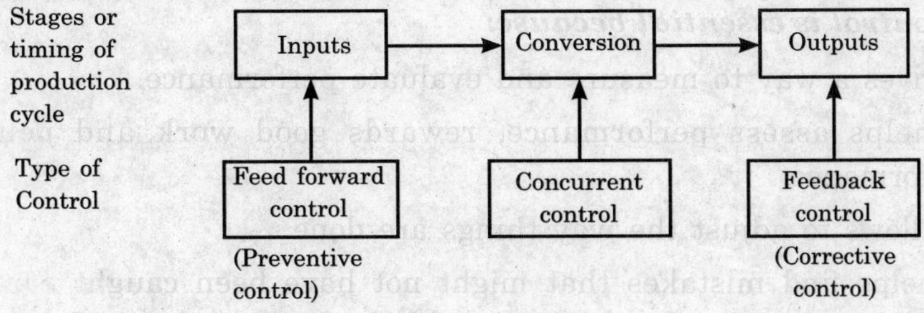

Types of Control

1. Feedforward Control: Feedforward control is a quality check on inputs, like men, machines, materials, and money. It helps to pick the best inputs to create products that meet the standards, for example, the material must be of the right quality. If a sample is approved, it is used in the production process. When it comes to choosing the right people for specific jobs, job descriptions and job specifications help control the selection process.

Feedforward control is about preventing problems. It predicts issues and stops them from occurring. Thus, it is also called preventive control or pre-control.

It aims to:

(i) Find the right inputs through proper planning and control systems.

(ii) Regularly check data to make sure it is used correctly.

(iii) Monitor variations between actual inputs and planned inputs to assess their impact on the outcomes.

(iv) Create plans to correct differences between actual and planned inputs.

2. Concurrent Control: Concurrent control is a hands-on way of managing things as it keeps a close watch on ongoing activities and helps decide if production should continue. For example, managers listen to the sounds of machines and watch how people work. If a machine is making strange noises, they fix or replace it before it makes faulty products. Likewise, if an employee's behaviour is not right at work, they address it before it harms productivity.

3. Feedback Control: Feedback control looks at the results, compares them to what was expected, and checks for the differences. It helps make sure that what happened matches the plan. While it cannot correct the past, it provides the foundation for future. It is also called post-action control.

Feedback control is essential because:

(i) It gives a way to measure and evaluate performance.

(ii) It helps assess performance, rewards good work and penalises poor performance.

(iii) It allows to adjust the way things are done.

(iv) It helps find mistakes that might not have been caught earlier through feedforward and concurrent controls.

(v) It forms the basis for planning. Plans can be adjusted, or new plans can be created.

In essence, it looks at past performance to guide future actions. While it cannot change what has happened, it helps avoid making the same mistakes in the future. Companies use multiple control systems at various stages of the production process.

20.6 BEHAVIOURAL ASPECTS OF CONTROL

The behavioural aspects of control understand that people often resist controls and looks for ways to deal with that resistance. The need for control is genuine, but sometimes people do not like it. They often mistrust and ignore controls because it can make people feel that they are losing their freedom. They like getting rewards for good results and blaming others for bad ones. They also tend to disagree with the rules, reporting, and costs linked to control systems, and sometimes even with the need for control itself.

It is important to understand that control does not limit their freedom. Some level of control is necessary and even wanted by most people. Control itself is not the problem; it is about finding the right balance between freedom and control. Too much of either can hurt performance. Managers need to think about how people will react to controls and find the right mix of freedom and control to encourage positive responses and reduce negative reactions.

The following methods help to facilitate control:

1. **Participative Standards**: When people participate in setting the standards, they are more committed to following them. This makes everyone understand the goals better and turns goals into practical criteria to judge performance.
2. **Positive Feedback**: Instead of punishing employees when they do not meet standards, managers should help them improve their performance.

3. **Coaching, Not Commands**: Managers should guide workers like coaches instead of just giving orders. They should be helpful rather than just pointing out mistakes in how things are done.
4. **Management by Objectives (MBO)**: MBO is a way to manage where specific goals are set together for the whole organisation, each department, and every person. These goals are used for planning, running the organisation, evaluating, and rewarding contributions. MBO encourages teamwork and makes control systems more acceptable.
5. **Human Resource Accounting**: This accounting recognises the importance of people in organisations. Instead of just focusing on financial reports for shareholders and the government, it looks at the people who make these reports and those who are directly impacted by them. Human resource accounting makes accounting reports more effective and gives people a sense of control. It looks at the costs related to factors like hiring, training, losses due to vacant positions, and separation pay when managing employees.
6. **Nature of Control:** When organisational operations and processes align with what people need, they tend to perform well. They are motivated and guided by their internal drive, rather than relying on external pressures. The way control works should match how people naturally are. Control should focus on meeting individual needs, not just what the organisation wants.

20.7 RESISTANCE TO CONTROL

People generally prefer controlling themselves rather than having others control them. They feel controls are imposed because they cannot be trusted. The resistance usually comes from the following reasons:

1. **Inappropriate Controls**: When controls do not match the goals or seem unrelated, employees resist controls. This usually happens when standards are set without participation from employees. They think the standards are based on opinions, not facts.
2. **Excessive Controls**: If there is too much control, it limits freedom and flexibility at work. People see it as restriction on their creativity and force them to follow rigid rules.

3. **Unrealistic Goals**: When standards are too high and seem impossible, employees may not try to reach them. Overbearing control can also stifle employees' creativity.
4. **Fear of Responsibility**: Employees who do not meet the standards resist control because it exposes their weaknesses. Both good and poor performers resist controls for different reasons – some want to protect their freedom, while others fear being held accountable.
5. **Changing Standards**: If the standards keep changing, it is hard for people to measure their performance against unpredictable targets. Thus, control measures would not help them achieve the goals.

20.8 EFFECTS OF RESISTANCE TO CONTROL

Resisting control can lead to the following problems:

1. **Work Delays**: When people are not happy with the control system, their performance suffers, causing delays in the operations.
2. **Attitude Change**: If controls are not set up properly, it can create negative attitudes and personal conflicts, thus, affecting the overall goals.
3. **Wrong Focus**: Too much control on quantity instead of quality, or the means rather than the goals, can make people behave in ways that do not align with the objectives. This is called "behavioural displacement," when people do things encouraged by controls and reward systems that are not in line with the organisational goals.

20.9 OVERCOME RESISTANCE TO CONTROL

Resistance to control can be overcome through the following measures:

1. **Explain the Need for Controls**: Employees should understand that controls are not just for achieving organisational goals; they also benefit them. Meeting standards can serve as a motivator.
2. **Change Attitude**: Viewing control as positive can change how employees feel about their work environment and superiors. It is crucial to focus control on the right areas – like physical, financial, and human resources – to shift the attitude from negative to positive.

3. **Realistic Control**: Having controls that are neither too lenient (under-control) nor too strict (over-control) is essential for achieving the goals. Under-control gives too much freedom, while over-control limits it. Realistic controls find the right balance to optimise performance.

   Reasonable Standards: The standards should be reasonable, practical and achievable. They should not be too high or too low.

5. **Evaluation of Controls:** It is important to evaluate the control process regularly. If the current controls do not work well, an alternate control system should be designed.

6. **Focus of Attention:** Controls should concentrate on results and improvements, not just how those results are achieved.

7. **Flexible Controls:** Even with good standards, the results might not be as expected. Managers should look at the standards which are adaptable. However, they should not keep changing the control system too often.

8. **Participation:** Involving employees in the control system helps people understand the standards better and evaluate their own performance. When people control themselves, it is the best kind of control.

9. **System of Reward:** Good performance should be rewarded to encourage the right behaviour. The organisational culture should promote cooperation, teamwork, communication, coordination, and motivation.

10. **Range of Control:** Despite a strong control system, there might still be deviations. Though managers can allow for a small range of deviations, the acceptable percentage of deviation depends on the product; for costly products like diamonds, there might be very little or no tolerance for deviations.

20.10 CONTROL PROCESS

The process of control involves the following steps:

1. **Determine the Areas of Control:** Every single activity cannot be checked in an organisation. The focus should be on the important areas that really affect how well the organisation does. These are called "key areas" that must work well for the whole organisation to be successful. This is called "critical point control." It helps to figure out the most important places that need attention.

2. **Setting Standards:** Standards are the specific criteria that tell how well employees are doing compared to what they should be doing. "Standard is a desired outcome or expected event with which managers can compare subsequent activities, performance or change."

   Standards are helpful because they:

   i. Help employees understand what they should and should not do in their work.

   ii. Show employees what their managers expect from them.

   iii. Let employees see how well they are doing.

   iv. Connect individual goals (what employees want) with what the organisation wants.

   As deviations form the basis for planning, standards should be scientifically framed. They should be:

   i. Easy to understand and possible to achieve.

   ii. Based on facts and evidence, not guesses.

   iii. Able to change if the situation changes.

   iv. Participative as employees should have a say in making the standards.

   v. Reviewed and updated when needed.

   Standards may be quantitative or qualitative. Quantitative standards (time, production, cost...) can be measured and qualitative standards (quality, behaviour...) are intangible.

3. **Measurement of Performance:** Performance is measured from time to time to see how good everyone is doing. It is simpler to measure numbers (quantitative) than qualities (qualitative). Personal observation, performance reports, etc. measure qualitative performance.

4. **Comparison of Performance Against Standards:** On comparing performance with standards, two possibilities emerge:

   i. If actual performance is equal to or better than the standard, managers reward the good work. The type of reward depends on what each employee needs.

   ii. If actual performance is less than the standard, the deviation may be significant or insignificant. If it is not significant (within an acceptable

range), they might just ignore it but if it is significant, top managers, following the "management by exception" rule, check only important parameters. "Management by exception is a control principle which suggests that managers should be informed of a situation only if control data show a significant deviation from standards".

5. **Correction of Deviations:** When there are problems, there can be two reasons: people not doing their job properly or the standards are faulty. The following corrective actions can be taken:

   i. ***Immediate action***: This corrects the problem right away to prevent bigger issues. It can involve solutions like hiring more staff, letting go of some employees, training the team, changing how leaders manage, or using different motivators.

   ii. ***Permanent action***: This action gets rid of the root cause of the problems, so they do not happen again. The issue may not be with how the standards are carried out, but with the standards themselves. Thus, managers might need to change the plans with a new set of standards.

20.11 FOCUS OF CONTROL

In big organisations, managers cannot watch every little thing by themselves. They focus on the most important areas that affect the organisational goals. These areas are the key areas or the critical points that require intervention of control system if not performing well. This approach is called "critical point control." It helps to focus on the most important parts to make sure the organisation is on track. The key areas are "those aspects of the unit or organisation that have to function effectively in order for the entire unit or organisation to succeed."

Peter F. Drucker identified eight key control areas:

- Market standing
- Innovation
- Productivity
- Physical and financial resources
- Profitability
- Manager performance and attitude

- Development, worker performance and attitude
- Public responsibility

Features of Critical Points

Critical point control has the following features:

1. They are the important areas that affect the entire operation. For example, in the production process, having the right quality of inputs makes the production process run smoothly. The quality of the output depends on the quality of the inputs.
2. They prevent problems, not correct them after they happen. They test a small production run to ensure quality before making the final products. Regular checks can help prevent losses.
3. They are not just about tangible things like production, sales, and profits but also involve intangible things like people working in the company, their skills, what motivates them, and their needs.

20.12 MANAGEMENT OR CONTROL BY EXCEPTION

Managers cannot oversee everything. Instead, they should focus on what really matters. If things are going as planned, there is no need to report it upwards. When there are noticeable differences (either good or bad), the matter should be reported to higher-ups. This approach is called 'management by exception,' where managers concentrate on important deviations rather than trying to monitor everything. It ensures that the most critical issues get the attention they need. "The more the managers concentrate control efforts on significant exceptions, the more efficient will be the results of their control."

Merits of 'Management by Exception'

1. It sorts out problems into two groups: the ones that really matter and the ones that do not need top manager attention.
2. It saves time, effort, and money because top managers deal with the important issues, not every little thing.
3. It helps lower-level managers develop by letting them handle everyday problems.
4. It optimally utilises resources because they focus on the most important decisions.

5. 'Management by exception' is closely related to 'critical point control.' Critical points show where to keep control, while the 'exception principle' helps to spot the important differences (deviations) that occur at the critical points.

20.13 EFFECTIVE CONTROL SYSTEM

1. **Forward-looking:** Control systems prevent repeating mistakes. They look ahead by giving data that helps in making plans.
2. **Multiple Controls**: A good control system controls production, inventory, sales, costs, and quality together. It spots issues in what is going in (before), what is happening now (during), and what comes out (after).
3. **Cost-effective:** The control system should focus on exceptional problems. Controlling exceptions at crucial points helps to use resources where they matter the most. Big organisations can use complex control systems, which are important for their work. High-precision fields like pharmaceuticals, engineering, and defence cannot afford even small errors, so they need good control systems.
4. **Timeliness:** When things go wrong, people need to report them as soon as possible. Waiting too long to act can be just as bad as not acting at all. Getting information quickly makes the control system work well.
5. **Adaptability:** A good control system should be adaptable to environment changes. It should have backup plans for unexpected situations.
6. **Focus on Important Areas:** Critical points help to use resources where they are needed the most. It makes the control system fast and cost-effective.
7. **Practical:** Testing performance in a pilot run with similar conditions can make the control system work better. It helps to make improvements before things happen.
8. **Organisational Climate:** The control system should match the organisation's needs and be easy to understand. If it is too complicated, it can make things confusing. Highly complex models can shift the focus from getting things done to understanding the system.
9. **Clear Standards:** The control system is good when the standards are clear, specific, measurable, and achievable. If the standards are unclear or based on personal opinions, they can lead to short-term gains instead of long-term success.

10. Focus on Important Deviations: Managers should pay attention to the deviations that affect efficiency. Small deviations can be left to be corrected themselves.

11. Positive Atmosphere: The control system should not stop creativity or limit how people work. It should let people have freedom in their actions. The focus should be on the work and not the way people do it. The system should encourage independence at work and be flexible to meet the needs of the people rather than forcing people to fit into the system.

Questions

I. Long Answer Questions

1. "Planning is looking ahead, and control is looking back." Comment.
2. Explain the importance and characteristics of a good control system.
3. Define controlling. Explain the essential requirements of an effective control system.
4. Explain the meaning, nature and importance of controlling function.
5. "Planning identifies actions and controlling sees that actions are carried out." Explain.
6. State the reasons for human resistance to control. Suggest ways to overcome this resistance.
6. Explain the meaning and steps involved in the process of control.
7. "Trying to control everything may end up in controlling nothing." Explain.
9. Explain the principle of critical point control. How can it relate to 'control by exception'?
10. 'Controls should aim at results, not people.' Discuss in the light of essentials of the control system.

II. Write short notes on:

(i) Management by exception

(ii) Pre-control and post-control

(iii) Critical point control

III. Multiple Choice Questions

1. The exception principle to control means

(*i*) Control over significant deviations

(*ii*) Control over all deviations

(*iii*) Control over no deviation

2. Principle of preventive control means

(*i*) Avoid the occurrence of deviations

(*ii*) Correct the deviations

(*iii*) None of these

3. Control over activities while they are in process is

(*i*) Feedforward control (*ii*) Concurrent control

(*iii*) Feedback control

4. Control over inputs is :

(*i*) Feedforward control (*ii*) Feedback control

(*iii*) Concurrent control

5. Control over key areas is :

(*i*) Control by exception (*ii*) Critical point control

(*iii*) Behavioural control

Answers

1. (i) 2. (i) 3. (ii) 4. (i) 5. (ii)

IV. Case Study

(I) Avon Co. Ltd.

Employees of Avon Co. Ltd. are self-directed to work. They assume responsibility for the assigned tasks and subordinate their individual interests in favour of company interests. Managers, therefore, trust them and share their workload with them. The CEO of the company wants to increase profits by 10% and tells the managing director of the company to take necessary steps. The managing director calls the general manager, Sales and asks him to plan his sales accordingly. The GM calls people of his department and says, The CEO wants 10% increase in profits and, thus, a consequent increase in turnover. "Since we have a system of self-direction and self-control, I leave it to you to think of ways to increase sales. Please report back to me by this weekend about how best can you increase the sales."

Questions

1. What kind of organisational set up is this?
2. Which type of control is followed by the company?

(ii) Our problems of control are over," said Venkatesh, the director of information systems, to Ramajayam, president of Elumalai Enterprises Ltd. "With our new computer installation, data gathering, departments and plant terminals, high speed printers, and cathode-ray-tube display stations, every responsible manager can find out what is happening in his or her area as it happens. Delayed reports can now be a thing of the past. I am sure you will find that the investment we have made in these systems is the best expenditure this company ever made. We will soon have real time control and we can manage to a desired standard, in exactly the way a thermostat keeps our offices at a desired temperature.

"I hope you are right," responded Ramajayan. "But I wonder."

Questions

1. What is real-time control?
2. Was Venkatesh right? Why or why not?
3. What would you suggest being done?

❑❑❑